Corporate Social Entrepreneurship

Business ethics teaching appears to have had little impact, particularly in the light of continued malpractice and misdemeanour in the form of financial scandals, environmental disasters and adverse consequences for communities. This timely book directly addresses a central question: is it that the existence of an ethical or an unethical climate influences behaviour, or, does the presence or absence of a moral character and personal values have the greatest influence on behaviour at work? Drawing on an empirically derived study and over thirty years of experience in both the public and private sectors, Hemingway proposes four modes of individual moral commitment to corporate social responsibility (CSR) and sustainability: the Active Corporate Social Entrepreneur, the Concealed Corporate Social Entrepreneur, the Conformist and the Disassociated. The discovery of the corporate social entrepreneur offers students and scholars a critical, alternative and optimistic perspective for the future of ethical business.

CHRISTINE A. HEMINGWAY FRSA is a Visiting Fellow at the International Centre for Corporate Responsibility at Nottingham University Business School. Prior to her academic career, she held senior managerial positions in blue-chip multinational corporations, including roles at Allied Lyons/Domecq, Reckitt and Colman and a subsidiary of the Total Oil group. She brings over thirty years of insight from both the public and the private sector to address the notion of social responsibility as a subjective state.

T0367725

Business, Value Creation, and Society

Series editors

R. Edward Freeman, *University of Virginia*
Jeremy Moon, *Nottingham University*
Mette Morsing, *Copenhagen Business School*

The purpose of this innovative series is to examine, from an international standpoint, the interaction of business and capitalism with society. In the twenty-first century it is more important than ever that business and capitalism come to be seen as social institutions that have a great impact on the welfare of human society around the world. Issues such as globalization, environmentalism, information technology, the triumph of liberalism, corporate governance and business ethics all have the potential to have major effects on our current models of the corporation and the methods by which value is created, distributed and sustained among all stakeholders – customers, suppliers, employees, communities, and financiers.

Published titles:

Fort   *Business, Integrity, and Peace*
Gomez and Korine   *Entrepreneurs and Democracy*
Crane, Matten, and Moon   *Corporations and Citizenship*
Painter-Morland   *Business Ethics as Practice*
Yaziji and Doh   *NGOs and Corporations*
Rivera   *Business and Public Policy*
Sachs and Rühli   *Stakeholders Matter*
Mansell   *Capitalism, Corporations and the Social Contract*

Forthcoming titles:

Hartman   *Virtue in Business*
Maak and Pless   *Responsible Leadership*
de Bruin   *Ethics in Finance*

Corporate Social Entrepreneurship

Integrity Within

CHRISTINE A. HEMINGWAY

CAMBRIDGE
UNIVERSITY PRESS

CAMBRIDGE
UNIVERSITY PRESS

University Printing House, Cambridge CB2 8BS, United Kingdom

Cambridge University Press is part of the University of Cambridge.

It furthers the University's mission by disseminating knowledge in the pursuit of education, learning and research at the highest international levels of excellence.

www.cambridge.org
Information on this title: www.cambridge.org/9781107007208

First published 2013
First paperback edition 2014

A catalogue record for this publication is available from the British Library

Library of Congress Cataloguing in Publication data
Hemingway, Christine A., 1960–
Corporate social entrepreneurship : integrity within / Christine A. Hemingway.
    pages   cm. – (Business, value creation, and society)
Includes bibliographical references and index.
ISBN 978-1-107-00720-8 (hardback)
1. Social entrepreneurship.   2. Social responsibility of business.   I. Title.
HD60.H45   2013
658.4′08 – dc23   2013005744

ISBN 978-1-107-00720-8 Hardback
ISBN 978-1-107-44719-6 Paperback

Contents

Figures

Tables

Foreword

Corporate Social Entrepreneurship: Integrity Within brings together a decade or more of Christine Hemingway's thinking about the place of individuals' responsibility within organisations as a vital component in wider corporate social responsibility. Hence the term corporate social entrepreneurship focuses on the ways in which individuals both limit organisational misdemeanours and champion social agendas in the context of profit-making.

Hemingway brings a particularly good vantage point to this endeavour. Her experience combines over a decade in business and over a decade in the academy, during which time she completed a PhD, here at the University of Nottingham's International Centre for Corporate Social Responsibility.

Hemingway's practical experience in a variety of industries informed her initial view that academics underestimate individual discretion within organisations in favour of structural accounts of business performance, be it financial or social. Moreover, her experience enabled her to win the participation of one former employer as her case organisation. This became an ethnography and contributes particularly to Part III of the present volume, 'Modes of moral commitment to CSR'.

Hemingway's doctoral experience enabled her to engage with the relevant literatures in order to propose and develop the corporate social entrepreneurship idea. Indeed she made the most of this and draws on a very wide set of literatures, particularly in management, philosophy and psychology to substantiate her approach, as set out in Parts I and II of the book: 'Values and corporate social responsibility' and 'Personal values and corporate social entrepreneurship'.

When Hemingway embarked on this project we thought it particularly timely in the wake of Enron and all that. Little did we anticipate the more profound relevance of her insights in the wake of the financial-sector crisis. Thus, the practical guidance on 'Developing a socially responsible organisational culture' (Part IV), particularly on how personal values can be encouraged in the cause of responsible business (Chapter 13), not only reflects Hemingway's concern for practice but also makes her contribution yet more timely than when she started.

Jeremy Moon
Professor and Director
International Centre for Corporate Social Responsibility
Nottingham University Business School
University of Nottingham

Preface

The topic of corporate social responsibility is centre stage. Indeed, the media have consistently reported corporate malpractice and misdemeanour, such as technical incompetence, which can result in disaster, to the detriment of local communities, and even tragic and far-reaching societal consequences. And so it seems that cutting corners and cutting costs has become the nature of modern capitalism, reflecting the insatiable drive of big business for ever-greater profits. Indeed, in the first published article on the subject of corporate social entrepreneurship, I posed the question: 'How much profit is "enough"?' (Hemingway, 2005: 237). At this time, many had perceived the market as getting out of hand. This caused me, the following year, to make reference to Adam Smith's metaphor for his view of the inherent fairness in free trade and market forces, and I wrote, 'perhaps the invisible hand has lost its grip'.[1] This was all prior to the financial crisis of 2008, caused by irregularities with regard to sub-prime mortgage dealings and compounded by lapses in corporate governance systems.

But the subject of social responsibility is not confined to corporate activity: it is also topical across a range of organisational domains. For example, the British Members of Parliament expenses claims scandal hit the headlines in 2010 and the world of sport has been dogged by betting-scam 'match fixing' in professional soccer, rugby and cricket. Even the role of the Church of England is under debate, highlighted by the 'Occupy the London Stock Exchange' protesters at St Paul's Cathedral. Nor can the media take the moral high ground when fraud cases abound, such as those in Germany, Italy and the US. Indeed,

---

[1] C.A. Hemingway, 'An Investigation into the Nature of the Relationship between Employees' Personal Values and Corporate Social Responsibility: Insights from a U.K.-based Multi-national Corporation,' PhD thesis upgrade document, presented to the Transfer Panel, December 2006.

the British tabloid press is currently undergoing a Government inquiry into media ethics, presided over by Lord Justice Leveson, as a result of telephone hacking. All this organisational scandal seems counter-intuitive, when we recognise that the majority of employees are not bad people and yet organisations and their employees continue to do bad things (Anand, Ashforth and Joshi, 2004). Nevertheless, fraud on the scale of Enron and Worldcom is not representative of corporate life. So we might regard a description of 'good' and 'bad' compa-nies as both reductionist and unrealistic. On the other hand, it was widely reported that the British media scandal was not perpetuated by a few 'bad apples', but was rife in the system. Consequently, we have seen public and political focus on *systemic* problems in wide-ranging organisational contexts such as those described above, as well as in the British National Health Service (NHS), in the Police and among care-home workers.

Consequently, corporate misdemeanour features heavily in the teaching of corporate social responsibility (CSR) or sustainability courses, through the use of moral dilemmas within case scenarios, or in business ethics teaching, by applying various ethical theories to those dilemmas in order to illustrate the 'things that can go wrong with business' and the range of consequences and possible solutions. Such teaching methods provide an accessible starting point to the subject of CSR, but they are clearly insufficient for our understanding of why misdemeanour occurs and what might constitute socially responsible behaviour in practice. So if CSR theory has tended to concentrate at the macro level, then this book draws attention to the micro (individual) and meso (relations, networks, alliances) levels, which are often the most important connection, illustrating the interplay between struc-ture and agency – particularly bearing in mind the void of qualitative research in moral decision-making activity (Siltaoja, 2006). Hence my motivation for this book and its alternative thesis regarding the per-sonal drivers of CSR.

So while close examination of organisational processes is clearly necessary, my argument here is that we also need to understand the motivations of employees – at all levels in the organisational hierarchy, in order to effect the required change. And so I have highlighted the largely uncharted field of ethical leadership in practice and the orig-inal notion of entrepreneurship in CSR, which centres not *just* upon preventing organisational misdemeanour, but also upon championing a sustainable social agenda, in addition to the profit-driven one. And I have drawn attention to the unexamined perspective that the CSR and sustainability agenda is not solely driven by governmental or economic pressures: it is also championed as a result of a personal morality, motivated by employees' own self-transcendent personal values, even if these dominant values are not representative of the majority of employees. Moreover, these personal values are exhibited as a moral character which motivates CSR, sometimes in an entrepreneurial manner, in the form of corporate social entrepreneurship. Furthermore, the organisational employee, at any level in the hierarchy, is a moral agent. This is despite a body of evidence which suggests that individual moral agency is sacrificed at work and is compromised in deference to other, structural pressures. Hence my thesis is consistent with the critical-realist philosophy, which recognises the dual forces of structure and agency, acknowledged in this book as important drivers of CSR, where the organisation represents the defining context, and within this my central proposition is that personal values represent a causal mechanism.

The notion of the corporate social entrepreneur emerged from a theoretical working paper which I published, over ten years ago, as part of the Hull University Business School Research Memoranda Series (Hemingway, 2002). In that first working paper, I discussed managerial discretion in CSR and argued that CSR can be motivated by an altruistic impulse driven by managers' personal values, in addition to the more obvious economic and macro political drivers for CSR. This reflected the traditional philosophical and business ethics debate regarding the moral agent. This working paper was followed by a second, co-authored with Patrick Maclagan, which I presented at the European Business Ethics Network Conference (EBEN-UK), in 2003 (Hemingway and Maclagan, 2003). In this conference paper, the concept of 'entrepreneurial discretion' as an overlooked antecedent of CSR was mooted and it was published the following year as a joint-authored article in the *Journal of Business Ethics* (Hemingway and Maclagan 2004). Consequently, I coined the term 'corporate social entrepreneur' (CSE) in the paper that I presented at the 17th Annual European Business Ethics Network Conference, at the University of Twente, Enschede, the Netherlands, in June 2004 (Hemingway 2004). In this paper, I conceptualised the notion of the CSE, differentiating this individual from other types of entrepreneur. The following year this paper was published in the *Journal of Business Ethics* (Hemingway 2005).

My theoretical starting point was Treviño's (1986) conceptual model of ethical decision making in organisations. This model (see Chapter 2), depicted ethical or unethical behaviour as the outcome of both individual and situational moderators of the ethical decision-making process. This reductionist view was problematic on a number of levels, not least because it presumed that the employee would actually recognise a potentially unethical situation. A second problem related to Treviño's assertion that 'business managers are not autonomous decision makers who look inside themselves to decide what is right' (Treviño, 1986: 609). And whilst I agreed that employees are not monadic individuals and operate in tandem with others in the workplace, discussing their tasks and projects as part of the daily operations of their own role, the notion of employee discretion was largely unexplored territory in organisation theory. Indeed, regardless of the arguments for and against bureaucratic controls in the workplace, where managerial discretion at work had been discussed it had generally been viewed as undesirable. This was because the dominant position from neoclassical economic theory was that to allow management the discretion to progress a social agenda was not in the interests of the shareholders of the company, whether or not the ends were for socially responsible purposes, or otherwise. Hence in the business ethics literature, the 'futility' of attempts to influence senior executives with regard to corporate social performance (Lovell, 2002b) and the amorality of business life has remained a dominant theme, compounded by research findings regarding the negative consequences for whistleblowers (Near and Miceli, 1996).

But management theory has overlooked social cognitive theory, which underlines our innate sense of social duty and the personal power of the employee as agent (Bandura, 1986, 1999; Schwartz, 2010), and so our understanding of ethical decision making in organisations remains fragmented. Indeed, recent meta-analyses of the behavioural ethics literature have criticised the field for its 'unsubstantiated assumptions' (Tenbrunsel and Smith-Crowe, 2008: 546) and inconclusive results (O'Fallon and Butterfield, 2005) – particularly as investigation has largely been confined to in vitro examination of the constructs that influence one or more of the stages in Rest's (1986) four-step process of regarding the moral nature of an issue, making a moral judgement, establishing moral intent and engaging in moral action, i.e. 'cutting up the process in successive phases' (Laroche 1995: 65) and often using student samples. This has failed to address the inherent complexity of behavioural ethics in situ and generated the criticism, directed at management scholars in general, of prioritising methodological rigour at the expense of the internal validity of results, thereby ultimately compromising the social usefulness of these studies (Hodgkinson and Starkey, 2011). And this theoretical and empirical reality did not reflect my own practical – and fallibly subjective – reality of three decades as an employee in public- and private-sector organisations. The latter included thirteen years as a corporate executive in seven different industries prior to the start of my academic career, which began later on in my life. And when I returned to the study of organisational behaviour, the rational models of ethical decision making struck me as both reductionist and improbable. As a management practitioner I had experienced and observed a good deal of autonomy as a budget holder, including the freedom to initiate opportunities for social good. And from a normative perspective, the potential for any corporate misdemeanour could arguably be greater if individuals are not allowed to take responsibility for their actions at work. This insight reflects Bhaskar's (1986) principle of hermeticism in the unity of theory and practice, which states that in order to effect transformation, scholars need to enhance their own reflexivity by distinguishing between what is empirical, what is actual and what is real. This does not accept that hermeneutics is exhaustive of social life and neither is it inconsistent with causal explanation (see also Archer, 2007; Sayer, 2000). And so my thesis is that personal values are an important driver of CSR and that they have been overlooked in preference to the more obvious, structural forces.

Hence, as a result of a study which was designed to examine social responsibility as a subjective state, this book provides new insight into what Maclagan (1998: 9) referred to as 'the logical relationship between values and action in organizations'. The investigation was executed via a form of ethnography, conducted over a three-and-a-half-year period between 2005 and 2008, within the headquarters of a division of a major UK-based multinational company. The findings from this investigation revealed four modes of moral commitment to CSR, refuting the consensus in business ethics regarding the homogeneity of management as an amoral group, and adding a unique dimension to the study of CSR and of behavioural ethics in organisations, via the agent employee.

Since that first working paper was published (Hemingway, 2002), significant academic interest has developed around the notion of corporate social entrepreneurship. Notably, scholars of social entrepreneurship from the Harvard Business School published a working paper in October 2004 (Austin et al., 2004), followed by two book chapters (Austin et al., 2006a; Austin et al., 2006b) and an article which compared corporate entrepreneurship and social entrepreneurship (Austin, Stevenson and Wei-Skillern, 2006). More recently, a Harvard Business School working paper (Austin and Reficco, 2009) was posted on a Harvard University Business School web page dedicated to the subject of the CSE (http://hbswk.hbs.edu/item/6153.html). Meanwhile, the Hemingway and Maclagan (2004) article has become the joint forty-fourth top-cited article of the *Journal of Business Ethics*, out of 4,747 papers published in the journal's thirty-year history, and was recognised in a book of their Citation Classics (Michalos and Poff, 2012). Significantly, the work at Harvard confined their notion of the CSE to management and was grounded in the fields of entrepreneurship and business strategy. This contrasted with my own multidisciplinary perspective, grounded in the critical-realist philosophy of research (Archer, 1995; Archer, 1996), recognising the transformative power of the employee as agent of corporate change via the psychological drivers for CSR. Thus momentum and interest from both academics and practitioners continues to build around this new topic, evidenced by some business consultancy start-ups dedicated to the practice of corporate social entrepreneurship. Also, Wikipedia's corporate social entrepreneur page has registered over 17,000 hits since it was launched at the beginning of 2010. So, as 'social capital has become eroded and capitalism implodes,'[2] this book is both timely and directly relevant to the contemporary business environment, because it provides students and scholars of environmental studies, sociology and business and management (including organisational behaviour,

---

[2] K. Starkey, 'Stranger in a Strange Land: Michel Foucault in the Business School', talk given as part of The Impossible Prison, an exhibition and seminar series by Nottingham Contemporary, Biocity, Nottingham, 24 November 2008.

work psychology, human resources, entrepreneurship, business strategy, business ethics and economics), with both a critical and an alternative perspective to supplement the dominant scholarly emphasis on the structural forces which drive practice in organisations. And with its emphasis on the employee as moral agent, this book refocuses attention on the role of the individual in corporate social responsibility. Moreover, it provides a new approach to the study of organisational decision making, by addressing a large gap in our understanding of the individual characteristics and behaviours that promote the development of CSR within organisations. This is in contrast to the more common focus on the subject, in terms of organisational rationale and activities. Hence this book presents an optimistic perspective for the future of business and thus provides us with insights to develop a better form of capitalism.

Overview

In the introduction to this book, the notion of CSR is unpacked via an examination of motives for CSR and the conflicting ideas regarding the social purpose of industry. Moreover, socially *ir*responsible behaviour, regardless of whether the locus of responsibility can be attributed to individual(s) or organisation(s), is regarded here as inherently connected. Indeed, sustained levels of corporate misdemeanour seemingly hit the headlines on a daily basis, keeping CSR topical in the minds of the general public. In addition, a newly found prominence of the business agenda, particularly UK-based business, is acknowledged. All this has also prompted a new impetus to formally integrate the subject into the curriculum of UK-based business schools (Moon, 2010), as well as to adopt it more widely in other academic disciplines. Thus the book begins, in Part I, by unpacking CSR, and highlighting the historically contentious and contested nature of CSR. Moreover, a political shift whereby CSR has become less contested, moving towards the business mainstream, is noted. This is consistent with realist social theory and its emphasis on transformative powers, in particular, Archer's (1995) morphogenetic theory. Thus the drivers of CSR are described in Chapters 1 and 2 in terms of structural and agential motivation.

Structural pressures from stakeholders can influence apparent pro-social corporate activity as part of the organisation's pursuit of economic efficiency (Batson, 1989; Feshbach and Feshbach, 1991).[3] Or CSR may already be ingrained as part of the organisation's culture. Hence the prosocial behaviour construct has been applied in organisation theory (Hannah, Avolio and Walumbwa, 2011; Hernandez, 2012) and is positioned in this book as synonymous with CSR. Thus in Chapter 3 it is shown that the individual's characteristics will influence their formally designated authority at work and facilitate their use of discretion with regard to CSR. In other words, a *single* locus of responsibility for CSR – the corporation – is called into question and the argument is made for the existence of individual champions. This is contrary to the usual ideas regarding notions of amorality and moral disengagement in the workplace. Indeed, corporate social entrepreneurship may well be motivated by consciously driven political reasons for personal advancement in addition to our innate sense of social duty. And so the relationship between our personal concerns – our personal values – and our behaviour is explained in Part II. In order to do this, literatures from philosophy, psychology and management are discussed in order to define values and determine their function.[4]

In Chapter 4, two key themes emerge: first, that values operate at different levels and that our personal values can be further categorised into our dominant individualistic (self-oriented) and collectivistic (social, or 'other'-oriented) values; second, that personal values act as drivers of our behaviour: for example, to behave in an entrepreneurial manner, for whatever end. This supports my

---

[3] The term 'prosocial' is used in developmental and social psychology to denote helping behaviour and is often used interchangeably with altruistic behaviour. See Chapter 2, where these distinctions are made explicit.

[4] The critical-realist philosophy of research that underpins this book is one that acknowledges the interconnectedness of different perspectives. This seems particularly true when examining the two fields of scholarship that represent CSR and values, both of which embrace a broad literature from a variety of academic disciplines. With regard to the study of values, a seminal quotation from Sherif (1936) in Hitlin and Piliavin (2004: 360) seems appropriate: 'Philosophers, psychologists and sociologists . . . have had a tendency to build up their own concepts, giving little or no attention to what their colleagues in other fields have been doing on the same problem. If the concept of value with which they are dealing reveals anything in common, a convergence combining philosophy, sociology and psychology may be fruitful in the development of a general theory of value.'

contention regarding personal values as a driver of CSR and leads to the introduction in Chapter 5 of the corporate social entrepreneur (CSE). He or she is motivated by a dominant sense of self-transcendent values and operates regardless of a perceived socially responsible context. However, taking responsibility per se is not enough. It is the taking of responsibility out of a sense of duty to others which is the subject of this book. Hence, in Chapter 6, the notion of a moral character which exhibits integrity is linked with motivation theory and discussed as key to corporate social entrepreneurship.

The nature of moral agency was explored empirically via an ethnography which was conducted within a division of a UK-based multinational corporation. This study is the subject of Part III. The purpose of the investigation was *to understand CSR as a subjective state* amongst a selection of corporate employees and to examine how personal values are articulated and their meaning and importance to these individuals. Hence, in Chapter 7, the methods employed for the collection of data are described. The tentative results of the study revealed four modes of moral commitment to CSR which are described in Chapters 8 to 11: the Active CSE, the Concealed CSE, the Conformist and the Disassociated. These four modalities illustrate the interplay between the powers of structure and agency in terms of the constraints on and enablements for corporate social responsibility between the organisation and the employee. More specifically, evidence is shown of integrity in action at work and the nature of the socially responsible actor.

Part IV of this book is concerned with drawing some conclusions from the empirical study – in particular, that employees' personal values moderated discretion at work. So the variability and ad hoc nature of the CSR which was found at the case organisation is discussed in Chapter 12. But on the basis of the investigation, I have proposed that fewer CSEs could be anticipated in an organisation with a less socially responsible context and greater passivity, and disengagement with CSR more prevalent amongst employees who would not wish to be perceived in the organisation as mavericks. However, the current economic crisis has highlighted the need for greater integrity amongst employees and thus the positions of Conformist and Disassociated are not sustainable. Finally, Chapter 13 delivers some practical guidance as to how employees' self-transcendent personal values should be levered and how employees can be empowered in the service of CSR. It is argued that as taking the initiative and pursuing opportunities are characteristic of leadership, and that these are virtues which may be taught and encouraged in the workplace, so the potential for significantly higher numbers of CSR leaders becomes apparent. These leaders may be developed as corporate social entrepreneurs.

It is prudent to define the terms that have been used in this book. Here, the terms 'ethical' and 'moral' have been used interchangeably, which is in common with much of the business ethics literature (e.g. Treviño, Weaver and Reynolds, 2006). Moreover, organisational ethics, social responsibility (SR), socially responsible behaviour (SRB) and prosocial behaviour are all regarded here as synonymous with CSR, because of their focus on the 'other'. Thus a CSR agenda can be expected to encompass sustainability, the latter incorporating environmental or 'green' issues. Moreover, despite the differences between the sociological and psychological connotations of individualism and collectivism (which are explained in Chapter 4), I have equated individualistic, self-interested or self-enhancement values, so too collectivistic, other-oriented or self-transcendent values.

Lastly, the publication of this book was preceded by a new reference work called the *Encyclopedia of Corporate Social Responsibility* (Idowu et al., 2013). Please note that the latter contains an entry on corporate social entrepreneurship (Hemingway, 2013), which was published in a substantially different form, but draws from some of the material contained within Chapters 3, 4, 6, 8, 9 and 10 and the Introduction to this book.

Acknowledgements

This work would not have been possible without the co-operation of the directors and the employees of the company in which the ethnography was based. Their time was very generously given and their candid responses were gratefully received.

I also wish to say thank you to all the folk at the International Centre for Corporate Social Responsibility (ICCSR), for their continued support of this research project. This began to take root over a decade ago, when I registered as their first PhD student at the Nottingham University Business School (UK). Enormous thanks also go to Christine Ennew and Andy Crane for their unfailing enthusiasm and encouragement regarding this difficult, complex and important research agenda.

In addition, thanks are owed to Margaret Archer and Kate Forbes-Pitt at the École Polytechnique Fédérale de Lausanne (EPFL) in Switzerland. First for making me most welcome at the Centre for Ontology in 2011 and second for very kindly giving me their time to coach and assist me with the communication of my research findings, within the context of the morphogenetic theory, and for helping me to develop my understanding of critical realism. The result of these worthwhile meetings was a paper that I presented five months later at the IACR Conference in Oslo, Norway (Hemingway, 2011)[1] and my significantly refined thinking, not least about the subject of this book. That said, if I demonstrate any misunderstandings, then these mistakes will be entirely down to me.

I am also indebted to the Work and Organisational Psychology Group at the Aston University Business School, for funding my visit to

---

[1] C.A. Hemingway 'Modes of Moral Commitment to Corporate Social Responsibility: Tentative Insights from a U.K.-Based Multi-national Corporation', presented at the 14th Annual Conference of the International Association of Critical Realism (IACR), Oslo University College, Oslo, Norway, 5–7 September 2011.

the EPFL. Particular thanks go to Pawan Budhwar for his tremendous encouragement and positivity.

I want to acknowledge Patrick Maclagan for his considerable time and depth of knowledge, which initially fuelled my own interest in morality at work and CSR in general, whilst we were members of the academic team at the Hull University Business School (UK), under the support and encouragement of the dean, Mike Jackson. Indeed, sections of our joint paper (Hemingway and Maclagan, 2004) have been reproduced throughout Parts I and II of this book.

Last but not least, I am enormously grateful for the friendship and steadfast support of John Smith, Becky Kavanagh, Ian Hadfield, Jane Chapman and Ian Chapman, all of whom went way beyond the call of duty after the rug had been pulled from underneath my feet. And in 2012, for the wise words of Joe Hemingway and Dirk Matten regarding my necessary 'purdah', in order to get the book written.

Introducing corporate social responsibility

A book about corporate social entrepreneurship cannot begin without some discussion of the wider corporate social responsibility construct in which it is embedded. Thus it is logical to begin this book by defining corporate social responsibility (CSR) and at the same time addressing the controversial debate concerning who should be responsible for social provision and how far this should extend, in terms of who and what should be included in it. However, my starting point is to look at some examples of corporate *ir*responsibility, in order to begin to address these normative questions about the role of business in society.

What is CSR and why is it necessary?

In contemporary capitalist society, corporations are ubiquitous and so they impact on everyone. Corporate social responsibility (CSR) is therefore a subject of interest to management practitioners and consultants and to the gamut of the academic business and management disciplines, as well as to the academic study of environmental science, law and politics and also to the general public. This is not least because of the prevalence of newsworthy examples of corporate *ir*responsibility (Hemingway 2005), which can provide an entry point for debates about the role of business in society.

A recent example of corporate misdemeanour was the case of Toyota GB. The management, based at headquarters in Surrey (UK), had decided to fine their car dealerships if a fault discovered by their mechanics was reported to the customer whilst the car was still under warranty. The warranty policy and procedures manual (seen only by the dealerships) stated that only faults that affect safety and reliability could be reported to customers. But the dealerships voiced their concerns to senior management that there was a grey area where other faults which could not be reported could indirectly affect safety and that the policy was unethical. Such managerial decisions, which were rescinded after the issue was broadcast in a Sunday newspaper (Insight, 2012), can be understood as a strategic need to reduce business costs. But this can sometimes involve cutting corners as a consequence of the imperative to increase profits, year on year.

Paradoxically (because it is another example of business cost), another contemporary issue in business ethics is excessive executive renumeration across both the public and the private sectors. This is currently being investigated in the UK by the High Pay Commission. Indeed, the so-called 'fat cat scandals' have been numerous, the most infamous example of this being the 'grotesque pension arrangements' of Sir Fred Goodwin (Paxman, 2009), who retired as CEO from the Royal Bank of Scotland at fifty years of age. With a reputation for cost cutting, Goodwin exited with a pension of £635,000 p.a. (£12,000 per week) for the rest of his life, after presiding over the bank's unprecedented annual loss of £24.1 billion – the biggest loss in British corporate history. Goodwin left 20,000 in danger of losing their jobs and the government with £325 billion of 'toxic assets' (Ginns, 2009). These may be seen as examples of corporations acting irresponsibly.

Thus CSR can be defined 'in terms of the social and environmental impact of systemic organisational activity' (Maclagan, 1999: 43). This thick construction was broadly illustrated by Gond (2006), whereby CSR represents the interface between business and society (see Figure 0.1 below).

Figure 0.1 also illustrates that there are other concepts related to CSR in the management literature. These are social responsibility, business ethics, philanthropy, corporate citizenship, corporate governance, corporate social performance, prosocial performance, socially responsible behaviour, cause-related marketing, sustainability and green business. There are other related terms. But here CSR is the generic term which I have used to discuss any activity at this interface between business and society, and therefore it also encompasses corporate misdemeanour and corporate irresponsibility. Thus the topical and political natures of corporate social responsibility are two important themes. This is because CSR encompasses normative and therefore inherently controversial arguments regarding the role of corporations in society. And these debates have produced three different perspectives on CSR: first, market fundamentalism, sometimes referred to as the theory of the firm, grounded in neoclassical economic theory; second, the business case for CSR, sometimes known as enlightened self-interest; and third,

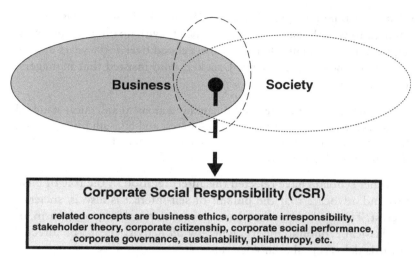

Figure 0.1 A simple representation of CSR (Adapted from Gond, 2006)

a multifiduciary perspective. At the core of these debates lies the voluntary, discretionary nature of CSR.

CSR may also be seen as a function of the corporation's changing environment, again producing controversial debates regarding who the corporation's responsibilities should extend to (Mitchell, Agle and Wood, 1997), against a background of growing corporate power and debates about globalisation (Achbar and Abbott, 2004; Held, 2002; Hertz, 2001). This has resulted in calls for corporations to take their social responsibilities as seriously as they pursue their economic objectives; in some cases, social responsibilities may be considered to be even more important (Carroll, 1979; Goodpaster, 1991; Klein, 2000). Indeed, capitalism's key tenet and what is seen as its sole focus, i.e. the maximisation of wealth, is considered by some to have gone too far, with the gap between the rich and the poor ever widening (Skidelsky and Skidelsky, 2012).

But these concerns are not new. For example, the economic historian Tawney emphasised 'the social purpose' as a duty of industry (Tawney, 1926: 242), and was highly critical of how he saw the development of industrialism, when he said that 'its teaching is that each individual or group has a right to what they can get, and denies that there is any principle, other than the mechanism of the market, which determines what they ought to get' (Tawney, 1926: 43). Tawney was greatly opposed to what he saw as a modern society with no limits on personal acquisition, sentiments that were also echoed over forty years ago by the management theorist Peter Drucker, who insisted that managers' responsibilities were:

for the public good, that he subordinate his actions to an ethical standard of conduct, and that he restrain his self-interest and his authority wherever their exercise would infringe upon the common weal and upon the freedom of the individual. (Drucker, 1968: 454)

But other scholars have rejected this interpretation of the role of business and advocate that the pursuit of self-interest is also in society's interest. These scholars align themselves with the theory of the firm, or neoclassical economic theory, whereby *all* activity has to be directed towards delivering shareholder value:

The classical view of the role of business in society is based on the economic principle that human well-being is served by the efficient use of society's resources and that the free enterprise system is the best means of achieving that efficiency. (Baron, 2003a: 645)

In this regard, CSR has been condemned as a 'fundamentally subversive doctrine in a free society' (Friedman, 1970: 8), or it may be dismissed as an inefficient way to run a business. For example, Baron referred to stakeholders as 'the non-market environment', which 'is populated by numerous interest groups and activist organizations that raise concerns about the practices of firms and pressure them to change those practices'. (Baron, 2003b: 108)

Another perspective on CSR is referred to as 'the business case', whereby CSR has increasingly been adopted as part of strategic business management practice. In these instances, CSR is often handled via public relations, whereby the focus of CSR is to manage stakeholder perceptions, the aim being for the corporation to be seen to be taking its social responsibilities seriously, in the long-term interests of the firm (Brown and Dacin, 1997; McWilliams and Siegel, 2001). Clearly, a strategic business perspective of CSR would adopt an instrumental, 'means-to-an-end', orientation, whereby the emphasis is on corporate image management with stakeholders, for competitive advantage. The business case, however, has increasingly been adopted by corporations who subscribe to the view that 'good ethics is good business'. This is also referred to as enlightened self-interest (Moir, 2001; Stormer, 2003), whereby greater emphasis is placed on the integration of CSR into the modus operandi of the firm, as well as into its corporate communications. Thus a stakeholder approach to CSR can be viewed in one of three ways: solely as a PR exercise, as business strategy or from a multifiduciary (social duty) perspective.

Third, the multifiduciary approach to business ethics and CSR (Goodpaster, 1991) is concerned with a firm's *duty* to its stakeholders. Here, the firm is regarded as having ethical responsibilities 'to do what's right and avoid harm . . . going beyond legal requirements' (Treviño and Nelson, 2004: 32). This may be understood as a different approach to capitalism. The approach emphasises a discourse with all the firm's stakeholders regarding what might constitute ethically correct corporate behaviour, because it is regarded as the morally right thing to treat all stakeholders fairly and not simply to include them for tactical reasons, due to a potential impact on the firm's commercial achievements (Maclagan, 1999).

Who is responsible for social provision and who and what should be included?

All this implies controversy with regard to the attribution of the responsibility for social considerations. Since the Thatcher years in the UK, government has increasingly sought the support of business for elements of social provision (Moon, 2004). However, this has attracted criticism from both the left and the right. On the one hand, the economist Milton Friedman (1970) expressed his view that social provision was the role of elected governments and that social responsibility was not and should not be a concern of business. Any suggestion otherwise, he said, was 'subversive' and a manifestation of socialism. On the other hand, the environmental and political activist George Monbiot (2000) worried about the idea of corporations subversively taking over the role of social provision that had traditionally been the domain of governments, observing this as an ominous shift of power, with corporations dictating and shaping new international legal frameworks:

Before long . . . only a minority of nations will lie outside a single, legally harmonized global market, and they will swiftly find themselves obliged to join. By the time a new world trade agreement has been negotiated, it will be irrelevant, for the WTO's job will already have been done. Nowhere on earth will robust laws protecting the environment or human rights be allowed to survive. Elected representatives will, if these plans for a new world order succeed, be reduced to the agents of a global government: built, coordinated and run by corporate chief executives. (Monbiot, 2000: 330)

Both scholars expressed grave concerns about governance issues, perceiving the shift of any kind of social responsibility from government to corporations as undemocratic. The influence of government as a driver of CSR will be dealt with more fully in the next section. But this also introduces a further facet to the notion of corporate social responsibility.

It is connected with the question surrounding the voluntary, discretionary element of CSR, in terms of actions that might *exceed* legal standards. For example, a firm's orientation towards CSR can be understood by examining its strength within or degree of adoption by the firm – is CSR regarded by a firm as part of its legal responsibilities, or part of a wider social duty? Is CSR regarded as strategically important? For example, is it socially responsible to comply with minimum health and safety or environmental standards? In this vein, Fred Goodwin's defence of his pension pot, referred to at the beginning of this Introduction, was that he had done nothing illegal. Similarly, UK Members of Parliament justified their highly extravagant expenses claims in the same way in their defence against charges of wasting taxpayers' money. This has led to CSR being described as either 'implicit' or 'explicit', determined by differing levels of formalisation of CSR within corporations either in terms of formal policies or strategies ('explicit' CSR), or in terms of an ad hoc approach ('implicit' CSR). The distinction stems from a comparison between corporate involvement in social programmes in the USA and Europe, due to established continental differences in both taxation levels and in the social provision provided by respective governments:

Many of the firm-based policies which in the USA are described as CSR are simply redundant in European institutional frameworks as it is mandatory or customary for corporations to fulfil such measures . . . [although] there is ample evidence that CSR in the 'explicit' sense is gaining momentum and spreading all over Europe (and beyond) . . . (Matten and Moon, 2004: 16)

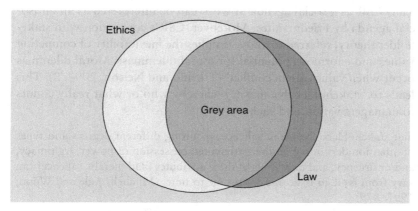

Figure 0.2 The relationship between CSR, ethics and the law (Crane and Matten, 2010, Oxford University Press)

Hence the concept of CSR may be perceived as having a longer tradition in the USA than elsewhere in the world. For example, the concluding chapter in Drucker's seminal text *The Practice of Management* is entitled 'The Responsibilities of Management' and serves to remind the reader that CSR is not a new idea. Drucker (an American) stated that 'Even the most private of private enterprises is an organ of society and serves a social function' (Drucker, 1968: 453). It appears that Drucker was an early protagonist of sustainability, in the enlightened self-interest (instrumental, or strategic) sense, because, he said, the adoption of a social responsibility in management is necessary 'for management's public standing, its success and status, for the very future of our economic and social system and the survival of the enterprise as an autonomous institution' (Drucker, 1968: 455). Consequently, CSR can also be understood in terms of *discretionary* or voluntary actions that anticipate public opinion, depicted as a 'grey area' by Crane and Matten (2010: 9). See Figure 0.2.

Hence the business ethicist Archie Carroll advocated business's responsibility in four forms: economic, legal, ethical and philanthropic, with philanthropic responsibilities described as 'purely voluntary' (Carroll, 1996: 35). Thus exceeding the requirements of the law remains a dominant feature of the CSR literature and it is an important theme in this book, because it signifies the inherent difficulties with CSR in that the values and objectives of society are varied.

Thus CSR as a social agenda at work can be interpreted as an antisocial agenda by Friedmanites. Moreover, CSR's connection with stakeholder theory, referred to above, implies the inevitability of competing values and enormous potential for moral dilemmas: 'Moral dilemmas occur when values are in conflict' (Treviño and Nelson, 2004: 3). This leads to 'stakeholder dynamism', whereby who or what really counts to managers varies, and such

that stakeholders change in salience, requiring different degrees and types of attention depending on their attributed possession of power, legitimacy, and/or urgency, and that levels of these attributes (and thereby salience) can vary from issue to issue and from time to time. (Mitchell, Agle and Wood, 1997: 879)

Clearly, then, in attempting to assess a corporate moral dilemma, or in a discussion of corporate rights and responsibilities, the social role of business has to be clarified by the participants, hence the idea of CSR as an *essentially contested* concept (Moon, 2002). That is, there are many domains of CSR, in terms of who affects and is affected by the corporation. Not only this, but as an academic discipline, 'the field of CSR is best described as being in a state of on-going emergence, one that lacks a dominant paradigm' (Lockett, Moon and Visser, 2006). In other words, 'CSR is a difficult concept to pin down' (Moon, 2004: 2). Therefore any interpretation of CSR is problematic, because it encompasses debates regarding what constitutes moral behaviour at work and what we mean by 'doing the right thing'. Nevertheless we can presuppose the existence of different levels of involvement in CSR, different motivations for that involvement and different values driving the particular type of involvement. This perspective is congruent with the idea of a stratified ontology, different levels of reality and the interconnectedness of the world, which is inherent within the critical-realist philosophy of research (Archer, 2000; Sayer, 2000). Thus, in Chapters 1 and 2, I have unpacked a combination of motives for CSR, themed under structural and agential forces. I begin with the structural drivers for CSR.

PART I

Values and corporate social responsibility

1 | *Structural drivers of corporate social responsibility*

CSR was defined in the introduction as a subject and field of study that sits at the interface between business and society. I also emphasised the contested, or controversial, nature of CSR, which connects to normative arguments about social duty and provision, allied to its discretionary or voluntary dimension. The complexity of motivations for CSR were outlined, which will now be examined in more detail. They are divided into structural motives (this chapter) and agential motives in Chapter 2. Here, the structural motives for CSR have been described in three parts: first, business strategy and stakeholder lobbying; second, business strategy and image management; and third, the organisation's own corporate culture. It is in these structural motivations that the political quality of CSR is most evident.

Business strategy and stakeholder lobbying

Corporate lobbying *by* stakeholders may be perceived as a structural influence for CSR, comprising inducements from governments and from public and institutional lobbying and activism (Baron and Diermeier, 2007). The lobbying *of* stakeholders by corporations is also significant.

Indeed, Moon (2004) described government as a significant driver for CSR in the UK. He referred to CSR as the new agenda for business, i.e. the sharing of responsibility for social provision between government and not-for-profit organisations as a result of governments being 'unable to govern responses to unemployment and economic development unaided' (Moon, 2004: 11). Furthermore, he explained how social changes in the post-war period led to the Thatcher, Blair and coalition governments being unable to provide for society's needs in the way previous governments had done via 'statism' in the pre-war period. Therefore successive administrations have persuaded business to become more involved with social issues, to take on many of the responsibilities that were previously expected of government, thereby shifting CSR from a paternalistic and philanthropic model, described above as implicit CSR, to a more explicit model of involvement, as seen in the USA. A mechanism for the British governments' encouragement for greater involvement in CSR has been soft legislation such as the OECD Guidelines for Multi-national Enterprises and the Ethical Trade Initiative.

Such partnerships are based on reciprocity, legitimising both government and business and motivated by concerns on both sides (Moon, 2004). For instance the strategic CSR agenda for business, whereby the corporate image is manipulated to avoid negative customer perceptions and market sanctions and diffuse the potential for negative media coverage. The motivation for government, argued Moon, has been to encourage the CSR agenda through fear of being perceived by the electorate as failing to provide adequate social provision and the possibility of ensuing social unrest. Interestingly, he identified a paradox, whereby the business case for explicit CSR may also be tempered by the firm through fear of customer backlash, i.e. the firm's anticipation that its attempts at social provision could be judged by the public as derisory. The implication of this is that social provision falls into a black hole, whereby neither government nor business accepts complete responsibility. Any reticence on the part of business towards CSR might also be fuelled by the conventional economic efficiency argument (Friedman, 1970). This would be in addition to resistance to potential increases in bureaucracy, as a result of the formalisation of corporate governance and the costs associated with such measures. Importantly, though, the *mandatory* American requirements for CSR, referred to by Matten and Moon (2004) in the introduction to this book, manifest as significantly different legislative frameworks for corporate governance between the USA and the UK. Nevertheless, in describing the formalisation of CSR by American corporations, Painter-Morland (2008) highlighted the prevalence of US ethics officers and their tendency to approach their role as one of compliance to the recommendations of the US Federal Sentencing Guidelines, as opposed to ethical leadership. The latter approach would involve a more proactive and holistic approach in the development of an ethical organisation and an interpretation of the spirit of those recommendations. Instead, the compliance approach has produced an ineffectual tick-box mentality amongst US ethics officers.

This serves to introduce my argument in this book that systemic forces for governance, such as legal frameworks, need to be bolstered by the vigilance and creative talent of employees. Corporate governance measures, whilst necessary, are insufficient. This theme is picked up again in the next chapter.

Indeed, Monbiot (2000) was cynical about business–government partnerships. He claimed that in its pursuit of global trade agreements, big business has managed to repeal much protectionist national legislation, whilst at the same time forcing governments to compromise their environmental and human rights legislation in their desire to attract and keep foreign investors. This amounted to a sell-out by many governments. He quoted Timothy Hauser, the US acting undersecretary of commerce (1997): 'We should put the business "horse" before the government "cart"', which, affirmed Monbiot, represents a real threat to liberal democracy:

There is, in principle, nothing wrong with global agreement governing fair trade. Fair, transparent rules are essential to prevent rich nations from crushing poor ones: the powerful have long insisted on freedom for their own traders and restrictions on the traders from weaker countries. But negotiations on such agreements appear, time and time again, to conform to a certain pattern: they are conducted in private by committees far removed from democratic scrutiny and control, providing splendid opportunities for lobbyists to infiltrate and direct them. Corporations have repeatedly steered and controlled such negotiations to ensure that they respond to their needs. (Monbiot, 2000: 304)

So, does a corporation's involvement with schools, or the sponsorship of university research or university departments (such as British American Tobacco's sponsorship of the International Centre for Corporate Social Responsibility at the University of Nottingham) represent a corporate takeover? This illustrates the controversial or contested nature of CSR.

Hence Monbiot advocated citizenship as the only way to curb what he saw as 'the corporate leviathan' (Monbiot, 2000: 360). This introduces public lobbying or activism as another means of imparting pressure on corporations for CSR. So in the introduction to this book I stated that CSR can be perceived as the right thing to do from different perspectives: as a public relations activity, as integrated into business strategy in pursuit of the 'win–win' outcome between business and society, or even as the firm's duty in a multi-fiduciary manner. But

whichever way we regard CSR, we have to understand it in terms of
the corporation's effect on – and also the influence on the corporation
from – stakeholder groups: consumers, the organisation's suppliers,
employees, NGOs/environmental activists and the local community
and other interest groups. These groups can 'raise concerns about the
practices of firms and pressure them to change those practices' via
corporate lobbying, demonstrations, boycotts and/or media coverage
and lobbying of government (Baron, 2003b: 108; Reed, 1999). Indeed,
anti-corporate activism was identified by Monbiot (2000) as a force
that caused big business and governments to modify their new multi-
lateral trade legislation, thereby safeguarding the environment and
human rights, which otherwise would have been under threat. As a
consequence, the corporation's CSR may be regarded as a reaction to
actual or anticipated stakeholder pressure from consumers:

Heinz's decision not to purchase tuna caught in purse seine nets served the
interests of various constituencies, and ethical consensus in society may well
have supported that decision . . . That Heinz took 2 years to change its policy
and not until it had become a boycott target suggests that its motive was to
reduce the pressure. (Baron, 2003a: 659)

Another manifestation of ethical consumerism and stakeholder pressure has been the growth of socially responsible investment (SRI) funds,
managed by the financial services industry, which assesses the risks
of the company's impact on society for individual and institutional
investors:

Historically, ethical investing meant avoiding things – polluters, tobacco
companies, businesses supplying armaments and so on. These days, ethical
investors are looking not just to avoid bad behaviour but to encourage
good. That means 'engaging' companies in active dialogue to persuade them
to improve their behaviour. (Connon, 2002: 39)

Examples of ethical investment and lobbying in action are the
FTSE4Good climate change criteria (Oulton, 2007) and the release
from prison of Aung San Suu Kyi, attributed to pressure 'brought
by a group of funds on the western companies that . . . operate[d] in
Burma' (Slavin, 2002). Most recently, the so-called Shareholder Spring
emerged in 2012, whereby a number of financial sector CEOs were
ousted as a result of revolts by shareholders, protesting at proposed
annual pay increases and excessive renumeration of company chiefs

in the light of their very poor company performance and poor share-holder returns (Mandoyan, 2012). But if economic efficiency and profit maximisation are compromised by CSR activity, why would anyone buy shares in a CSR company?

The answer is that some people derive satisfaction from the CSR orientation of the firm, in the same way that buying a fairly traded chocolate bar or engaging directly in social good makes us feel good. This might be motivated by altruism, sometimes known as prosocial behaviour (Bierhoff, 2002), or it might be psychological egoism, i.e. motivated by self-interest to impress others, or to make ourselves feel good (Maclagan, 1998: 30). So not all shareholders view CSR in terms of cost to the business. Indeed, the growth of ethical consumerism in the UK bears witness to the popularity of the principle of 'supporting a cause'. This was valued at £43.2 billion, i.e. a growth by value of 47% since 2005 and 9% year on year over the last two years, despite a 2% fall in UK household expenditure over the last year (Co-operative Group, 2010 and Anderson, 2007). And SRI is paralleling this growth: green and ethical funds were worth £19.3 billion in 2009. Thus it is my contention that this growth may also reflect a social change, which we could regard as a shift in personal values. Nevertheless, it would be nonsense to underestimate the dominance of the commercial impera-tive and economic motive behind any corporate activity. Hence all of the motives for CSR discussed above could be attributed to the rise of CSR on the corporate communications agenda. Indeed, marketing communications represent the most prevalent vehicle through which we observe CSR and the ensuing publicity generated can sometimes be perceived as the sole reason for the organisation's apparent prosocial activity, regardless of whether CSR is or is not an integral part of the modus operandi of the firm.

Business strategy and corporate image management

The business case for CSR is that the concern of management is to maximise shareholder value. As such, '"the business case" . . . considers CSR as part of the process of adding value to the corporation' (Moon, 2004: 3). This perspective represents the strategic approach to CSR and it involves the management, or manipulation, of stakeholder groups. Here, the motive for CSR is the long-term sustainability of the business, and/or because 'being seen to be doing' CSR will facilitate stake-holder management. But it requires a degree of investment, whether for short-term tactical purposes or as part of a longer-term, strategic plan. Indeed the evidence is inconclusive as to whether engaging in CSR can actually improve the profitability of the firm (Barnett, 2007), although Orlitzky's meta-analysis of the relationship between corporate social performance and financial performance showed that 'they are positively correlated, most likely because social performance helps enhance corporate reputations, and, to a lesser extent, improve managerial learning and internal efficiencies' (Orlitzky 2008: 127).

With regard to business sustainability, the reciprocal partnerships between government and big business that were described above represent one facet of CSR, concerned with the facilitation of the organisation's continued license to trade. Indeed, according to Davis (2005: 87), 'From a defensive point of view, companies that ignore public sentiment make themselves vulnerable to attack.' Moreover, the social legitimacy imbued in firms through its CSR was examined by Kell and Ruggie, who ascribed 'the corporate interest in business ethics and good citizenship' to the necessity for corporations to be able to integrate 'the increasing number of diverse cultures of their officers and employees' as a result of their global operations (Kell and Ruggie 2001: 326). Similarly, Moon attributed business community involvement to issues of recruitment, the economic development of the area and business's anticipation of threats of social upheaval (Moon, 2002). In these instances, the firm needs to publicise its activities and to be *seen* to be engaging in CSR. It is thus notable that the Confederation of British Industry (CBI), the UK organisation of employers, defined CSR as 'the extent to which companies should promote human rights, democracy, community improvement and sustainable development objectives throughout the world' (Confederation of British Industry, 2001a). The phrase 'the extent to which' underlines my point regarding the voluntary, discretionary nature of CSR and thus the likely variation in its implementation. As the CBI's mission is 'to help create and sustain the conditions in which business in the UK can compete and prosper' (Confederation of British Industry, 2001b), the trade-off for the CBI is the balance between being seen to be supporting human rights and other CSR initiatives, and at the same time not alienating other parties such as the governments of undemocratic regimes, in order that its members should have access to global markets. This apparent ambiguity illustrates the business sustainability orientation and the complexities involved in adopting a stakeholder approach. It also suggests that in terms of the motivation for CSR, its application is open to interpretation and that not all companies may be proactively responsible, i.e. take responsibility for their activities regardless of public opinion. Thus an alternative approach to CSR is a reactive, or image-management 'responsive' level of commitment (Carroll, 1979; Wood, 1991).

From this perspective, CSR is a response to the competitive environment and the demands on managers from various stakeholder groups (Menon and Menon, 1997; McWilliams and Siegel, 2001). It may also entail manipulation of those stakeholder groups in order to seek the survival of the firm (Anastasiadis, 2006; Desmond and Crane, 2004: 1228). Similarly, the inclusion of stakeholders in corporate affairs and CSR reporting was identified as 'mechanisms by which the organisations satisfy (and manipulate)' pressures on them to demonstrate satisfactory CSR performance (Gray, Kouhy and Lavers, 1995: 65). Hence CSR disclosure and reporting, such as The Sunday Times Corporate Responsibility Index (Stone, 2007), may be cynically viewed in terms of corporate image management, a strategic marketing activity. Here the tools of marketing communications are employed, notably public relations activity, in order to improve the competitive position by delivering the messages designed to create or maintain a good image (Adkins, 1999; Darby, 1999). Consequently, with regard to CSR, the marketing literature concentrates on marketing's role in the management of stakeholder (especially customer) perceptions and CSR's effect on the (corporate) brand (Sen and Bhattacharya, 2001). 'Doing good deeds' produces a positive public relations story and the widespread adoption of marketing communications for this purpose by the top British companies has led to the commercialisation of CSR and the growth of a CSR industry. Indeed, Friedman acknowledged the public relations role of CSR: 'this is one way for a corporation to generate goodwill as a by-product of expenditures that are entirely justified in its own self-interest', although he also denounced this as 'hypocritical window dressing' (Friedman, 1970: 6).

Worse, it has also been argued that corporations adopt CSR to cover up the impact of corporate misdemeanour. Sceptics have accused companies of taking a public ethical stance in order to project a good image, regardless of their unpublicised unethical practices (Caulkin, 2002). John Monks, general secretary of the British Trades Union Congress (TUC), 'questioned the CBI's commitment to corporate social responsibility', saying that most firms had adopted it as a 'fig leaf to avoid awkward questions at annual general meetings' (Macalister, 2001). An example of this from the USA was the discredited company Enron, which, while continuing to use three different sets of accounts, also gave its four-page ethical code to all new employees to sign on their first day. It also had a community relations department and was the largest corporate contributor in Houston, Texas (Davis, 2002). Enron was cited as an example of a company that used 'good causes to buy reputation, in the way it uses politicians to buy power and auditors to buy shareholder value' (Caulkin, 2002).

A concern for corporate reputation at the expense of everything else illustrates responsiveness as opposed to responsibility: doing such things as product recall because they are expedient (Reidenbach and Robin, 1991: 278). Indeed, Desmond and Crane referred to the 'blind faith' of economic egoism; that is, the pervading economic morality of the firm: of delivering enhanced financial performance at the expense of any other kind of morality (Desmond and Crane, 2004: 1228). Comparative sentiments have been expressed by economists as well as business ethicists. For example, the political philosopher Michael Sandel claimed that we have moved from a market economy to a market society, where people are mainly motivated by money (Sandel, 2012), and a critique of market fundamentalism was produced by the financier George Soros (2008). So whilst Jones (1995) advocated that the relationship between stakeholder groups and the firm must be based on mutual trust and co-operation (as opposed to opportunism) in order to facilitate competitive advantage, his perspective remains an instrumental, or consequentialist, approach to stakeholder theory and CSR. This can be contrasted with the multi-fiduciary, deontological approach from moral philosophy:

> We need to make a distinction between good as a means and good as an end. If something is valued for its own sake, it is good as an end, intrinsically good. But if a thing is valued for the sake of something else which it produces, then it is good as a means. (Raphael, 1981: 34)

Therefore a discussion of strategic motives for CSR may be conflated with the argument that the motivation for engaging in CSR is always driven by some kind of self-interest, in contrast to the possibility of an altruistic or idealistic impulse among business leaders or managers. But there is also a middle ground of enlightened self-interest: whereby 'the business case' for CSR is motivated by the win–win of social good for its own sake, *combined* with the motivation for positive benefits for the corporation. And whilst Rollinson observed that 'it is always difficult to tell whether behaving ethically towards external stakeholders is prompted by altruism or self-preservation' (Rollinson, 2002: 44), my contention is that reductionist debate of an either–or nature is unrealistic as well as futile. This will be elaborated in Part II.

However, in many cases nowadays, and with the growth of the CSR movement, the likelihood is a combination of these two motives, in the sense of enlightened self-interest. Thus, to recap, the concept of psychological egoism ('feeling good by doing good') has already been acknowledged in this chapter and cited as one of the motives for CSR. Further to this, prosocial behaviour, which may or may not be regarded as altruism, is discussed in Chapter 2. Moreover, the firm may have a reputation for philanthropy, which has been assimilated into its corporate values and manifests as part of the organisation's culture. This is considered next.

Organisational culture

According to Treviño, ethical decision making in organisations may be partly influenced by situational moderators such as the immediate job context, the characteristics of the work and the organisational culture. Most adults, she said, are susceptible to situational variables that either restrict or encourage, because most adults operate at the conventional level of cognitive moral development, i.e. compliance (see Chapter 2 for a fuller explanation of this). Treviño's view supported the idea that most managers may be amoral (Carroll, 1987), perhaps displaying pragmatism and conformity in order to achieve organisational ends. Hence one can expect the organisational (and thus the industrial and legal) environment to influence the degree to which individuals are encouraged to take CSR initiatives (see Leidtka, 1989; Reidenbach and Robin, 1991), thereby supporting the notion of the individual's environment as constraining or enabling (Archer, 2003).

Moreover, Treviño described the organisational culture as having 'a profound effect on ethical/unethical behaviour in most people' (Treviño, 1986: 614). She defined organisational culture in terms of the normative structure ('how we do things around here'), referent others (influential people in the organisation), levels of obedience to authority and the levels of ascription and adoption of responsibility for consequences. 'How things are done' included how suppliers and employees are treated and involvement with the local community, for example. Indeed, many corporate reputations for socially responsible activity have been acquired as a result of philanthropic activities: arguably the most obvious example of so-called altruistic values in CSR are historically associated in British and American history with the Quakers.

In particular, 'Quakers became known for integrity both in personal relationships and in business affairs; they honoured contractual promises and they maintained fixed prices for goods' (Murray-Rust, 1995) (see Chapter 6 for an exposition of the role of integrity in CSR). Well-known British corporations with Quaker origins are the philanthropic chocolate manufacturers Rowntree, Fry and Cadbury (the Quakers approved of drinking chocolate as a healthier alternative to alcohol). However, Rowlinson and Hassard presented a more critical perspective on the motivations of the early philanthropists, ascribing the 'invention of the Cadbury corporate culture' to books and articles that were specifically commissioned by the Cadbury family for public relations purposes. Also, particular labour management practices of the firm were 'developed . . . in response to contemporary social movements rather than Quaker inspiration', and evidence appears to show that working conditions at the Cadbury company were no different to those of other companies (Rowlinson and Hassard, 1993: 311). At this point it is necessary to acknowledge the scholarly debate with regard to whether or not a corporate culture exists.

Treviño's (1986) perspective of an organisational culture was echoed by Hoffman: 'As organisations form a structured set of norms and values, a collective evolves in the form of organisational culture' (Hoffman 1993: 12). This can be contrasted with the notion that organisations 'don't have values; senior managers do. And they vary. Hence there is no such thing as organizational culture but cultures' (Furnham, 2005: 29). Indeed, the myth of 'a single coherent organization' was argued via a study of a UK college of higher education, when senior management had attempted and failed to change the status of the college to that of university (Humphreys and Brown, 2002: 430). But Fiol differentiated between 'culture as observable manifestations' and 'cultural belief systems' or 'culture as deep meanings' (Fiol, 1991: 196).

Fiol identified three broad schools of thought in the organisational culture debate. First, the 'culture pragmatists' are those scholars who

describe culture change as a result of observing the existing manifestations of organisational culture, such as Peters and Waterman (1982),
or Alvord, Brown and Letts (2003) in the arena of social change.
A second group, the 'culture purists', 'argue that cognitive processes
reside in and are ruled by deeply ingrained repetoires that are beyond
conscious manipulation' (Fiol, 1991: 192). A third approach requires
accessing 'webs of meaning' and 'peoples' understanding of themselves
in relation to the system' (Fiol, 1991: 200). Fiol quoted Fiol and Dunbar (1990): 'a common set of core values underlies and governs the
meanings of even the most behaviorally diverse firms' (Fiol, 1991:
202). Indeed, using qualitative marketing research, business strategists
or corporate marketers can produce common organisational cultural
themes perceived and agreed by employees as representative of a
common culture. This is the same process adopted by the academic
researcher, who builds common or overriding themes up from the literature in a subject, or, from qualitative data, in the development of
theory.

Three aspects are apparent here. First, a distinction needs to be
made between the existence (or not) of a corporate culture and, if it is
believed to exist, the question raised is whether or not corporate culture
change is possible. The business strategist would not attempt culture
change without first understanding the nature of the existing culture, in
order to build the new strategy based on existing organisational values,
thereby aiding the adoption of the new plan by the employees. The
importance of establishing the essence of the existing organisational
culture as a starting point upon which to build a new strategy is evident
in the mantra of the business strategist: 'Where are we now, where do
we want to be and how do we get there'. Moreover, the necessity of
employee 'buy-in' to the success of any planned organisational change
is prevalent in the transformation literature (and seems to be a stage
that was overlooked by the college managers in the 2002 Humphreys
and Brown study) (Fisher, 1986; Irvin, Pedro and Gennaro, 2003;
Lacey and Andersen, 2004: 6).

Second, in attempting to establish whether organisational culture
exists, or whether organisational change is possible, there may be
greater validity in comparing 'apples with apples' and investigating
either public sector *or* private sector organisations and not general-
ising across the sectors. For example, one might expect the existence
of a more coherent organisational culture within a corporation than

within a public sector organisation, by virtue of the former's longer association with the principles of business strategy. Third, one could speculate that the acceptance and adoption of organisational values may be higher amongst corporate staff than amongst public sector organisation staff, for reasons akin to ideas regarding the notion of career choice and personality type (Hardigan, Cohen and Carvajal, 2001; Holland, 1985; Rubinstein, 2003). For example, stereotypes regarding respective professionals in both the public and private sectors may or may not involve relative differences in employees' levels of dynamism or creativity, their resistance to change, or their levels of compliance. Nevertheless, my presupposition here is of the existence of organisational (corporate) culture as an antecedent of ethical behaviour at work. And that organisational culture may be a manifestation of organisational values, which, in the case of a multinational company, can be influenced by the personal values of the owners or CEO, the industry (category) values, the home country and the local community (Agle and Caldwell, 1999) – see Chapter 4 for a fuller explanation of a value. Certainly, organisational culture and CSR have been linked in the management and marketing literatures (Agle, Mitchell and Sonnenfeld, 1999; Maignan, Ferrell and Hult, 1999).

I have now described the structural forces for CSR – such as overtures from and to governments, the public, consumers and other stakeholder groups – and how CSR can be embodied as part of the firm's (or industry's) culture. These structural forces were also described as predominantly economically motived. However, my central concern is with the *actions* of employees, and so my thesis states that personal values combine with personality variables, in addition to the impact of the wider cultural and organisational context, to determine an individual's unethical behaviour, or, conversely, to drive CSR. Thus, in the next chapter, the notion of the employee as moral agent is explored more thoroughly.

2 | Agential drivers of corporate social responsibility

My thesis is that the obvious structural influences for CSR are not the sole drivers of CSR decision making in private sector companies, even if they appear to be the most obvious. Indeed, the critical-realist philosophy of research encompasses ideas regarding the dual powers of structure and agency, causation and generative mechanisms that influence phenomena. And whilst the structural forces described in the last chapter are significant, it is the notion of individual moral agency, or a moral character, as an influence for CSR which is my own particular focus.[1] So, by way of introduction to this chapter, my starting point is Wood's reference: 'Ethical training, cultural background, preferences . . . and life experiences . . . that motivate human behaviour' (Wood, 1991: 700). This supported Treviño's social interactionist theory of ethical decision making in organisations (Treviño, 1986), which incorporated both individual and situational moderators, to combine with the individual's stage of cognitive moral development (Kolhberg, 1969) to result in ethical or unethical behaviour. So, too, we might regard these factors as relevant to corporate social entrepreneurship. Consequently, in what follows, I have highlighted cognitive moral development, personality and personal values as important agential moderators of a dominant focus on the self or other. Moreover, within the agential context of an 'other' orientation, the chapter sets out the relationship between helping behaviour, prosocial behaviour and

---

[1] The notion of moral agency taps into traditional philosophical debates regarding character and free will. But it is not within the scope of this book to present a synopsis from the philosophical literature, such as the ideas of David Hume. However, the connection with virtue ethics is discussed in more depth in Chapter 6. My thesis also applies to organisations in the public and voluntary sectors, where the necessity for taking the CSR initiative and the entrepreneurial drive to see through such initiatives to completion are needed equally.

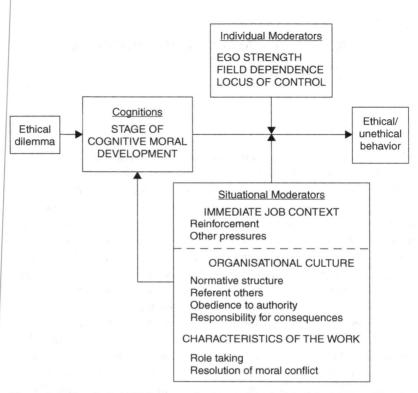

Figure 2.1 Treviño's (1986) interactionist model of ethical decision making in organisations (courtesy of Academy of Management Review)

altruism – constructs which are all relevant to the notion of corporate social entrepreneurship.

Cognitive moral development and personality characteristics

Treviño's (1986) person–situation interactionist model of ethical decision making in organsations is presented in what is widely regarded as a seminal article in the business ethics literature. Treviño's argument was that the individual's response to an ethical dilemma can be explained by the interaction of individual and situational components to produce ethical or unethical behaviour (see Figure 2.1).

Individual moderators of ethical behaviour were cited as the personality characteristics of ego strength, field dependence and locus of control. Ego strength indicated strength of conviction, field dependence the degree to which others' opinions are sought (thus linked with notions of autonomy), and locus of control the extent to which the individual takes responsibility for their actions. Moreover, situational moderators were described as the immediate job context, the organisational culture and the characteristics of the work itself. However, the ethical decision-making process, postulated Treviño, hinges upon the individual's stage of cognitive moral development (CMD), a theory developed by Lawrence Kohlberg (1969).

Kohlberg's (1969) study was based on fifty-eight boys of between ten and sixteen years of age interviewed at three-year intervals over a twelve-year period. It was developed from the influential psychological studies of intellectual and moral cognitive development by Freud (in 1924), Piaget (in 1932) and Erikson (1950) (see Eysenck, 2004: Chapter 16), all of whom had proposed sequential, hierarchical models of learning and human development. The relevance of CMD theory to the subject of business ethics was highlighted by Maclagan (1998: 22), who described CMD thus:

Kohlberg's proposition is that people can progress, from childhood onwards, through three levels of cognitive moral development, each divided into two stages. Such development refers to persons' capacity to understand the concept of morality, and ultimately to be able to engage in ethical reasoning... this means a progression from self-interest, through appreciation of, and conformity with, the moral values and norms of society and support for members of one's immediate circle, to greater independence of mind and potential for the questioning, on ethical grounds, of organizational purposes and activity.

Indeed, the business ethics scholars Crane and Matten applied the theory of cognitive moral development to the business context and provided an example to illustrate each of Kohlberg's six stages (see Table 2.1).

But Kohlberg's work is not without its critics, a point which was also highlighted by Treviño (1986). For example, Gilligan (1982) produced further insight with regard to gender differences in moral response, although her association of the caring trait with women has been similarly controversial. Moreover, Maclagan suggested that Gilligan's results might have identified 'different ways of thinking, a masculinity–femininity distinction... rather than gender as such'

Table 2.1 *Kohlberg's stages of cognitive moral development (1969)* *(Source: Crane and Matten, 2010: 154, Oxford University Press)*

Level	Stage		Explanation	Illustration
I Preconventional	1	Obedience and punishment	Individuals define right and wrong according to expected rewards and punishments from authority figures.	Whilst this type of moral reasoning is usually associated with small children, we can also see that businesspeople frequently make unethical decisions because they think their company would either reward it or let it go unpunished.
	2	Instrumental purpose and exchange	Individuals are concerned with their own immediate interests and define right according to whether there is fairness in the exchanges or deals they make to achieve those interests.	An employee might cover for the absence of a co-worker so that their own absences might subsequently be covered for in return – a 'you scratch my back, I'll scratch yours' reciprocity.
II Conventional	3	Interpersonal accord, conformity and mutual expectations	Individuals live up to what is expected of them by their immediate peers and those close to them.	An employee might decide that using company resources such as the telephone, the Internet and e-mail for personal use whilst at work is acceptable because everyone else in their office does it.
	4	Social accord and system maintenance	Individuals' consideration of the expectations of others broadens to social accord more generally, rather than just the specific people around them.	A factory manager may decide to provide employee benefits and salaries above the industry minimum in order to ensure that employees receive wages and conditions deemed acceptable by consumers, pressure groups and other social groups.

III	Postconventional	5	Social contract and individual rights	Individuals go beyond identifying with others' expectations, and assess right and wrong according to the upholding of basic rights, values and contracts of society.	The public affairs manager of a food manufacturer may decide to reveal which of the firm's products contain genetically modified ingredients out of respect for consumers' rights to know, even though they are not obliged to by law, and have not been pressurised into this by consumers or anyone else.
		6	Universal ethical principles	Individuals will make decisions autonomously based on self-chosen universal ethical principles, such as justice, equality, and rights, which they believe everyone should follow.	A purchasing manager may decide that it would be wrong to continue to buy products or ingredients that were tested on animals because he believes this doesn't respect animals' rights to be free from suffering.

(Maclagan, 1998: 32). (See also Chapter 4 regarding Hofstede's masculine–feminine distinction.)

Pertinent to this book, however, Kohlberg argued that the majority of people function at Stages 3 and 4 of his model (conformity with societal groups and laws), thereby operating at the conventional level of cognitive moral development. This was also supported in Weber's (1990) study of management, cited by Treviño, who observed that *most* business managers operate at the conventional, and not the post-conventional, stage:

> most business managers reason at the conventional level of cognitive moral development... This means that their decisions about what is morally right are highly influenced by what significant others think, say, and do. Thus, business managers are *not autonomous* decision makers who look inside themselves to decide what is right. Rather, they look to relevant others in the social context (e.g., peers, leaders) for cues. (Treviño, 2002: 223, my emphasis)

Importantly, an individual operating at the postconventional level, Kohlberg said, would have awareness that others have different values, and at Stage 6 they would practice what might be regarded as a deontological stance regarding the adoption of universal principles – regardless of context and the majority opinion – even if this means violating the law (Treviño, 1986: 605). These individuals would be reasoning autonomously. This is particularly significant and it implies a strength of character, particularly when we think of large organisations, maybe in the business context, where employees do not operate monadically. Furthermore, cases of employees who cited their independent thought and action were found in the empirical study which is described in Part III of this book – for example, the individual who exhorted co-workers to 'think for yourself' when she overheard racist comments at work (see Chapter 9). Other employees have been observed to exercise their discretion in the pursuit of social responsibility, as evidenced in the study of change agents in the workplace (Drumwright, 1994; Fineman and Clarke, 1996; Menon and Menon 1997; Meyerson, 2001; Wood, 1991). So on the assumption that the majority of employees of a firm may be functioning at the conventional level of cognitive moral development, one might expect those functioning at the postconventional level to be the minority. Nevertheless, this notion of the principled individual has informed the ideas contained in this book, even though CMD was not explicitly part of my investigation. Thus we return to Treviño's social interactionist theory (1986).

The ethical decision making of 215 MBA students and their responses to reward system pressures was empirically tested in an Australian study (Ashkanasay, Windsor and Treviño, 2006). The study examined the participants' levels of cognitive moral development (CMD), their belief in a just world (BJW) and their understanding of organisational norms of reward or punishment. BJW is a belief in justice, whereby the good will be rewarded and the bad will be punished. According to the researchers, people with a high BJW believe that life is fair and that when things go wrong it is their responsibility to change matters. Those with a low BJW are said to 'see themselves as victims of an unjust system' (Ashkanasay, Windsor and Treviño, 2006: 5), comparable to those with an external locus of control (LOC) who believe that they are unable to affect their circumstances (reminiscent of Archer's 'fractured reflexives' – see Chapter 4 below). So whilst BJW and LOC were described as 'theoretically and empirically distinct', the researchers did not explain their preference for testing BJW, and the results were mixed:

for high CMD managers, higher levels of just world beliefs and higher levels of expectancy that the organization condones unethical behaviour both resulted in more ethical decisions. For . . . [low CMD] managers, higher levels of just world beliefs and higher levels of expectancy both resulted in less ethical decisions. There was no effect of just world beliefs or expectancy for the mid-CMD managers. (Ashkanasay, Windsor and Treviño, 2006: 12)

The finding that there was no correlation between BJW and CMD is curious. Indeed, those respondents with *high* BJW and low CMD made fewer ethical choices. Consequently the researchers speculated that the low-CMD managers may well have interpreted 'getting what you deserve' and 'a just world' in terms of opportunism and an attitude of 'every man for himself'. Perhaps LOC would have been a more illuminating measure to use than BJW, if the notion of taking responsibility for one's actions is the common thread between the two concepts. However, in the same study, both Kohlberg's theory and Treviño's (1986) hypothesis that low-CMD individuals would be most influenced by perceptions of a reward or punishment system were supported. Indeed, the respondents were found to have

a propensity to behave unethically if they thought that their superiors at work would condone unethical behaviour. Yet 'high CMD
managers... made even more ethical decisions when they found
themselves in an unethical organisational environment' (Ashkanasay,
Windsor and Treviño, 2006: 13). This finding indicates the possibility of a principled employee using their discretion, regardless
of organisational constraints, and is significant to the subject of
this book about corporate social entrepreneurship. Nevertheless, the
Ashkanasay, Windsor and Treviño study leaves questions unanswered
regarding the underlying motives of the high-CMD managers.[2]

Further to this, Wood, in her conceptual paper, referred to 'principles... [that] motivate human and organizational behaviour' (Wood,
1991: 713). Moreover, there was empirical support for the notion
of the employee as moral agent, taking a different stance from the
'espoused company position'. Here, Harris and Crane highlighted
managers' *personal beliefs* in the adoption and implementation of a
green organisational culture (Harris and Crane, 2002: 227–8).[3] All this
supports Desai and Rittenberg's perspective that it is individual managers who 'often shape the moral environments in which they work'
(Desai and Rittenberg, 1997: 3). But outside management theory the
notion of agency is not just confined to managers (see Archer, 2007).
This implies the necessity to delve further, using different perspectives
found in the social sciences, such as psychology, social psychology and
moral philosophy, to examine ideas of value and prosocial behaviour,
or even altruism.

---

[2] Haidt (2001) provided a robust critique of rationalist decision-making models
in moral psychology, which has received much support in the business ethics
literature (e.g. Treviño, Weaver and Reynolds, 2006; Tenbrunsel and
Smith-Crowe, 2008). Consequently, I have argued elsewhere that the time may
be right for a substitution of CMD in behavioural ethics theory in favour of
personal values. I also advocated a greater use of ethnography to bolster the
current lack of phenomenological insight in this area, in order that scholars can
begin to model behaviour in organisations more accurately (Hemingway,
2012b).

[3] This is not to equate beliefs with values. The latter are described in Part II
below in terms of their nature and structure. A value is more immutable than a
belief and is regarded by some psychologists and sociologists as the core of our
sense of self (Hitlin, 2003).

Personal values and the possibility of altruism

Schwartz and Bilsky stated that there are common threads in all the definitions of values: 'values are (a) concepts or beliefs, (b) about desirable end states or behaviours, (c) that transcend specific situations, (d) guide selection or evaluation of behaviour or events, and (e) are ordered by relative importance' (Schwartz and Bilsky, 1987: 551). As Rescher believed, 'values... manifest themselves concretely in the ways in which people talk and act' (Rescher, 1969: 5). This view of a value as a principle or norm that guides behaviour was supported by Jacob, Flink and Schuchman, (1962), who referred to values as 'the normative standards by which human beings are influenced in their choice among the alternative courses of action they perceive' (cited in Harrison 1975: 117). Indeed, the normative aspect to personal values was endorsed by Hitlin: 'The primary content of a value is the type of goal or motivational concern it expresses' (Hitlin, 2003: 119). Also by Maclagan, who emphasised the subjective nature of personal values: 'if... whatever is of particular importance to people may be of some moral significance to them, then by the same token, person's values, whatever they are, may have some bearing on moral issues as they see them' (Maclagan, 1998: 10).

In this light, we might regard the term 'moral values' as tautological. Now this creates significant implications for many of the business ethics constructs that are preceded with the 'moral' or 'ethical' premodifier, such as moral imagination – or even moral agent – suggesting the potential for value judgements on behalf of some scholars and generating questions of construct validity. So whilst I have described these theoretical and methodological problems elsewhere (Hemingway, 2012), Maclagan's (1998) philosophical insight aligns with the discussion in the introduction about the tremendous difficulties in trying to establish what constitutes organisational moral behaviour.

Even so, managers' personal values have been widely investigated both in general (England, 1967; Lincoln, Pressey and Little, 1982; Bigoness and Blakely, 1996) and in specific contexts, such as in marketing (Fritzche, 1995; Rallapalli, Vitel and Szeinbach, 2000) and corporate social performance (Swanson, 1995; Wood, 1991). Indeed, this body of literature is pertinent to my argument that employees' personal values and their personal interests in a particular social cause can be a

motivating factor for CSR, in addition to other, structural forces such
as corporate strategy. For example, Wilson speculated that 'a new,
younger generation of managers is emerging, educated to the needs of
their fellow citizens and the planet and anxious to do the right thing'
(Wilson, 2002: 8). This echoed the findings of a Conference Board
report (1991) of corporate practices in the US, Canada and Europe:
'Social Responsibility appeared to be internally driven through younger
managers and their families who are making demands on top management that previous generations would never do' (Hoffman, 1993: 16).
Indeed, demand for undergraduate and postgraduate courses in CSR
continues, whilst there has been a wave of cinematic films with a
CSR theme on general release in recent years: *Erin Brockovich, Blood
Diamond, The Constant Gardner, Syriana, The Corporation, Super-
size Me, McLibel*, etc., etc., perhaps reflecting changes in British and
American social values.[4] Arguably, these managers and potential managers reflect changing national expectations of business (Matten and
Moon, 2005). Indeed, Kahle, Poulos and Sukhdial linked personal values and social values very closely, claiming, 'Values are . . . integrally
connected to social change', and 'values are individual representations
of societal goals. As elusive societal goals change, individuals' values
will sometimes lead and sometimes reflect this change' (Kahle, Poulos and Sukhdial, 1988: 35). Thus Giacomino, Fujita and Johnson
referred to cross-cultural studies conducted in the 1970s and 1980s
that showed significant differences between the values of managers in
both an Eastern and a Western work context. The researchers differentiated between managers who valued individuality (in the USA) and
Japanese managers who valued 'socially oriented activity', and found
that the Japanese managers in their study had a 'personal' focus linked
to their moral values, such as honesty and broadmindedness, over
goal-oriented values such as ambition and logic (Giacomino, Fujita
and Johnson, 2000: 15). Interestingly, their research 'suggested an
impending convergence between Eastern and Western work values',
particularly amongst the younger age groups. More ambiguously, the
findings of Bigoness and Blakely were mixed with regard to 'support to both those who believe that values are becoming increasingly

---

[4] The University of Nottingham Business School has successfully incorporated
film screenings into its curriculum for students of CSR (Bondy, Crane and
Browne, 2004).

homogeneous across nations and to those who believe that value differences continue to exist across cultures' (Bigoness and Blakely, 1996: 748). These mixed results in the cross-cultural study of values lead Schwartz to conclude, 'There is substantial agreement about the nature, functions, and content of individual values. This is not the case for culture-level values' (Schwartz, 2011: 313).

However, there may be some evidence to indicate that personal values and possibly social values could be shifting, particularly in the West. For example, Kahle, Poulos and Sukhdial conducted a comparative study of personal values in the USA over a ten-year period and they found a shift: 'more Americans were concerned with a sense of accomplishment and warm relationships with others' (Kahle, Poulos and Sukhdial, 1988: 41). Also in the USA, Macchiette and Roy reported changes in consumer values in terms of 'America's concern with social responsibility', reflected in consumer purchases (Macchiette and Roy, 1994: 63). Indeed, Rescher referred 'to a shift from the Protestant Ethic of "getting ahead in the world" to the social ethic of "service to one's fellows"' (Rescher, 1969: 124). This view was endorsed by Archer (2012), whose longitudinal UK-based study identified a shift from 'autonomous reflexivity', with its emphasis on social mobility, towards a dominant mode of 'meta-reflexivity', characterised by critique of self, market and the state. This shift represents what she described as a new epoch, postmodernity (Archer, 2012), and echoes Inglehart's (1997) thesis regarding a shift from materialist (modernist) values towards 'postmaterialism' and postmodern values. Indeed, the notion of a plurality of social values compares with empirically derived findings regarding the structure of human (personal) values (Schwartz, 2006). And with regard to questions of social change, the growth of 'fair trade' (ethically and sustainably marketed) products in the UK has shown an exponential increase from sales of £195 million in 2005 to £863 million in 2009 and record sales of £1.17 billion in 2010, according to the Fairtrade Foundation. The move by many large consumer brands, such as the confectionary product Kit Kat, to fairly traded ingredients has been attributed to 'rising consumer interest and public pressure'; there is a similar story in the USA, where sales were valued at $1.2 billion for 2009 (Relaxnews, 2011). According to the UK's *Independent* newspaper, 'Fairtrade is on a roll because it is tapping into the public mood. Most people do not want to buy goods with a high social price tag' (Lamb, 2002). Thus, even though 'tapping into the public mood' is precisely what a marketing-oriented company would do, my premise is that not all socially responsible activity by corporations is solely driven by commercial objectives. Moreover, social values are likely to affect corporate values (espoused or otherwise, see the 'Organisational culture' section in Chapter 1), not least because 'employees bring their values [including consumer values] into the work setting' (Robertson, 1991: 120).

Indeed, empirical evidence supports the view that CEOs and senior management tend to establish the ethical norms for corporations (Agle et al., 1999: 507; Desai and Rittenburg, 1997: 796; Robin and Reidenbach, 1987; Treviño, Butterfield and McCabe, 1998). However, it would be nonsense to assume that all employees' values are inherited from senior management, rather like some kind of organisational DNA (Hemingway and Maclagan, 2004: 38). For example, when senior management attempted to impose a new set of organisational values and change the status of a UK college of higher education to that of university status, the change was unsuccessful and 'organisation socialisation' was not found to have taken place (Humphreys and Brown, 2002), hence the earlier discussion, in Chapter 1, of scholarly debate surrounding the possibility of organisational values and an organisational culture. Furthermore, the problems in attempting to distinguish organisational from individual values (and other types of value) and a deeper exposition of the function and structure of values will be discussed in Chapter 4.

Even so, I have emphasised that the empirical study of values is notoriously difficult. Furthermore, Hitlin and Piliavin criticised scholars of sociology for their 'cursory understandings of values, imbuing values with too much determinism or viewing them as too individually subjective' (Hitlin and Piliavin, 2004: 359). Not surprisingly, then, there has been a relatively sparse literature regarding the influence of employees' personal values on the activities of the firm, most notably in the business ethics literature. However, even if a direct link between values and behaviour is hard to find in organisation theory, the 'green' literature has shown that CSR can be the result of *championing* by a few managers, due to their personal values and beliefs, despite the risks (in terms of commercial and subsequent personal outcomes) associated with this (Andersson and Bateman, 2000; Drumwright, 1994; Fineman and Clarke, 1996; Menon and Menon 1997). Moreover, Drumwright's findings showed that *middle managers* were often the socially responsible change agents and that 'the all-out support of top management is not necessarily a requirement for the success of socially responsible buying' (Drumwright, 1994: 17).

The buying behaviour of these change agents was described as 'rooted in a commitment based on a complex and often difficult process of moral reasoning' (Drumwright, 1994: 4). Furthermore, not all of Drumwright's managers were operating in a climate that was sympathetic to socially responsible buying for other than the structural reasons described in Chapter 1 above. Some were 'moving beyond their formal job responsibilities' (Drumwright, 1994: 12), i.e. acting autonomously and using their discretion in the workplace, claiming that they were acting in terms of 'the right thing to do', which also just happened to provide a competitive advantage. One employee confided that her socially responsible values stemmed from her hippy days in the 1960s (Drumwright, 1994: 5). But this subject might have claimed a religious motive, as religion has been linked with philanthropy, one of the domains of CSR (Carroll, 1979).

Indeed, Rice underlined the importance of religious values to international business practice and recommended that business professionals need to examine a firm's religious philosophy, or its 'ideal set of ethics', in order to understand its business culture in practice (Rice, 1999: 356). Moreover, the notion of *Ren* in Chinese religion is translated thus: 'Human-heartedness, or loving benevolence toward other humans; a pivotal ethical notion in Confucianism' (Smart, 1989: 106), and the importance of helping other people less fortunate than oneself can be found in the major religions of Buddhism, Judaism and Islam (Rice, 1999; Smart, 1989: 63). Therefore religious or spiritual values can be viewed as a motivator of philanthropy, or CSR (Pruzan, 2008), although it could also be argued that the religious motive is itself driven by reasons of self-interest, for example to secure a place in Heaven (Christianity), or to practice Karma (Hinduism, Buddhism and Jainism). However, not all 'moral values' are religiously motivated, even though moral teaching is evident in many of the major religions. Also, Rescher differentiated moral values from other categories of values: notably social values, political values, religious or spiritual values and sentimental values (Rescher, 1969: 16). Any one of these categories of values could be a driver of CSR. Furthermore, as motives (and their underlying values) can be mixed in business decisions (Batson, 1989; Di Norcia and Tigner, 2000: 2–3), those

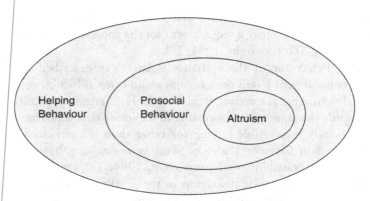

Figure 2.2 The relationship between helping, prosocial behaviour and altruism (Bierhoff, 2002, Psychology Press/Taylor & Francis Group)

motives considered in this chapter, so far, are not seen as mutually exclusive.

However, as pointed out in Chapter 1 above, strategic motives for CSR may be conflated to argue that the motivation for engaging in CSR is always driven by some kind of self-interest (Moon, 2001), such as psychological egoism (Baier, 1993), and that idealism, or altruism, do not have any place in CSR. Psychological egoism can be contrasted with naked self-interest where, for example, people follow a grasping, materialistic path in the organisation's political jungle. Psychological egoism is, in essence, the view that *all* our actions can be traced back to self-interest, for example feeling good (or avoiding guilt) by doing good (Hemingway and Maclagan, 2004), or to the idea of 'emotional contagion', whereby sympathetic behaviour results from our innate drive to understand the other's position, because we see others as extensions of ourselves (Ring, Lipinski and Braginsky, 1965). Once again, the inherent methodological complexity surrounding the notion of complete self-sacrifice is obvious and no doubt is the reason why the business and management literature, including business ethics, seems to find it very difficult to use the A-word (altruism). However, the field of psychology is not so coy.

For example, Bierhoff differentiated between altruism, prosocial behaviour and helping behaviour, although he also used these concepts interchangeably (see Figure 2.2).

Bierhoff described the distinctions thus:

'Helping' is the broadest term, including all forms of interpersonal support. The meaning of 'prosocial behaviour' is narrower, in that the action is intended to improve the situation of the help-recipient, the actor is not motivated by the fulfilment of professional obligations, and the recipient is a person and not an organisation. The term 'altruism' refers to prosocial behaviour that has an additional constraint, namely that the helper's motivation is characterised by perspective taking and empathy. (Bierhoff, 2002: 9)

Indeed, other scholars have identified that altruism does not necessarily imply total self-sacrifice. This is an important alternative perspective, particularly if we apply it to the business context to challenge the dominant notion that all business behaviour is self-interested: 'Altruism is the quintessence of prosocial behavior. When used in its most restricted sense, it denotes self-sacrifice. When more broadly applied, it connotes cooperation, generosity, and helping behavior' (Feshbach and Feshbach, 1991: 190). Certainly, prosocial behaviour and helping others are commonly associated with CSR (see most corporate websites, with their emphasis on their community involvement). Batson (1989) provided further guidance, here, in his exposition of the role of personal values in prosocial motivation (see Chapter 4 below for an expansion on the psychological processes that have been connected with moral sensitivity). Nevertheless, the purpose of the investigation which informed this book was not to empirically establish the existence or not of 'pure' altruism. Instead, the aim was to investigate social responsibility as a subjective state in the form of a small exploratory study. The findings of this study revealed four modalities or modes of moral commitment to CSR. These included corporate social entrepreneurs who were characterised by perspective-taking and empathy and a drive to help others (see Part III).

Therefore, in the second part of this book, the notion of an individual's personal social orientation, or 'other' focus, is discussed in greater depth, in a discussion regarding self-transcendent personal values and the idea of a moral character. At this point, however, I would like to highlight the distinction made by Maclagan (1998) when he differentiated between a social orientation and a service orientation. The former would be someone who simply likes being with people, as in a social situation, an interpretation which was articulated by one of the 'conformist' employees as part of this particular investigation (see Chapter 10 below). Contrastingly, an individual with a sense of duty to others is identified as having a service orientation (Maclagan, 1998: 20). My own presupposition is that a sense of duty is inherent within the description of a social orientation, or the term 'social values'. Thus my argument refers to *an individual who operates at work driven by their dominant personal values, which may, in some cases, take precedence over conflicting situational influences.* Importantly, though, one may infer that CSR driven by personal beliefs would depend upon the amount of autonomy associated with the individual's role in the organisation, or upon the opportunity to influence events through organisational political processes, or 'entrepreneurial discretion' (Hemingway and Maclagan, 2004).

Of course, this discretionary process can enable 'unethical' managers to influence events. My focus, however, is on the exercise of individual choice and the articulation of personal values as a driver of CSR. This, too, was a concern of the economist Milton Friedman, who referred to the idea of a corporate executive engaged in CSR as acting 'in some way that is not in the best interests of his employers', and denounced this as 'spending someone else's money for a general social interest', an argument that continues over forty years later (Friedman, 1970: 3, 4; *The Economist*, 2001). Surely, the crux of this argument is this: we cannot expect *any* employee to completely maximise the profitability of the business. Where is the line drawn with regard to acceptable and non-acceptable costs? Are managerial expenses or the office Christmas party a waste of shareholders' money? This is the domain of corporate governance, which has become even more topical in the light of controversial staff bonuses and the current financial crisis. So my argument is that *personal discretion is used – or a personal agenda will be progressed at work – to some degree.* Nevertheless, regardless of the continuing moral or normative debates regarding the obligations of business, my thesis is that CSR can be driven by well-intentioned, 'ethical' managers (who might be regarded as 'unethical' by supporters of Friedman). And so the concept of agential discretion and its significance will be dealt with more fully in the next chapter, along with the notion of a championing of CSR.

3 | Moral agency and discretion

Duty or disengagement?

In this chapter I set out how the individual's characteristics will influence their formally designated authority at work and facilitate their
use of discretion, thereby producing a degree of autonomy *within* the
confines of the organisation. This leads to a discussion of the controlling mind in social responsibility (or misdemeanour) and motives
for helping. Thus the argument is made for the existence of individual champions of CSR, regardless of whether or not this is formal
policy. However, this is contrary to the notions of amorality and
moral disengagement in business ethics, which have been attributed
to social pressures and conflicting workplace demands. Indeed, social
entrepreneurship may well be motivated by consciously driven political reasons, for personal advancement, in addition to a sense of social
duty. Hence a *single* motive and locus of responsibility for CSR –
the corporation – is called into question, due to the connections
between organisational and individual values.

Employee discretion in corporate social responsibility

So far in this book, I have argued that employees may exhibit their
personal values through CSR, regardless of any formally appointed
role autonomy, although one would anticipate greater role autonomy
higher up the organisational hierarchy. And in describing 'the principle of managerial discretion', Wood quotes Carroll (1979) regarding
managers as 'moral actors': 'A company's social responsibilities are not
met by some abstract organizational actor; they are met by individual
human actors who constantly make decisions and choices, some big
and some small, some minor and others of great consequence' (Wood,
1991: 699). This raises the question that being responsible for one's
own decisions and the use of discretion at work is for what end? Moreover, the notion that managers might not always operate in a rational
manner was identified much earlier by Berle and Means (1932), who

saw a divergence of interests between the ownership and the control of the 'quasi-public corporation'. They gave the example of a manager who might 'maintain labor standards above those required by competitive conditions' for 'reasons of professional pride' and therefore be in opposition to the interests of the owners (Berle and Means, 1932: 124). This was also a concern of Milton Friedman, who worried about executive autonomy and argued that if the executive engaged in CSR, then 'the corporate executive would be spending someone else's money for a general social interest' (Friedman, 1970: 4).

A specific case of the observation and personal use of managerial discretion occurred during my own previous career in marketing management. In a range of different industrial contexts, I witnessed an ad hoc approach with respect to requests for sponsorship and varying degrees of involvement in local community projects. Indeed, I was responsible for my own marketing budget and I once selected the National Society for the Prevention of Cruelty to Children (NSPCC) as the beneficiary of a promotion attached to a packaged branded food product, although I could have selected a commercial partner for, say, a competition, such as a holiday firm or music publisher for giveaways. Here was an example of cause-related marketing (Adkins, 1999), because I justified my choice of promotion on the basis that it would be a win–win outcome for both the charity and my brand and thus my employer. Therefore, regardless of my reasons for taking that particular decision and the likelihood of psychological egoism operating on my part, this example accords with the idea of the agent using their discretion for socially responsible ends (Carroll, 1979; Swanson, 1995; Wood, 1991). But the concept of discretion requires further consideration.

Discretion is defined in the *Oxford Concise Dictionary* as 'the freedom to decide what should be done in a particular situation'. But in an organisational context there may be at least *three* types of discretion: formal discretion, unintended discretion and entrepreneurial discretion. First, formal discretion is where one is explicitly given the authority to use judgement or initiative within broadly defined guidelines, as in the example of my selection of the children's charity as the beneficiary of the on-pack promotion, which was paid for from my marketing budget, when I worked for a publicly listed company. Second, unintended discretion may occur in all sorts of ways, but could be envisaged where there is ambiguity in the language of guidelines and directives (Selznick, 1949: Chapter 2) or, where the individual faces conflicting demands in their role (Frank, 1963; Drumwright, 1994). Third, entrepreneurial discretion is manifest where the individual consciously decides to ignore perceived organisational constraints and goes ahead anyway (Hemingway and Maclagan, 2004: 39). Consequently, whilst there is a case for organisational control, in order to prevent unethical employees abusing their right to act autonomously in their appointed role (see Chapter 4 below), there are still inherent difficulties. Differing degrees of bureaucracy, allied to organisational or departmental culture, or the management style of the line manager and their own personality, will affect the categorisation into types of discretion in this way, i.e. one person's tightly controlled employee may be perceived as a 'loose cannon' by another. Significantly, all three modes of discretion are also potentially linked with CSR, as a result of the relationship between CSR and personal values.

However, if employees do have the freedom to use such discretion with regard to the allocation of resources, or the time to champion CSR, tension and conflict may develop when they wish to support a different 'cause' than has been directed by their manager. Or, other managers may not want to engage in CSR at all. Not everyone will agree on what the 'right' activities are. Indeed, Buono and Nichols observed with regard to corporate social responsibility 'that there is intellectual agreement on many issues of fact, but intense disagreement over priorities' (Buono and Nichols, 1985: 68), thereby supporting the notion described in the introduction to this book that CSR is inherently 'contested' (Moon, 2002: 3). Thus in various ways participation in the organisational political process also allows for influence, which may provide a channel through which personal values can inform CSR. This brings into focus the point that key individuals may be instrumental in formulating and implementing companies' formalised CSR policy, or, its ad hoc CSR activity: 'Corporate social responsibility may be viewed as a process in which managers take responsibility for identifying and accommodating the interests of those affected by the organisation's actions' (Maclagan, 1998: 147).

Once we construe CSR in this manner, the importance of individuals' values and motives is raised again, and in particular, the *corporate* as opposed to the *individual* status of the ensuing initiative is called into question. Thus, in a theoretical framework, two key dimensions were specified for the analysis of CSR in practice (see Figure 3.1).

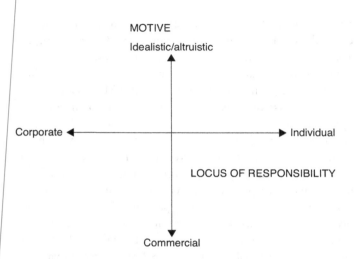

MOTIVE
Idealistic/altruistic

Corporate ◄——————————————————► Individual

LOCUS OF RESPONSIBILITY

Commercial

Figure 3.1 A framework for analysing CSR (Hemingway and Maclagan, 2004)

First, the motivational basis: is this purely commercial, or is it multi-fiduciary or idealistic? Second, the locus of initiative and responsibility: is this corporate (as in the definition of CSR) or individual? Thus the position in the top right-hand quadrant is akin to Kant's ideas of 'purposive' freedom, whereby autonomy allows us to use our judgement to turn away from self-interested behaviour, for the good of humanity. Indeed, Curtis (2001: 4) argued that agency refracts a pre-existing responsibility to other people. Purposive freedom also links with scholarly ideas about the concept of integrity, which is explored in greater depth in Chapter 6 below. Importantly, though, I have already advocated the likelihood of mixed motives (Batson, 1989), and in Part II we see that the individual possesses a combination of individualistic and collectivist values, although particular values might be dominant and operative. Furthermore, I have already asserted that we possess a set of personal values, or personal priorities, which may or may not overlap with organisational values. Thus, on the theoretical basis that CSR functions at the *interface* between business and society (see the introduction to this book), the attribution of a single motive for CSR is reductionist. However, whilst a socially responsible action might be located on Figure 3.1, this may well be context-specific. Furthermore, on the basis of the transitive dimension of knowledge (Archer, 1995; Fleetwood, 2004), one might expect a shift in position over time, as a consequence of the development of knowledge and more widespread CSR education. This will be elaborated further in Part IV.

But my focus in this book is upon the employee as agent, who uses their discretion to champion CSR. Nevertheless, whilst I have equated different types of discretion with the subject's sense of autonomy, the recurring theme of the controversial nature of CSR continues, along with its inherent link to ideas regarding control of – and by – management. Indeed, the motives for CSR have been unpacked in the preceding chapters and so a second important facet of CSR, the locus of responsibility, is now introduced. Nevertheless, it is still tempting to conflate ideas of autonomy with the individual, although this also contrasts with the ideas of the philosopher Hegel, who believed that autonomy could only be achieved through our cultural institutions (Church, 2012). Thus a seemingly paradoxical question is introduced, regarding whether or not we can attribute agency to an institution. Therefore the next section begins by addressing the traditional business ethics debate regarding the possibility of corporate, as opposed to individual, moral agency. This discussion leads to a connection with ideas regarding different levels of values, and then to moral disengagement. As a psychological response to the drive for survival, moral disengagement can occur either consciously as part of organisational politics, or subconsciously, to avoid cognitive dissonance and to preserve the sense of self. I will then return to the idea of a sense of duty to society, citing the whistleblower as an example of a moral agent whose values may not permit moral disengagement in the face of what is perceived to be misdemeanour. Thus we see that arguments for autonomy tend to connect with arguments for control, to prevent either institutions or individuals behaving as they like, to the detriment of others.

Corporate moral agency or human sympathy?

The scholarly debate on corporate moral agency (Ranken, 1987) is closely associated with problems surrounding the culpability of a company in cases of gross negligence or corporate manslaughter. It was summed up like this: 'Corporate moral agency enables the possibility of describing an event in two ways: first the intentional action of the individuals, and second, the intentional action of the corporation for which the individuals work' (Soares, 2003: 145). But corporate guilt is very difficult to establish, particularly if we bear in mind the multifarious nature of a company's internal decision structures

(French, 1979; Moore, 1999). Indeed, UK law in this area is also very complex.

Prior to 6 April 2008, UK law stated the necessity to pinpoint 'a controlling mind', or a senior individual who had breached their duty of care, before a company could be prosecuted under common law for manslaughter. Now the law has changed. But the previous legislation still stands, in cases where it can be shown that conduct or events that contributed to the offence occurred before 6 April 2008. If, however, they occurred on or after this date, then the Corporate Manslaughter and Corporate Homicide Act 2007 (CMCHA) is now applicable:

Therefore if the breach of duty is alleged to have occurred before 6 April 2008, for example where a building has been defectively wired or a person has been exposed to asbestos many years ago, the common law applies. (Crown Prosecution Service, 2013)

This is of great concern to those who claim that governments allow corporations to behave as though they are above the law (Monbiot, 2000). Hence Maclagan (1999: 44) proposed that to establish responsibility in organisations one must 'consider the values, motives and choices' of those who are involved in policy formulation. So where individuals are either involved in misdemeanour, or clearly championing CSR, a question is raised whether attributing these initiatives to the corporation is valid. The key question seems to be this: can a corporation be regarded as a moral agent, as though it has a mind, or can moral action only be acknowledged as the behaviour and responsibility of the individual? Accordingly, Ranken observed,

Whatever qualities we attribute to that artificial being [the corporation], surely it cannot be supposed to have a capacity for human sympathy. It must therefore lack the independent *internal* motivating force which is precisely what we rely on when we speak of a person of good character ... (Ranken, 1987: 635, original emphasis).

Now the philosopher Hegel advocated that institutions had agency and that there is ethical life, or *Sittlichkeit*, within institutions (Neuhouser, 2000). And whilst it is hard to believe that anyone would advocate that institutions have consciousness independently of the people who populate them, Hegel was probably referring to what we understand as the organisational culture when he referred to the ethical life of an institution and the 'types of human intersubjectivity' generated within institutions, where people come together. This is akin to the notion of collective power within organisations (Redding, 2006), i.e. that they are more than the sum of their parts:

A corporation, for example, endures even after particular members of that corporation have moved on and others have replaced them. In some sense, it remains the same corporation. What Hegel calls 'ethical life' (*Sittlichkeit*) is for him embedded in that institution – i.e., is not reducible to the persons. In this way, a particular corporation can be said to have a history, during which it pursued this or that policy, for example, with this or that rationale, which is documented in this or that archive, etc. (Orange, 2007)

Certainly, the influence of organisational – or group – culture on individual behaviour cannot be dismissed (see Chapter 1 above). Therefore, whilst the debate over moral agency has primarily been concerned with responsibility for misdeeds or unethical outcomes, the relevance of this debate with respect to CSR remains. Thus it follows that the idea of 'the controlling mind' can equally be applied in the context of CSR, as it is in the context of corporate misdemeanour. And I have already pointed out that employee discretion in pursuit of a social agenda has also been classed as misdemeanour by some scholars (Baron, 2007; Cespa and CeStone, 2007; Friedman, 1970). But the question remains: what are the drivers behind deliberate acts of misdemeanour, or CSR. Indeed, Victor and Cullen (1988) acknowledged the need for an examination of individuals' ethical behaviour *within the context* of the organisational climate. And so the notion of a locus of responsibility may be unhelpful, due to the difficulties involved in separating out the origin of the belief in CSR, or social value.

The interconnectedness of structure and agency: whose values?

In her discussion of the 'dimensions of values', Scott (2000: 515) highlighted the complexity involved in attempting to answer this question regarding the separation of value ownership. Indeed, for Scott, the meaning of a moral value is situation-specific, determined by the value category (saliency of), agent (level of discretion), object (proximity to), effect and intention (to harm or to help). Moreover, value ownership was addressed by Agle and Caldwell (1999) in their research into values in business. The researchers examined over two hundred papers taken from seven management journals published between 1989 and 1999, plus additional articles cited in the bibliographies, in order to produce a framework based on different levels of values. These levels were identified as individual, organisational, institutional, societal and

global. Institutional values included the 'values of professions, industries, societal institutions such as business, government, and labor, and
so forth' (Agle and Caldwell, 1999: 331). Indeed, the authors argued
for the importance of specifying the precise level of analysis in order to
avoid affecting the validity of values research, and they advocated that
researchers distinguish the *personal values* of those involved with CSR
decision making from *corporate values*. Thus the potential is implied
for a qualitative methodological approach to tease out these nuances,
as opposed to the dominant quantitative methodological approach in
management research.

Nevertheless, epistemological and methodological problems are
intrinsic to any attempt to separate levels or sources of values. This
was indicated in a study of managers' perceptions of a green culture: 'many managers ... are likely to see their change possibilities
constrained by the values underlying the system in which they operate'
(Harris and Crane, 2002: 230), thereby concurring with Solomon's
view: 'It is hard to find a manager who does not feel the pressures
of careerism or suffer some contradiction between obligations to the
company and his or her sense of personal integrity' (Solomon, 1992:
5), or the sentiment that Conscience 'is often the victim of the need to
maintain organisational and personal relationships' (Fisher and Lovell,
2003: 26). These problems are reflected in the management literature,
which has largely ignored the possibility of individual agency and is,
arguably, compounded by the view that some managers may be, or
appear to be, amoral. Indeed, Carroll made a distinction between the
immoral, amoral and moral manager, pessimistically claiming that
'the vast majority of managers are amoral' (Carroll, 1987: 12), arguing for the development of a moral conscience and a 'sense of moral
obligation' amongst managers (Carroll, 1987: 14). However, the
organisational context may require employees to *act* as if they are
amoral and perhaps to behave differently than they might act outside
the workplace (Fisher, 1999; Harris and Crane, 2002; Lovell, 2002a).
This, then, introduces the subject of moral disengagement (Bandura,
1999) or moral myopia.

Moral myopia and muteness

An amoral person may appear to be morally mute. This is said to occur
when an employee decides to keep quiet and not speak out in situations

where they may disagree with circumstances at work that produce an ethical dilemma and when their ability to act as a moral agent is severely compromised, through fear of marginalisation at work, or more serious consequences (Bird and Waters, 1989; Harris and Crane, 2002; Lovell, 2002a). Harrison was pessimistic about the possibility for individual moral agency:

The bulk of the evidence suggests that the values of managers have a strong organizational orientation. Therefore it seems rather doubtful that in the event of a conflict of values, the personal values of the manager would take precedence over organizational values. It is more likely that the manager would accommodate his personal values to the purposes of the organization in such a way as to further his [or her] own aspirations. (Harrison, 1975: 130)

This idea suggests a conscious decision on the part of the employee, for reasons of organisational politics. Indeed, citing Miriam Beard, Walton (1988: 41) referred to managers as 'moral eunuchs'. But moral muteness may also occur for subconscious reasons as part of the sub-ject's personality, such as their levels of field dependency or obedience to authority (see Chapter 2 above). Furthermore, due to the connection between the nature of personal values and emotion (Hitlin and Piliavin, 2004), a rationalised economic argument is arguably easier to articu-late than an alternative position which is connected to a deeper-seated personal value. Or the employee may be oblivious to any particular ethical issue in the first place (Hemingway, 2012; Palazzo, Krings and Hoffrage, 2012).

Hence moral muteness is an important concept, because it implies complicity in unethical situations, regardless of a business context. It was illustrated by social psychologists in both the Milgram experi-ment, with regard to obedience to authority, and the Stanford prison experiment (Zimbardo, Maslach and Haney, 2000). In the Milgram study, the *majority* of subjects delivered the final, lethal electric charge to the 'student' (an actor) when they had been told to do so by the 'professor'. And in the Stanford prison experiment, the good guards failed to report their more brutal colleagues to the researchers in charge of the experiment, their silence making them complicit in the unnec-essarily bad treatment of the poor students who had been randomly selected as prisoners (Zimbardo, Maslach and Haney, 2000). These studies are commonly discussed in business ethics courses to illustrate the compromises of individual morality in situations of social pressure, or group-think (Janis, 1982; Maclagan, 1998: 117). Indeed, 'ordinary' peoples' complicity in atrocity was illustrated in the autobiography of an Auschwitz survivor, described by the book's reviewer:

He is wary of 'generalisations' about the Holocaust, or glib answers to 'how could it happen?' He has seen such atrocities happen again in Europe, and at first hand in El Salvador in the 1980s, working for the United Nations. As in Nazi Europe, the people committing the atrocities were 'for the most part not sadists, but ordinary people'... (Hart, 2009).

So even though the corporate context is banal by comparison with the Holocaust, my point relates to the significance of structural pressure and its influence on human behaviour. Moreover, the desire to be seen to be 'fitting in' with a prevailing amoral organisational culture has been evidenced by management researchers, who have identified the perceived futility of attempting to influence top management to co-operate in a socially responsible manner (Collins and Ganotis, 1973; Lincoln, Pressey and Little, 1982; Lovell, 2002a), or who have found that ethical arguments and moral discourse are 'reframed' into the more commonly accepted commercial language of business organisations (Andersson and Bateman, 2000; Catasus, Lundgren and Rynnel, 1997; Crane, 2000; Crane, 2001; Desmond and Crane, 2004; Fineman, 1996: 488; Lovell, 2002b; Watson, 2003 (see also Chapter 10 in Part III below, where examples of passive behaviour were articulated by the 'conformist' subgroup). Thus it comes as no surprise that the headline-grabbing examples of corporate misde-meanour continue to emerge, if corporations are largely populated by amoralised managers (Carroll, 1987; Crane 1998) in a modern business world that 'places business needs above individual morality' (Hendry, 2004: 181). Indeed, a study of advertising executives found 'significant numbers of practitioners either do not see ethical dilemmas that arise, or their vision is short-sighted' (Drumwright and Murphy, 2004: 7), thereby supporting the idea of moral myopia as opposed to wickedness (Solomon, 1992: 3):

While some people fail to see the moral dimension of problems at all, others have distorted moral vision that results largely from rationalization or from an unwillingness to focus on the problem so that it is seen clearly. The rationalizations contribute to and reinforce the perceptual problem. (Drumwright and Murphy, 2004: 11)

But is the alignment between personal and organisational values the result of the individual's rational choice (Hemingway and Maclagan, 2004: 40)? This introduces the connection between values and emotion and the role of psychological drivers involved with the process of moral agency.

Psychological processes and the relationship with moral sensitivity

In the previous section, the question was posed whether the alignment of personal with organisational values was produced by a conscious, rational choice on the part of the individual, or might it entail a process of subconscious dissonance reduction, whereby individuals may change their beliefs and values as a necessary part of the process of resolving organisational–individual value conflicts (Festinger, 1957; Hemingway and Maclagan, 2004; Lovell, 2002a; Lovell, 2002b)? In such a situation, a degree of anxiety may result from the internal conflict (Leidtka, 1989: 807), and this may be resolved through some kind of justification process and psychological adjustment of personal values. Social psychologists have referred to this as 'negative state relief', whereby prosocial behaviour is believed to be a side effect of egoistic mood management and 'the reduction of unpleasant feelings' (Bierhoff, 2002: 151–3). Thus, in a situation where organisational and personal values are in conflict, the individual can, literally, *re-evaluate* in order to produce a congruency of values and avoid cognitive dissonance, thereby preserving their sense of self (Hitlin, 2003; Rowe, 2009). Such psychological motives were also unpacked in Batson's flow-chart of egoistic and altruistic paths to helping, reproduced as Figure 3.2. Here, Batson proposed two paths based on egoistic motives, and one (Path 3) empathetically evoked altruistic motivation to help. In Path 3, the individual adopts the perspective of the other, in the manner of emotional contagion, which I referred to in Chapter 2).

But what determines the egoistic or altruistic response? Zahn-Waxler (1991) identified feelings of guilt or empathy as facilitators. And for Ranken these emotions are key to our understanding of socially responsible behaviour and therefore morality: 'Must we not respond affectively to the good and harm that comes to others, before we can recognize it as morally relevant?' (Ranken, 1987: 635). However, Feshbach and Feshbach (1991) pointed out that whilst they observed empathy as a mediating process between aggression and

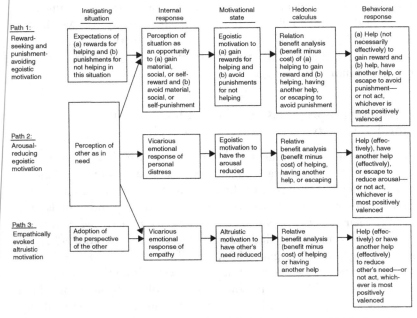

Figure 3.2 Egoistic and altruistic paths to helping (Batson, 1989, Lawrence Erlbaum/Taylor & Francis Group)

altruism in young children, the empathetic response did not necessarily lead to altruistic behaviour. Indeed, Batson also proposed a fourth, deontological motive, whereby the individual internalises the principle of helping:

these people may grow beyond instrumental morality and come to value justice – or mercy or thoughtfulness – not because of the rewards or punishments they anticipate for compliance with this principle (as on Path 1) but as an abstract principle in its own right. If so, then it is the moral principle itself that is valued. (Batson, 1989: 225)

This perspective parallels Kohlberg's postconventional Stage 6 of cognitive moral development, described in Chapter 2.

But in a discussion of CSR or moral disengagement, we need not necessarily assume a conflict of values between the organisation and the employee (Holland, 1985; Siltaoja, 2006). Moreover, an Australian study, Feather (1986) found that schoolchildren were happier and more satisfied with their school than those children whose value priorities were discrepant with those they attributed to the school. And in a management context, Sen and Bhattacharya (2001) cited research indicating that where there is overlap between organisational and employees' values, the employee tends to demonstrate a preference for, and commitment to, that employer. They referred to 'employee identification' thus:

We find that akin to consumers' perceptions of congruity with brands on self-relevant dimensions, their [employees'] perceptions of congruence between their own characters and those of relevant companies (as conveyed by their CSR actions) can also be a source of self-definition. (Sen and Bhattacharya, 2001: 16)

This indicates the importance of a congruency of organisational and individual values with personal identity, which may enhance organisational effectiveness. Indeed, the notion of an individual's 'fit' with their organisation was investigated empirically, whereby personality characteristics (not personal values) and organisational cultural diagnosis were measured by employee self-report, in two different types of firm. These results were tested against co-worker's ratings of their colleagues' influence at work in order to assess the individual's perceived effectiveness (Anderson, Spataro and Flynn, 2008). Thus any congruency between organisational and individual values introduces the notion of authenticity: 'we feel authentic when we behave in keeping with our values' (Hitlin, 2003: 123). It also implies a link between job satisfaction and CSR, which is highlighted at the end of Chapter 6 below in an explanation of integrity.

Despite all this, notions of organisational/individual immorality and amorality, combined with the prevalent examples of corporate misdemeanour, some of which were cited in the introduction to this book, lead us to look for the mechanisms for the control of organisational power (Marcuse, 1969: vii), and also for controls within organisations, in order to prevent individuals from abusing their power (see Mitchell, Agle and Wood, 1997: 863). Indeed, developing the ideas of Nietzsche and Habermas, Foucault regarded power as inherent in our relationships with other people, in terms either of games of power, or of 'the more obvious states of domination', when people abuse their power (Rabinow, 2000: xvii). This is also the domain of the critical management theorists (Legge, 1998; Thompson, 2004). And whilst Foucault's ideas about power and their relevance to management and organisation theory are not my specific focus (see McKinlay and

Starkey, 1998), which presupposes the idea of employees overcoming organisational constraints and working within the boundaries of the system, Foucault's ideas regarding 'the self as a practice of freedom' and moral conscience are pertinent to my argument and are discussed in Chapter 6 below.

This introduces another dimension to the notion of rationality which was discussed above in the context of 'weighing up' a situation which causes moral myopia and the ensuing justification (Anand, Ashforth and Joshi, 2004; Drumwright and Murphy, 2004). Conversely, some scholars regard rationality as an important safeguard against unethical behaviour. Hence bureaucratic management structures have been connected to ideas of rational management and control and the maximisation of efficiency to prevent individuals from pursuing their self-interest (Weber, 1947). However, the Weberian perspective omits the importance of personal values as a mediating force that may produce the *moral sensitivity* advocated by Moberg and Seabright (2000), or, alternatively, misdemeanour. Indeed, Moberg and Seabright argued in favour of a combination of rationality *and* the organisation's sense of community, i.e. 'moral inclusion and perspective-taking' (Moberg and Seabright, 2000: 859), whereby employees may be sensitised towards ethical issues in order for them to critically evaluate appropriate courses of action. Paradoxically, then, amorality has been a criticism levelled at bureaucracy, accusing it of dehumanising the workplace with an 'unhappy separation of reason and emotion, pleasure and duty ... deemed to be inimical to individual liberty, personal responsibility and other "enterprising" virtues' (Du Gay, 2000: 66).

This critique includes the charge in contemporary practical management that a formalisation of procedures and control can stifle the necessary creativity and innovation to produce a sustainable competitive advantage. This produced a shift from the scientific management school, with its emphasis on control, to the human relations school of management, with its ideas regarding flexibility, team-working and empowerment. And to illustrate the apparently dysfunctional nature of the bureaucratic management structure, Hendry referred to Dalton's studies (1959) of American manufacturing firms in the 1940s and 1950s, whereby the inefficiencies of bureaucratic structures frustrated managers to the extent that they had to resort to breaking the rules and being dishonest in order to get the job done. However, other managers began 'to advance their own interests against those of the organisation' (Hendry, 2004: 64).[1]

This brings our discussion back to my fundamental presupposition, that employees (management or otherwise) do not always act rationally in the interests of the shareholders of the company (Berle and Means, 1932; Gabriel, Fineman and Sims 2000). Indeed, Maclagan cited Child, 'who highlighted the arbitrary nature of managerial decisions and organisational strategy' (Maclagan, 1998: 146). This critical perspective was echoed by Soares, who differentiated between corporate goals and 'the temporary, conflicting self-interests of managers and directors' (Soares, 2003: 145). Now, the deployment of organisational politics at work to further one's career, or one's perceived status, has been well documented (Bailey, 2001). The difficulty, though, is in establishing whether those engaged in pursuing a personal agenda are acting solely to increase their own level of perceived power, or whether these employees actually believe that achieving their desired ends will be in the best interests of the organisation (Martin, 2001: 871). Thus an apparent dichotomy between self-interest and helping others is a recurring theme: whether we are examining the corporate motives for CSR, or are questioning an idealistic personal motive, 'much of organizational life, whether we like it or not, is based on self-interest' (Eisenhardt, 1989: 64).

But Silverman's assertion is more nuanced, stating, 'There is a basic conflict between the needs of individuals and the goals of organisations' (Silverman, 1970: 77). And if this *is* the case, then Hendry's view of a 'bi-moral society' – whereby 'we have two conflicting sets of guidelines for living', first a '"traditional morality" of obligation and [second] a "market morality" of self-interest' (Hendry, 2004: 2) – sounds plausible, implying that some people may be driven by a sense of duty (whether to the firm or to a wider society), whilst others may be driven more by self-interest. However, in Part II below I will argue that this apparent values dichotomy is more likely to be the exception than

---

[1] Using a rereading of Marx, Adler (2012) described both the enabling and the constraining functions of bureaucracy. On the one hand bureaucracy can empower employees through their wider participation and empowerment in decision making and fairness through policy and procedure, enabling advancement. On the other hand is Weber's perspective of the 'iron cage', whereby employees are exploited as a result of the bureaucratic system. These realities, argued Adler, produce employee ambivalence towards bureaucracy.

the rule, and that one would more realistically expect the majority of individuals who champion CSR at work to be driven by a combination of motives (Batson, 1989). But exceptions were also found as part of the exploratory investigation which was conducted as part of this study. In other words, the outcome of a 'rational' justification can produce any outcome across a range of behaviours, from passivity to prosocial or antisocial behaviour (Hemingway, 2012).

Further to this, the notion of cognitive scripts or schema have been discussed in the business ethics literature in the context of moral myopia and unethical behaviour (Gioia, 1992). Indeed, Hitlin (2003) cited Schwartz (1996) with regard to 'scripted responses' being employed in the absence of a conflict of values. Moreover, support for the 'altruistic self-scheme' (i.e. altruistic self-concept) has been described in the social psychology literature (Bierhoff, 2002: 96). Hence psychological processes can produce a moral orientation (Maclagan, 1998: 21), which will be perceived by others in terms of immorality, amorality or morality. And my contention is that our guidelines for living, referred to by Hendry (2004), or our personal concerns which give us our personal identity (Archer, 2012), equate to our personal values. These were introduced in Chapter 2 above, within the context of agential drivers of CSR. So this is a thesis about the power of agential reflexivity, and my point is this: that the employee's level of involvement in CSR will *always*, in part, be determined by their own personal values.

Now our discussion has returned to the idea of the contested nature of CSR, in terms of whether it is inherently driven by self-interest or by Hendry's notion of the traditional morality of obligation and thus the controversial relationship with business. In support of the latter multi-fiduciary perspective on CSR, Handy normatively advocated 'the quest for a purpose in our own lives ... the quest has to be an attempt to leave the world a little better than we found it ... Our duty to others is founded on our duty to ourselves' (Handy, 1998: 63). This is achieved via 'proper selfishness', whereby

we are inevitably intertwined with others ... it's proper to be concerned with ourselves and a search for who we really are, because that search could lead us to realize that self-respect, in the end, only comes from responsibility ... for other people and other things. (Handy, 1998: 86)

But this is not an original perspective. Indeed, Hendry's concerns regarding the decline of the traditional morality of obligation were articulated much earlier by Tawney, when he rallied against the withdrawal by both the state and the church in the eighteenth century, which, he said, had previously maintained 'a common body of social ethics'. This resulted in 'a decline of [social] purpose' in favour of 'the growth of private rights and private interests . . . so that government passed into the lethargic hand of classes who wielded the power of the State in the interests of an irresponsible aristocracy' (Tawney, 1926: 12). Thus, with the onset of the Industrial Revolution, the rights of the individual became paramount and service to society became 'a secondary consequence' (Tawney, 1926: 23). The result, he said, was our 'acquisitive society', whereby rights are deemed to be more important than duty. A society based on a sense of duty as opposed to rights, however, would be a 'functional society'. And so in the wake of the global financial crisis and renewed debate about the role of capitalism, Tawney's ideas may be regarded as premonitory. Hence, having a sense of obligation may explain the existence of the whistleblower (Miceli, Near and Dworkin, 2008; Stansbury and Victor 2008), assuming that he or she is driven by a sense of moral outrage and social duty, although there is also the possibility that the whistleblowing has been wholly or partly prompted by a desire for revenge due to personal disappointment. Therefore the employee's sense of autonomy to use their discretion and to take responsibility for progressing a social agenda at work, will be considered next.

PART II

Personal values and corporate social entrepreneurship

4 | The relationship between personal values and behaviour

Personal values have been acknowledged as important components in the process of human perception (England 1967), not least because of their connection to our our emotions and our social norms (Jacob, Flink and Schuchman, 1962). This indicates the significance of values as an integral facet of human decision making (March and Simon, 1958: 11). In what follows, a value is defined as a cognitive structure which combines with our emotion and plays a pivotal role in our decision making and subsequent actions. Here we see parallels with personality characteristics, although personal values are defined by scholars as standards of conduct. This connects the study of value with ideas about morality, including virtue ethics theory. Moreover, some scholars differentiate between a personality characteristic or trait and a personal value on the basis of what is thought to be the more enduring nature of personality compared with values. This is a moot point, however, with relatively little empirical investigation of values in business and management compared with the vast literature on personality. Furthermore, a personal value, or standard of conduct, is thought to function as part of our survival mechanisms, driving behaviour as an expression of the self and *also* in the interest of the welfare of the group. Hence the notion of individualistic and collectivistic values emerges in both psychology and sociology. However, whilst the individual is likely to possess a combination of values, the idea of either *dominant* individualistic or collectivistic values that emerge in particular circumstances has significant support in the social psychology literature. Importantly, though, values are not immutable and *re-evaluation* as a result of our experiences seems to occur in some individuals: a phenomenon which was reported by some of the subjects who participated in the empirical part of this investigation (see Part III). Nevertheless, the incommensurability of value, in terms of difficulties in interpretation and measurement, compounded by the notion of values operating at different levels, is noted in this chapter.

Defining personal values

The study of value has traditionally had its roots in philosophy as the study of axiology. It can be traced back to the teachings of Socrates, Plato and Aristotle in the form of virtue ethics (O'Hear, 2000; Raz, 2003). In this context, values have been described as: 'things of the mind that are to do with the vision people have of "the good life" for themselves and their fellows' (Rescher, 1969: 5). Moreover, adopting the ideas from ancient philosophy, Wojciszke (1989) connected personal values with the concept of the ideal self and Wright described values 'that define the positive goals in life' (Wright, 1971: 201). Thus we can regard a personal value as a standard of conduct: 'A value is a conception, explicit or implicit, distinctive of an individual or characteristic of a group, of the desirable, which influences the selection from available modes, means, and ends of action' (Kluckhohn, 1951: 395; see also Meglino and Ravlin, 1998). Indeed, Rokeach (1973) was unequivocal regarding the antecedent influence of values on behaviour:

To say that a person has a value is to say that he has an enduring prescriptive or proscriptive belief that a specific mode of behavior or end-state of existence is preferred to an opposite mode of behavior or end-state. This belief transcends attitudes toward objects and toward situations; it is a standard that guides and determines action, attitudes toward objects and situations, ideology, presentations of self to others, evaluations, judgments, justifications, comparisons of self with others, and attempts to influence others. Values serve as adjustive, ego-defensive, knowledge, and self-actualizing functions. (Rokeach, 1973: 25)

Hence Hitlin and Piliavin (2004) added that values give meaning to action. These perspectives denote the normative role of values and indicate that our dominant personal values represent our ideas about morality, which links back to the discussion in the introduction to this book about the contested nature of CSR. Moreover, in the previous chapter regarding moral duty and moral disengagement, I described personal values as an (overlooked) agential power that constrains and enables socially responsible activity at work, because they play a key role in 'directing behavioral choices' (Wojciszke, 1989: 248).[1] Indeed,

---

[1] Note that Archer's disenfranchised fractured reflexives supported Wojciszke's (1989) view that not *everyone* has a working personal value system that motivates their behavioural choices.

there is substantial empirical support from the psychology literature regarding the pivotal role of values in attitude formation and our subsequent behaviour (Agle and Caldwell, 1999; England, 1967; Lusk and Oliver, 1974; Williams, 1979). And even though the early axiologists did not differentiate between a value and an attitude (Rescher, 1969: 51), scholars now estimate that whilst we hold thousands of attitudes, there are just forty to sixty personal values (Rokeach, 1973: 11; Hitlin, 2003). These are formed as a result of reward, punishment or deprivation, primarily from our parents (Williams, 1979; Wright, 1971), but they may be modified or reordered as a result of our reflections on our experience (Archer, 2012; Hitlin and Piliavin, 2004).

This implies that our personal values can function as a heuristic device or decision-making shortcut (Fisher and Lovell, 2003: 113). Hence senior managers were observed to be mediating green stakeholder influence by applying their 'interpretive frames' (Fineman and Clarke, 1996: 727), and also personal values were seen to operate as important determinants for top management in their choice of corporate strategy (Guth and Tagiuri, 1965; Olson and Currie, 1992). Indeed, the function of values as a behavioural catalyst has also been observed via studies of the personal choices of respondents with regard to a wide variety of activities, such as choice of occupation (Guerrier and MacMillan, 1981), or the propensity to cheat. Empirical studies described how some union leaders had different values to managers, whilst common sets of values were found amongst different groups of people such as church attendees, students who cheated in examinations and anti-Semites (Rokeach 1973; Williams, 1979). Furthermore, predictions regarding both managers' success at work and also their ethical behaviour at work were found to be reliable (England, 1973).[2] Nevertheless, it is important to point out that our values are not the sole antecedents of our actions: they connect to our emotion and combine with other motives (Hitlin and Piliavin, 2004: 380). Indeed, some scholars have cautioned against overemphasising the predictive nature of values and ignoring the influence of other determinants of behaviour, such as (structural) environmental influences (England, 1967; Hitlin, 2003; Meglino and Ravlin, 1998; Williams 1979: 28).

---

[2] In England's (1973) study, nineteen out of twenty-five predictions about how managers with certain values could be expected to behave at work were supported by the data.

Furthermore, the function of our values, in motivating the individual to 'achieve satisfactions and avoid dissatisfactions' (Rescher, 1969: 9), has been attributed by scholars as a survival mechanism through defining the sense of self and also in terms of group welfare. The self-identity function of values is discussed next.

Values and personality: self-identity function

Human beings are driven to re-enforce their sense of identity (Erikson, 1994; Piliavin, 1989), and values function in this process of defining and redefining our sense of self: protecting and enhancing our self-esteem (Rokeach, 1973; Wright, 1971). Indeed, using the Schwarz values instrument (Prince-Gibson and Schwartz, 1998), Hitlin found values to be a predictor of identity, describing them as at the core of self-identity, which is affected by and affects social identity: 'Our values lead to experiences of personal identity, which in turn lead to reflexive constructions of various role-, group-, and value-identities' (Hitlin, 2003: 122). He also referred to 'situationally relevant identitites' as an intermediary force that affect behaviour, rather than there being a simple cause-and-effect relationship between values and behaviour (Hitlin, 2003: 128). Indeed, the connection between personal values and the identity confirmation of the self was also articulated in the management literature by Watson:

For any individual to give an account of themselves and their life, they are bound to give some indications of what values they hold or, in so far as these may differ, what values they wish to be seen as holding by those they are addressing. To say who you are is closely related to saying what it is you 'believe in'. (Watson, 1994: 74)

But the idea that identity is simply a 'presentation' of the self was heavily criticised on epistemological grounds by Margaret Archer, who attacked this traditional view of identity as reductionist:

Goffman intrigued us for two decades with the outer doings of his feisty subject, who insouciantly disported himself in the interstices of society. But the presentation of the self was all about presentational acts in everyday life and the account was confined to these public outworkings, for the shutters came down on the self whose inner deliberations generated these performances. Goffman left us with two questions. How could subjects perform socially with such virtuosity if society were merely a stage-setting for the conduct of their private business, and who was the mysterious self who could set up and impose this private agenda? His origins, properties and powers remain immured behind the brick wall. Goffman owed us an account of the self, but left the bill unpaid, for the sources of the self remained completely shrouded. (Archer 2000: 317)

For Archer, it is the agential power of reflexive deliberation which produces the subject's modus vivendi. And through her empirical investigation, she discovered that, in late modernity, the subject's self-image need not necessarily result from the responses of others to our actions (Archer, 2012; Piliavin, 1989). Thus, for Archer, *our sense of self is more than our social identity.* It is continually tested in a 'morphogenetic sequence' until we find a role in life that we find worthwhile and that satisfies us. This is not simply a case of accepting what life throws at us; it is the dynamic human *process* of engaging with the natural, practical and social orders 'in which structure conditions agency, and agency, in turn, elaborates upon the structure which it confronts' (Archer, 2000: 306). This may result in 'unscripted role performances' which, in time, may change role expectations.

For example, Archer referred to the aloof professor of the past who nowadays might be considered by some to be poor at his or her job, on the strength of this. A similar anecdotal point was made about British general practitioners, referred to as 'the arrogant and unconcerned conventional doctors one used to come across thirty years ago' (Bennett, 2005: 603), and might also be applied to the police and other authority figures in the UK, whose role may be seen to have changed over the years. To ascribe this role modification simply to public sector attempts to adopt a business model and move towards 'a customer focus' would be to deny that some people are personally motivated to be helpful towards others at work, also that '"structure" and "agency" are distinct strata of reality' (Archer, 2003: 2). Thus, according to Archer, we are 'quintessentially evaluative beings', a view of identity that gives a far greater weight to the force of agency than is found in management theory. For example, Fiol described identity as 'peoples' understanding of themselves in relation to the system/s' (Fiol, 1991: 200). Yet it is possible for us to understand ourselves *despite* the system, a practice which is advocated through meditation and/or prayer in much Eastern and Western religious philosophy. Hence the importance of reflexivity as a mechanism for agency is revisited in Chapter 6 below.

The effects of CSR on employee identity were described by Gurney and Humphreys (2006) in their study of Laskarina Holidays. Drawing upon Sheth, Newman and Gross's (1991) categories of value, the researchers observed that the employee is 'a fully fledged consumer in search of meaning and self-fulfilment' (Gurney and Humphreys, 2006: 85). Here we see a marketing perspective, whereby a product (or service, in this case) comprises tangible and intangible attributes that constitute a 'bundle of benefits' in the mind of the consumer. According to buyer behaviour theory, the same psychological processes will occur regardless of the stakeholder status of the individual, as part of human cognition. So from this perspective, the reputation of Laskarina Holidays for 'social and environmental initiatives' (Gurney and Humphreys, 2006: 88) constituted the intangible elements of brand image, generated by the cognitive associations produced as a result of the activities of the company. In this particular case, the value was derived by employees.[3]

Other scholars have emphasised structural forces that constrain the employee as agent. For example, Marxist-inspired scholars have blamed capitalism for damaging modern subjectivity. And within this perspective, we might judge unethical employees (perhaps stealing from their employer, or making the case for an excessive bonus) as consumers seeking to satisfy their desire for enjoyment through expensive consumer products, in order to feed their unattainable sense of fulfilled identity (Böhm and Batta, 2010). This also accords with the idea of self-selection and employment (Holland, 1985), whereby individuals choose a career, or select a specific industry or vocation, that reflects their own personal values. For example, Baron (2005) argued that corporations may employ and train individuals who want to address social issues through their work: a notion evidenced by the targeting and recruitment of the University of Warwick's sociology graduates by the global investment banking and securities firm Goldmann Sachs, for their highly lucrative positions based in the City of London. See also the introduction to this book regarding the arguments whether this recruitment policy might be an attempt at a public relations 'whitewash', or part of a long-term strategic move on the part of

---

[3] See Keller's (1993) model of customer-based brand equity, whereby the reputation or first-hand experience of a brand can create both positive and negative associations in the mind.

the company to develop a more socially responsible corporate culture from within.

Furthermore, self-*esteem* requires that we continually *validate* or confirm our values. Meglino and Ravlin cited the work of Kluckhohn (1951): 'any actions that are inconsistent with these values will result in feelings of guilt, shame, or self-depreciation ... Thus individuals will exhibit value-related behavior in private in order to avoid negative internal feelings' (Meglino and Ravlin, 1998: 356).

Worse, compromises made as a result of external pressure may result in damage to our sense of personal identity (Archer, 2000: 305), although this is not to suggest that we are necessarily and consciously 'in touch' with what our values actually are. Indeed, it has been suggested that managers are unlikely to have articulated them (Sull and Houldner, 2005). Hence it is worthwhile, at this point, to distinguish between values, desires, attitudes, personality characteristics or traits, and our beliefs. The distinction may lie in the relative robustness of our desires, attitudes, personality characteristics or personal values, or how deeply held they are within the psyche.

According to Frankfurt, animals have what he called 'first-order' desires to act, but only humans have 'second-order' desires and volitions, the volition being the mechanism to act which is mediated by emotional feelings of guilt or conscience (Frankfurt, 1988). Archer equated this distinction with our ability to be reflexive: i.e. the strongest urge does not necessarily prevail (Archer, 2003: 29), unless in the case of very young children, or the subgroup of people called the 'fractured reflexives' (Frankfurt called them 'Wantons'): unfortunates who are unable to be reflexive and thereby do not possess the drive to cope with life. Thus our personal values are not to be confused with our desires. According to Frankfurt, our desires may be overruled by our behaviour, for example in a 'Type A situation', where we would blame our external circumstances for our behaviour and feel that we had no choice but to act (Frankfurt, 1988: 48). And so I equate our personal values with what Archer referred to as our ultimate concerns, evolved via our ability to be reflexive (Archer, 2000; Archer, 2003). They are more deeply rooted than our desires and are connected to our emotions (Michie and Gooty, 2005; Schwartz, 2010), and thus provide the *reason* for the first-order desire to act, or the reason for the second-order volition (our sense of 'better judgement'). This is distinct from the more salient desire, or want, which is also instrumental to our behaviour and also value-expressive; so, too, the subject's attitude towards an object and is instrumental to an act, or the intention to act

Values focus on ideals; attitudes are applied more to concrete social objects ... The general consensus is that values hold a higher place in one's internal evaluative hierarchy than attitudes. Compared with attitudes, values are more central to issues of personhood ... and are less *directly implicated* in behavior ... [Moreover,] values are more durable than attitudes. (Hitlin and Piliavin, 2004: 361, added emphasis; see also Fishbein and Ajzen, 1975: 15)

With regard to personality characteristics or traits, Jacob, Flink and Schuchman (1962) conceptualised personal values as components of personality. More recently, however, scholars have distinguished values from personality characteristics:

Personality is an 'individual's characteristic patterns of thought, emotions, and behavior' ... Compared with values, which can evolve over time ... personality indicates more stable patterns of behavior ... Further, personality traits are observable and are used to predict future behavior ... Indeed ... personality may be more observable than values are. (Anderson, Spataro and Flynn, 2008: 704)

Further refinement was provided by Hitlin and Piliavin (2004), in suggesting the differences between personality traits and values: 'Traits are enduring dispositions; values are enduring goals. Traits may be positive or negative; values are considered primarily positive' (Hitlin and Piliavin, 2004: 361). The implication here is that whilst both attitudes and values are subject to change, (Fishbein and Ajzen, 1975; Rescher, 1969: 139), attitudes are likely to be less robust than personal values, i.e. less deeply held (Hitlin, 2003). Norms, which are often equated with beliefs, are likely to be even more transient than attitudes (Wojciszke, 1989). Thus in the empirical investigation of corporate social entrepreneurship, which is discussed in Part III below, I have distinguished personal values and personality traits. So whilst I have cursorily identified some of the distinctions between the various psychological elements that affect motivation, it is the *combined* effect of these various forces on our behaviour that is important. And in returning to the role and strength of our personal values in self-identity, a significant methodological difficulty for the empirical study of values is apparent, resulting in fewer behavioral studies of values compared with other psychological constructs (Hitlin and Piliavin, 2004: 361). This incommensurability of values is important and consequently is discussed further over the next two sections, first in terms of values operating at different personal levels (in addition to the idea of different macro levels that was introduced in Chapter 3), and second in terms of different ideas regarding how values are structured.

However, in addition to reinforcing our self-image, the moral nature of values causes them to function 'in the interests of society' (Rokeach, 1973: 9), and so it is this second purpose of our personal values which is discussed in the next section, specifically the notion of values that serve self-interest and those which may serve a social welfare function. And it is these 'other'-oriented, or collectivist, values that are of particular interest here as an overlooked driver of CSR.

Group survival function: self-enhancement (or individualistic) values and self-transcendent (or collectivist) values as theoretical opposites

Nietzsche's central thesis was that the psychological drive to esteem and value objects is linked with our 'will to power' and self-preservation, which he said was the essence of the human condition. But in addition to self-enhancement, psychologists have ascribed a social function to personal values: 'Values are cognitive representations of three types of universal human requirements: biologically based needs of the organism, social interactional requirements for interpersonal coordination, and social institutional demands for group welfare and survival' (Schwartz and Bilsky, 1987: 551). Thus a dual purpose to the function of values emerges: enhancement of the sense of self, which was discussed in the previous section, and also the welfare of others. What ostensibly appears, to some, to be a dichotomy of personal values is significant, although I will elaborate how the dichotomous perspective is incomplete. This is the notion of values as individualistic (self-oriented) or collectivist (other-oriented). In support of this apparent duality, Rokeach described values as having either a personal focus or a social focus, and as self-centred or society-centred (Rokeach (1973): 9). Also, England (1973: 84) referred to values as being individualistic or group-oriented, with 'hard' (such as aggressiveness, achievement, competition) and 'soft' values (such as tolerance or compassion). And Meglino and Ravlin referred to 'people with high concern for others' (Meglino and Ravlin, 1998: 375).

However, the terms individualistic and collectivistic values return this discussion to the potential for confusion regarding the *ownership* of a value. This problematic aspect of the study of values was identified in the last chapter by way of reference to Agle and Caldwell's (1999) meta-analysis of research on values in business and is elaborated further below. Is the locus of responsibility for the action a result of values operating at the macro, meso or micro levels? This problem regarding the ownership of a value is exacerbated if the terms individualistic and collectivistic have differing connotations. Indeed, Kim et al. (1994) identified that individualism and collectivism dimensions (I-C) have been adopted in both psychological and sociological studies. For example, Hofstede's seminal study into cross-cultural values identified nations with a relative emphasis on either individualistic or collectivistic values:

'Individualism' pertains to societies in which the ties between individuals are loose: everyone is expected to look after himself or herself and his or her immediate family. 'Collectivism' as its opposite pertains to societies in which people from birth onwards are integrated into strong, cohesive groups, which throughout people's lifetime continue to protect them in exchange for unquestioning loyalty. (Hofstede, 1980: 51)

Indeed, the incommensurability of values is evident if we look at family security as an example. Hofstede regarded family security as a facet of individualism. Contrastingly, Schwartz and Bilsky's (1987) comparative study (using teachers and student teachers in both Germany and Israel) identified the value of family security as collectivistic. In fact, Schwartz and Bilsky (1987) incorporated both Rokeach's (1973) personal-values instrument and Hofstede's (1980) interpretation of I-C into the development of their own values instrument, which was used in their cross-cultural study of personal values. Schwartz and Bilsky (1987) described the I-C dimension as the 'interests served' of a value. Here, the values of *ambition*, or *pleasure*, were connected with an individualistic interest, whereas *responsibility* or *helpfulness* served the collectivist interest. Other values, such as *wisdom*, function to serve both types of interest (Schwartz and Bilsky, 1987: 551). However it is Schwartz and Bilsky's 'motivational domain' of a value that is of particular significance.

Schwartz and Bilsky's six motivational domains (goals) of personal values encompassed the human drives for enjoyment, achievement, self-direction, restrictive conformity, maturity and the prosocial. The last domain was described as 'a positive, active concern for the welfare of others' (Schwartz and Bilsky, 1987: 552) and encompassed Rokeach's personal standards of helpful, forgiving and loving, and goal of equality. Thus, for Schwartz and Bilsky, collectivistic values included the three motivational domains of security and restrictive conformity, as well as the prosocial values. The I-C distinction might also be compared with the two character orientations of 'having' and 'being', whereby 'having' is a concern for acquisition, possessions and display of status, whereas 'Being entails the abandonment of egocentricity, selfishness and the desire for possessions . . . an ethic of responsibility' and 'some concern for others, a tendency towards altruism' (Maclagan, 1998: 72).

It is also interesting to note that Hofstede declared that he had *not* identified altruism as a feature of collectivism in the cultural context. Instead, countries with more 'feminine' characteristics, on his masculine–feminine dimension (characterised by, for example, nurturing and an emphasis on relationships), would be more appropriate, he said:

there is no relationship between cultural collectivism and altruism, as some researchers have postulated. Collectivism is not altruism, but in-group egoism. In a collectivist society, a poor relative can expect to be helped, but not necessarily a poor stranger. Whether a stranger can expect to be helped depends on the society's degree of 'femininity'. The Good Samaritan does not represent the collectivist society, but the feminine one. (Hofstede, in Kim et al., 1994: xiii)

Indeed, the altruistic dimension was investigated as part of a later study of cross-cultural values, conducted in individualistic countries that differed in their masculinity (Canada and the USA) and femininity (Norway and Denmark). The researchers also added the additional variable of gender. Charity advertising messages were shown to business school students and tested for any gender differences in the two with regard to two aspects: First, whether the students felt more motivated by an egoistic appeal ('the desirability of donating money that will benefit oneself as well as helping others'), or an altruistically oriented advertisement ('the desirability of helping or benefiting others in need'). Second, the study aimed to establish the students' perceptions as to where the moral obligation for charity should lie. Should the charity message be aimed at individuals or at the government? The mixed results challenged the idea of gender stereotypes and supported the idea of variability within cultures:

> members of individualist cultures will prefer self-focused appeals, whereas those in collectivist cultures will prefer other-focused appeals. Similarly, research on gender often assumes traditional sex roles for women and men. Findings show that women across cultures prefer other-focused or altruistic appeals and men prefer self-focused or egoistic appeals . . . our research challenges these views. (Nelson et al., 2006: 53)

However, as part of their discussion, Nelson et al. also acknowledged the cultural differences between Europe and the USA regarding perceptions of individual or state responsibility for social provision (Nelson et al., 2006: 45), believed to have affected the responses. This facet of CSR was discussed earlier, in the introduction to this book. Hence, and in support of the idea of mixed motives (e.g. Batson, 1989; Di Norcia and Tigner, 2000; and Schwartz and Bilsky, 1987: Chapter 2), Hofstede later addressed the critique that his research had categorised nations as either individualistic or collectivistic. And he agreed that at the psychological level (as opposed to the sociological level of his own research) individuals can possess both individualistic and collectivistic values. He also said, 'I found that a single, bipolar, dimension is a useful construct (that is, conceptual tool) for subsuming a complex set of differences' (Hofstede quoted in Kim et al., 1994: xi). Thus, at the individual or psychological level, Hofstede recommended that a multidimensional model of individualism–collectivism (I-C) would be preferable to a unidimensional one. This more nuanced approach parallels the discussion in Chapter 3 above (see Figure 3.1) regarding the motivation and the locus of responsibility for CSR.

At this point, it is necessary to highlight uncertainty with regard to age (and/or life stage) as antecedent factors in the deployment of collectivistic values. For example, in the Nelson et al. (2006) study which was described above, students – as opposed to more experienced subjects – were surveyed for the purposes of establishing gender or culture differences in a self- or other-orientation. But this may not be appropriate for investigation into corporate social entrepreneurship. For example,

Hitlin's empirical study into personal identity (discussed in the previous section) found 'that younger volunteers tend to be motivated more strongly by interpersonal relationships than by a sense of obligation to the community (which motivates older volunteers)' (Hitlin, 2003: 132). Moreover, Jacob, Flink and Schuchman referred to 'the modification over time of patterns of values and beliefs . . . the capacity for change seems to vary among individuals and according to age . . . [and a] congealing of values and beliefs as the person grows older' (Jacob, Flink and Schuchman, 1962: 26). Indeed, Rokeach (1979) described a change in values with age from the instrumental values (means) to the terminal (ends). And in their meta-analysis of values research, Hitlin and Piliavin declared, 'There is some evidence for age-graded systematic changes in value structure' (Hitlin and Piliavin, 2004: 374). So taking into consideration the concept of cognitive moral *development* (see Chapter 2 above) and the notion of a mature and more sophisticated character (see Chapter 6 below), these theoretical perspectives indicate that the use of students as a proxy for managers in values research might be a compromise too far: 'results of a study on volunteerism indicate that the motives of younger and older volunteers may differ, with older volunteers being more altruistically motivated' (Bierhoff, 2002: 72; see also Hemingway, 2012). Hence the literature on personal values indicates that investigation into the nature of the relationship between personal values and CSR would have enhanced validity by using actual employees in their corporate context as opposed to using student subjects. On the other hand, Schwartz declared, 'People form values in adolescence that change little thereafter' (Schwartz, 2006: 6) – see Chapter 7 below for a discussion of the methodology which was adopted for my own exploratory investigation into corporate social entrepreneurship. Consequently, I return to the notion of other-oriented or collectivistic values, which was introduced, above, with reference to the work of Shalom Schwartz, and the six motivational domains of values (Schwartz and Bilsky, 1987).

Prince-Gibson and Schwartz (1998) increased the motivational domains from six to ten. They also replaced the interests-served categories of values (I-C) by two dimensions: (i) openness to change and conservation and (ii) self-enhancement and self-transcendence. This is illustrated by Figure 4.1, known as the Schwartz values theory.

It is an important theory, which reflects substantial empirical support for 'ten motivationally distinct value orientations that people in

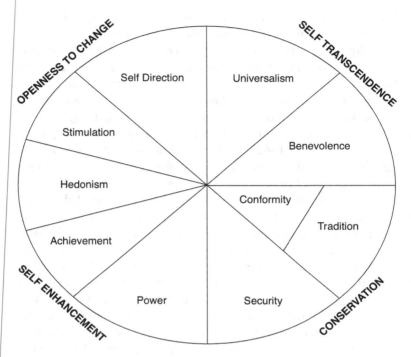

Figure 4.1 Schwartz's (2010) theoretical model of relations among motivational types of values (reprinted with permission from the American Psychological Association)

all cultures recognise' (Schwartz, 2006: 1) and that are 'dynamically related to one another' (Schwartz and Bilsky, 1987: 561).

The circular structure in [Figure 4.1] portrays the total pattern of relations of conflict and congruity among values postulated by the theory. The circular arrangement of the values represents a motivational continuum. The closer any two values [are] in either direction around the circle, the more similar their underlying motivations. The more distant any two values, the more antagonistic their underlying motivations. (Schwartz, 2006: 2)

Thus the self-transcendence values appear in direct opposition to the self-enhancement values (comprising the values of achievement and power). Here, self-transcendence encompasses the motivational domains of universalism and benevolence and is conceptually aligned with the notion of social responsibility. Benevolence is defined in terms of values that 'preserve and enhance the welfare of those with whom one is in frequent personal contact', and 'universalism' as 'tolerance and concern for the welfare of all others'.[4] So self-transcendence 'reflects a preference to achieve the welfare of a broad social group even at the expense of personal well-being versus self-enhancement motivated to achieve personal self-interest at the expense of the welfare of others' (Lan et al., 2007: 124).

Consequently, the notion of self-transcendence is of particular interest to this discussion of corporate social responsibility, where we might expect employees who are motivated to perform some social good to be driven, in part, by their other-oriented values. Of course it is a matter for debate whether or not those with such an orientation are driven by a genuine concern for others, or whether the altruistic drive is purely a function of self-interest. Indeed, I have been arguing throughout this book that one would not expect an either/or situation in terms of an individual possessing solely self- or other-oriented values. Moreover, Maclagan refuted Kluckhohn's idea (1951) of 'a simple dichotomy between altruistic good and egoistic evil' (Maclagan 1998: 29) which was discussed in the context of mixed motives in Chapter 2 above. Furthermore, this notion precisely parallels another conflationary perspective which conceptualises CSR as either market fundamentalism (theory of the firm) or multi-fiduciary duty (see the introduction to this book). It may also encourage a reductionist attribution of value to either structure or agency. However, my thesis is that the deployment of an individual's dominant values produces a context-dependent moral orientation, although a general predisposition towards either self or others might be observable (Hemingway, 2005; Hemingway, 2012; Rosenthal and Buchholz, 2002). Nevertheless, the Schwartz values theory indicates that a sense of our social duty is as much part of the human condition as is self-preservation. Indeed, other social psychologists, such as Bandura (1999), whose work on moral disengagement emerged from his research into childhood aggression, have described our sense of social duty as innate. Yet, as I have already pointed out, the relationship between altruism and self is a highly complex area and so the purpose of the empirical study which informed this book was

---

[4] Hofstede used the term 'universalism' differently and in the contexts of ethnocentricism and of 'applying general standards' across cultures. His use of the term was in order to reflexively illustrate the danger in cross-cultural research and anthropology of the researcher imposing his or her own values on the subjects of study (Hofstede, 1980: 33 and 45).

not to try and establish whether *true* altruism is possible (see Baier, 1993; Wright, 1971: Chapter 6).

So it is apparent from the discussion above that scholars have theoretically and empirically identified values as drivers of our behaviour, which operate via our expressions of the self (Piliavin, 1989). All this implies that there are inherent epistemological, ontological and therefore methodological problems associated with the study of values. Furthermore, the scope for error may also be compounded if values operate at different levels. This notion of categories of personal values is now continued further.

Different levels of personal values

In the section above, I discussed personal values from both sociological and psychological perspectives. Different categories of values were also identified in the previous chapter, such as social values, political values, religious/spiritual values and sentimental values (Rescher, 1969: 16). Additionally, Rokeach's (1973; 1979) values instrument was categorised into moral, competence, personal and social values (Fisher and Lovell, 2003: 111). Moral and competence values encompassed Rokeach's *instrumental* values (how we should live and behave) and personal and social values referred to Rokeach's *terminal* values (the ends or purposes that we should be striving for). Rokeach's distinction between instrumental and terminal values is discussed further in the next section. Other categories of values include theoretical, economic, aesthetic, social, political and religious (Allport, Vernon and Lindzey, 1960). Unsurprisingly, then, Agle and Caldwell (1999) warned of the potential for confusion in failing to distinguish between values that operate at different levels.

Their framework identified individual, organisational, institutional, societal and global values (Agle and Caldwell, 1999). This conforms with the critical-realist philosophy of research, which assumes a stratified ontology and different levels of reality (Sayer, 2004) and the morphogenetic idea that: individuals 'develop values which shape and are shaped by societal and organisational norms' (Hoffman, 1993: 10). Hence it is unrealistic to ignore the structural influences of organisational, industrial, national and regional values. For example, CSR has been described in terms of its personal importance to executives in

India, for deeper cultural and religious reasons, compared with Western countries (Budhwar and Varma, 2011). Moreover, the importance of the corporate context to ethical/unethical decision making within the firm, with its unique corporate culture and ethical climate, has also been acknowledged by scholars of management and business ethics (Anand, Ashforth and Joshi, 2004; Treviño, 1986). However, the limitations upon the scope of this book dictate that my focus remains on the employee as agent of CSR.

Furthermore, it is interesting, at this point, to draw a parallel between the confusion between macro levels of values identified by Agle and Caldwell and also the potential for confusion already identified above, in terms of values that operate within the micro (employee) and meso (firm) levels, and the likelihood of the individual possessing a combination of individualistic and collectivist values in their cognitive repertoire. This is akin to the idea of the psychological 'evoked set' (March and Simon, 1958: 10; Howard and Sheth, 1969). In practice, an example of mixed motives was demonstrated by the retail manager who claimed to be driven by a moral compass at work and who appeared to champion various CSR initiatives. This manager declared how she had progressed a new opportunity to sell fresh food whilst she also acknowledged the likely adverse effects of this move on local grocery businesses (Watson, 2003). The subject justified her action on the grounds of her duty to her employer (to increase profitability). However, there is an equally likely scenario that this individual also perceived her duty to herself, i.e. being seen by her employer as the originator of a new commercial opportunity.

This connects with a third potential source of confusion in the study of values; that is, in distinguishing between the values expressed by the individual and those *dominant* values that actually drive behaviour (Meglino and Ravlin, 1998; Wright, 1971), i.e. espoused versus in-use values (Argyris and Schon, 1978). Indeed, England's (1978) Value Framework differentiated between 'conceived' or 'expressed' values and 'non-relevant' or 'weak' values. Non-relevant or weak values 'would have little or no impact on behavior', whilst conceived values 'may be translated from the intentional state into behavior'. Conceived values were further categorised into operative (high probability of being translated into actual behaviour), intended (moderate probability) and adoptive values. Adoptive values were described as less a part of the personality structure of the individual and affect[ing] behavior largely because of situational factors' and so we might expect the majority of employees who are complying with CSR initiatives to be acting as a result of their adoptive values. According to England, *all* personal values are potential values (England, 1978: 36). Therefore, if 'some values clearly dominate over others' (Guth and Tagiuri, 1965: 125) then this implies a hierarchy of values (Mele, 1995: 145) or a meta-order (Williams, 1979: 25), with dominant values occupying a central or core space in the individual's psyche (Maclagan, 1998: 97; Williams, 1979: 33). For example, the retail manager in Watson's study appeared to demonstrate her collectivistic values: 'She appears interested in helping to make changes in the world – to make it a better place, in her own value terms' (Watson, 2003: 175). Yet her dominant in-use values may well have been the more individualistic values of ambition, social recognition and/or family security.

Another facet of this potential confusion lies in the 'fact–value distinction', defined as part of a normative–empirical split in business ethics. Essentially, Rosenthal and Buchholz (2002) differentiated between a value as a fact ('what is') and a normative value judgement ('what ought'). This distinction resonates with the distinction between espoused and operative (or in-use) values. For example, if I were a subject participating in a study of personal values and were asked to use a values instrument, I might select 'capable' as a standard of conduct which is most important to me, but in fact I might lack confidence and be the sort of person who gives up on a task and possibly relies on others. My response would mislead the researchers, because I aspire to be regarded as a competent person. And so the challenge for the researcher of values lies in trying to establish the dominant values that actually drive our behaviour, because a key methodological issue is the normative content and the centrality of personal values to our self-identity in terms of who we are and who we wish to be. However, 'we can assume that expressed values are not unrelated to operative ones, particularly if these expressed values are . . . under conditions in which the subject has every reason to be sincere and truthful' (Wright, 1971: 197). Hence the problem remains: which personal values might act as a catalyst for the championing of CSR? As noted above, this implies considerable methodological difficulties, not least due to the conflicting ideas with regard to how values are structured.

The structure of values and implications for a methodological approach

The idea of systematic ordering, or a prioritising of our values, is reflected in the notion of a values system, which, according to some scholars, comprises two related sets of values. Whilst Rescher discussed our fundamental, 'intrinsic' values (Rescher, 1969: 18), Rokeach called these 'terminal values', or our ultimate, desired 'end-state of existence' values (Rokeach, 1968: 551), for example *health*.[5] (See the Appendix for the lists of Rokeach's terminal and instrumental values.) Rokeach called his second set of values the 'modes of conduct', or instrumental values. Instrumental values (a term also used by Rescher, 1969), are the mechanisms that we use to achieve our long-term, terminal goals (values), such as being *self-controlled*, or *courageous*, for example. Hoffman described Rokeach's value classification as follows:

> Rokeach offers a breakdown into two main types of individual values: terminal (or ends) values and instrumental (or means) values. The former refers to beliefs or conceptions about ultimate goals or desirable end-states of existence that are worth striving for (such as happiness or wisdom); the latter refers to beliefs or conceptions about desirable modes of behaviour that are instrumental to the attainment of desirable end-states (such as behaving honestly or responsibly). (Hoffman, 1993: 11)

Rokeach estimated that we possess thirty-six values and the Schwartz values survey (SVS) recognises fifty-seven (Schwartz, 2006). Interestingly, the number of estimated values in Confucianism was given as 'approximately fifty', although they were referred to as 'virtuous items', e.g. moderation, humour, justice, respectfulness, etc. (Zhang, 2002: 225). (The connections between value and virtue are discussed in Chapter 6.) Importantly, with regard to our portfolio of values, scholars have suggested that we all possess more or less the same set of values. According to Rokeach, 'the number of human values are small, the same the world over, and capable of different structural arrangements' (Rokeach, 1979: 2). This notion of a limited number of personal values parallels the idea that we experience a limited repertoire of emotions. Conversely, from a Christian perspective, the

---

[5] In Rokeach's form D version of his value survey (1973), the terminal value *happiness* was later replaced by *health* in the form G version. Similarly, the instrumental value *cheerful* was replaced by *loyal*.

Catholic priest is unlikely to hear anything new as he ministers to the same sins in the confessional (Greene, 1971). Indeed, the connection between value and emotion was already made in the last chapter. But with regard to the distinctions between people, the differences may lie in our differing priorities, or the relative weightings that we attach to our values (Hoffman, 1993). Consequently, Meglino and Ravlin (1998) highlighted two major differences in the understanding of how values are structured. First, values are understood in relation to each other: they are hierarchically organised and possibly traded off against each other (Rokeach, 1973; 1979; Schwartz, 2010). Second, they exist independently and function as 'equal in their intensity' (England, 1967; Lusk and Oliver, 1974). This disparity signals the problematic nature of studying values, sometimes referred to as their incommensurability.

The incommensurability of values concerns the notion that there is no common measure for a given value, also that they can be perceived as incomparable due to their circumstantial quality (Hsieh, 2007). This importance of context whereby prima facie duties may be over-ridden by other ethical demands was explained by Maclagan (1998: 35). Moreover, citing Dancy (1993), Maclagan argued that an ethical decision is made via the process of 'defeated reasons', i.e. that the deployment of the selected prima facie duty is via a process of elimination of the remaining duties, depending upon the salient aspects of the situation at the time of the decision. Thus I am connecting a prima facie duty as the chosen course of action (Maclagan, 1998: 35) and the dominant personal value that is activated, even though activation 'may or may not entail self-concious thought about the value' (Schwartz, 2010: 230). Thus my thesis centres upon the notion of particular values being held more centrally than others (in most people) and also deployed as a matter of personal principle, or a sense of duty. This suggests a positivist position, whereby values are a fixed entity, and 'reality exists independently of the observer, and hence the job of the scientist is merely to identify . . . this pre-existing reality' (Easterby-Smith, Thorpe and Lowe, 2002: 34). However, the problem of equivalence (Feather, 1986), or the potential for different interpretations of a given value, once again highlights the inherent methodological difficulties with the empirical study of personal values. Nevertheless, this need not be an insurmountable empirical problem, as advocated by Feather (1986: 276), who cited Rokeach: 'the psychological significance that a particular value has for a person is far more important than its semantic meaning'. Thus the study of values is 'reminiscent of earlier debates in the psychological literature (e.g., the concern with nomothetic versus ideographic methods in the study of personality)' (Feather, 1986: 275). So whilst a nomothetic or quantitative study would be used in order to predict or control, the idiographic, qualitative study, undertaken in order to describe and understand, was selected as the most appropriate choice of method for the exploratory study which formed the basis of this investigation into corporate social entrepreneurship.[6]

Further to this, the clinical psychologist Dorothy Rowe acknowledged the incommensurability of values due to contextual influences and the notion of espoused values reflecting our self-identity (although she equates virtue with value):

An exercise I have used a great many times in workshops is where I give the participant a list of the ten most common virtues – truthfulness, generosity, loyalty, courage and so on – and ask them to rank them in order of importance. Ten virtues allows for 3,628,800 possible permutations. I cannot recall any two of my workshop participants ever coming up with the same list. Even when two or three people agreed on what was the most important virtue, when I asked each one, 'Why is this virtue important to you?', each person gave a different answer. This answer was linked to how the person saw himself, or wished to see himself, something which would emerge in the discussion over the whole day. The values which different people give to the common virtues explain why a person may behave badly in certain situations but not in others. A man might be unfaithful to his wife and steal from his boss, but be utterly fearless in the face of danger. Knowing that he was a liar and a thief did not trouble him, but to know himself to be a coward was unendurable. (Rowe, 2009: 153)

Significantly, then, the choice of nomothetic or idiographic method is rooted in contrasting epistemological perspectives. And the dominance of quantitative methodological approaches in the study of personal values reflects a positivist epistemology, whereby it 'is possible to obtain hard, secure objective knowledge' (Carson et al., 2001: 6). However, if values are not necessarily knowable as 'materially real', like a tree or a mountain, for example (Fleetwood, 2005), then this implies the appropriateness of an alternative methodological approach, such as an

---

[6] The point being made here refers to the dominance of quantitative research study in psychology, which has a much longer history in that field than studies which have adopted qualitative methods.

attempt to access the different meanings that people may attach to particular values, at specific points in time. Indeed, it has already been suggested that the positivist approach in the study of business ethics 'fails to get to grips fully with the issues of moral meaning' (Crane, 2000: 32). Moreover, due to the highly personal nature of values in terms of their centrality to our sense of identity, one could argue that the traditional quantitative approach lacks the required sensitivity needed to establish such nuances. So if, as Guth and Tagiuri (1965) suggested, managers interpret company strategy and match company resources and opportunities according to their own values, then a research emphasis on interpretation and meaning in a study of the role of personal values in the workplace would be highly appropriate to 'focus on the ways that people make sense of the world especially through sharing their experiences with others via the medium of language' (Easterby-Smith, Thorpe and Lowe, 2002: 29). Hence the research design of the study which formed the basis of this investigation into corporate social entrepreneurship was geared towards accessing employees' reflexive thoughts; their own 'commentaries':

> Since our highest concerns are about what we value most, then reflection is about which commentaries are the best guides to what matters most to us. Rather than trying to rationalise our first-order emotions, we evaluate them as guides to the life we wish to lead, and thus end up embracing some and subordinating others. (Archer, 2000: 223)

Furthermore, Treviño highlighted a gap in the business ethics literature regarding the cognitive processes that take effect when employees are faced with ethical dilemmas, calling for an investigation into employees' 'personal ethical standards' (Treviño, 1986: 604). And the gap is even wider in terms of our understanding the behaviour of those employees who progress a socially responsible agenda at work, for example economists' vague description of agency as 'warm glow preferences' (Baron and Diermeier, 2007a: 542). This is despite the calls of scholars of organisation over fifty years ago, who advocated further research into the cognitive factors affecting organisational behaviour:

> there has been less concern with cognitive than with other phenomena in organization . . . In particular, empirical evidence of a reliable and persuasive

kind is almost nonexistent – a complaint we have made throughout this volume, but which applies with special force to the topic of cognition. (March and Simon, 1958: 210)

This brings us back to the empirically little-understood notion of moral character. Therefore the literature on personal values from social psychology has provided a foundation upon which to investigate the notion of entrepreneurial drive in the pursuit of any of the domains of CSR and the concept of corporate social entrepreneurship tentatively moves some way towards closing this gap.

5 | *The corporate social entrepreneur*

In the previous chapter, I described how personal values function both as part of our self-identity and for group cohesion and its survival. Moreover, I argued that *dominant* and activated values function as catalysts to our behaviour. In particular, I highlighted the notion of individualistic (or self-enhancement) values and collectivistic (or self-transcendent) values, whilst emphasising that we would generally not expect an either/or situation. Furthermore, in Chapters 2 and 3, I explained how other individual characteristics moderate our innate sense of social duty (Bandura, 1999; Schwartz, 2010), which may produce the entrepreneurial discretion to act in terms of antisocial or prosocial behaviour, or even altruism.

The purpose of this chapter, then, is to define the corporate social entrepreneur (CSE) and to explain how it is different from the 'regular' entrepreneur, the intrapreneur, the policy entrepreneur and the public or social entrepreneur. But I begin by unpacking entrepreneurial discretion a bit further, through an examination of entrepreneurial values in terms of the characteristics and activities of entrepreneurship in general. This is necessary to an understanding of the entrepreneurial drive behind some acts of CSR. However, despite our innate social values, not everyone acts as a corporate social entrepreneur. In fact, on the basis of our understanding of moral muteness in the workplace, we might expect the CSE to represent a significant minority (see Chapter 3). Therefore this chapter culminates with a theoretical model which represents four hypothesised modalities, or predispositions towards CSR.

Entrepreneurial values

A review of research into the personality characteristics and values of the entrepreneur found them to be 'vastly different' from the personal values of managers and revealed some debate as to whether the personal values of male and female entrepreneurs may be different (Fagenson, 1993; Olson and Currie, 1992). However, some common themes emerged. Entrepreneurs were characterised as creative and imaginative people, high in social competence, with a prevailing need for autonomy, freedom and independence in order to escape from 'organizational constraints limiting their creativity and potential', (Chapman, 2000: 99; see also Burgelman, 1983; Corman, Perles and Vancini, 1988; Longenecker, McKinney and Moore, 1988). The entrepreneur's need for autonomy was also highlighted by Shane, when he emphasised the importance of personality characteristics to the development of a theory of entrepreneurship (in addition to other structural and agential forces): 'researchers have identified five aspects of personality and motives that influence the exploitation of entrepreneurial opportunity: extraversion, agreeableness, need for achievement, risk-taking and independence' (Shane, 2003: 97). Indeed, scholars of entrepreneurship have identified such characteristics as a dominant sense of responsibility and a drive to be in control, or the possession of an internal locus of control, as typical of the entrepreneurial character (Chapman, 2000; Corman, Perles and Vancini, 1988; Olson and Currie, 1992; Shane, 2003: 108). This connects with the notion of autonomy which has been a presupposition throughout this book so far, inherent within notions of agency. Furthermore, autonomy has also been identified as a facet of integrity, which is discussed in Chapter 7 below.

Other psychological antecedents of entrepreneurship were identified as intuitive decision making, often 'when there is little historical information to guide those decisions'; overconfidence; and a strong sense of self-efficacy and self-esteem (Shane, 2003: 117). These are potentially negative aspects of a personality, whereby an entrepreneur with an internal locus of control and desire for autonomy could be perceived as a 'loose cannon', pressing ahead regardless of the consequences. Combined with any Machiavellian tendency, whereby the end justifies the means, this behaviour might be regarded as reckless and therefore unethical, regardless of whether or not the objective is to achieve a socially responsible result – for example, the policy entrepreneurs described as at times 'motivated by thinly veiled self-interest, these innovators used ethically questionable strategies to achieve their personal and organizational objectives' (King and Roberts, 1992: 175).

Entrepreneurs seek constant challenges, which may explain their well-known tendency towards opportunism (Shane, 2003). But their drive to accomplish may be connected to a need for personal fulfilment with regard to intellectual and professional goals, which, if achieved, gives the entrepreneur a sense of self-respect (Chapman, 2000; Fagenson, 1993 and Olson and Currie, 1992) and may be valued by the individual as more important than making money (Corman, Perles and Vancini, 1988; Guerrier and MacMillan, 1981: 26). Empirically derived examples of those displaying entrepreneurial drive were the managers who championed green initiatives, without feeling the need to use commercial rhetoric (Crane, 2000; Gurney and Humphreys, 2006). They may also have been demonstrating a sense of duty and obligation to society. Therefore the notion of employees not always conforming to the requirements of the firm and the application of entrepreneurial discretion, as described in Chapter 3 above, is not only important in an analysis of corporate wrongdoing, it is also relevant to the study of CSR.

Indeed, business ethicists and management theorists have argued that some managers may exercise moral discretion in the course of carrying out their work (Carroll, 1979; Drumwright, 1994; Swanson, 1995; Treviño, 1986). First, citing Carroll (1979), Wood (1991) argued that managerial discretion is one of three key principles of CSR, referring to managers as 'moral actors' within the organisation. Second, the concept of a moral actor was supported empirically by Drumwright, who, across a variety of business functions, identified managers who initiated and championed some environmentally motivated buying decisions (Drumwright, 1994). Similarly, the CSR change agents, who selected an initiative based on their 'personal interest and sphere of influence' (Cramer, Jonker and Van der Heijden, 2004: 218). Third, even if they were found to be minority players within the organisational arena (Crane, 2000; Harris and Crane, 2002), the activities of environmental champions have been documented in the management and green literature (Andersson and Bateman, 2000; Dillon and Fischer, 1992; Elkington and Burke, 1989; Fineman and Clarke, 1996; Walley and Stubbs, 1999). My argument, then, is that such champions are likely to operate at a *variety of levels* within the organisational heirarchy: from manual workers or clerical staff to junior management through to directors. And they may not necessarily be the most senior executives to set the moral tone of the corporation. For example, a study of German managers observed a higher social orientation amongst lower-level managers than amongst middle managers (Marz, Powers and Queisser, 2003: 7).[1] Moreover, these champions may not even have a high profile within the firm, unlike Drumwright's 'policy entrepreneurs', working 'to put issues on the corporate agenda' (Drumwright, 1994: 4).

Indeed, personality characteristics were found to be more effective in terms of ability to influence others (an entrepreneurial characteristic) than formal authority or performance in the job itself, particularly when the personality characteristics fitted with the organisational culture (Anderson, Spataro and Flynn, 2008). And whilst the difference between personality and values has already been noted, I have also argued that personal values, in addition to other individual and situational forces, drive socially responsible behaviour. Therefore, employees such as these might be expected to operate either *overtly* or *covertly* as corporate social entrepreneurs (CSEs) within the business context. But the notion of a CSE who identifies and progresses opportunity within the corporation for socially responsible activity has received little attention in the entrepreneurial and business ethics literature, although there have been calls for research to identify different types of entrepreneur (Ucbasaran, Westhead and Wright, 2001: 70).

A typology of entrepreneurship

Entrepreneurial activity was defined by Low and MacMillan (1988) as 'the creation of new enterprise' (cited in Davidsson and Wiklund, 2001: 81), and is synonymous with 'the relentless pursuit... [and exploitation] of opportunity' (Alvarez, Barney and Anderson, 2012; Chapman, 2000: 98). The 'regular' entrepreneur has been most commonly associated with SME's with regard to new business start-ups and also management buy-outs or buy-ins, and, less flatteringly, with a spontaneous, intuitive management style and possibly a disregard for detailed analysis (Corman, Perles and Vancini, 1988; Shane, 2003). Particularly since the high incidence of 'dotcom' failures in the 1990s, the term 'entrepreneur' has, sometimes, been associated with the high

---

[1] For a contrasting view which argues that the adoption of a moral corporate culture has to be embraced by top management in order to be effective, see also Agle, Mitchell and Sonnenfeld, 1999; Robin and Reidenbach, 1987.

rate of new business failure, due to the founders' poor management skills, sometimes attributed to lack of business qualifications or business experience (Lussier, 1995; McCarthy, 2003; Perry, 2001).

Entrepreneurs were typically considered as business leaders until the 1980s, when the term 'intrapreneur' was coined (Pinchot, 1985). The terms 'intrapreneur' and 'corporate entrepreneur' have been used synonymously and generally refer to corporate managers who exhibit entrepreneurial spirit in terms of idea generation, creativity and drive in the course of carrying out their work: marshalling resources and influencing and championing 'new ideas from development to complete profitable reality' (Kuratko, Montagno and Hornsby, 1990: 50). Intrapreneurship is associated with either new product development (Kolchin and Hyclak, 1987: 15) or 'the creation of semi-autonomous units within the existing organization' (Kuratko et al., 1990: 50). This relatively new term reflected calls in the late 1970s and 1980s for corporate managers to develop initiatives supported by a move away from hierarchies towards flatter organisational structures and less bureaucracy, in order to foster a culture of innovation against a background of fierce competition from the Japanese and the so-called 'Asian tigers' (Dent, 1999).

In such an increasingly complex business climate, the classical management techniques involving the *control* of workers endorsed by the scientific management school (to boost efficiency and productivity) were regarded as *in*efficient compared with the newer ideas of the human relations theorists. Here, increased autonomy and greater responsibility through job enlargement (Argyris, 1957) and enrichment (Herzberg, 1966) were advocated for job satisfaction and the retention of staff. Decades later, as 'rationalisation' in business became the focus, management theory embraced these ideas of self-control, creative thinking and taking the initiative: what became known as 'thinking outside the box' (although allowing workers to take the initiative had already been advocated by Fayol in 1916; see Pugh, Hickson and Hinings, 1971). These newer approaches were designed to enable the organisation to achieve its goals through the deployment of employees with greater levels of responsibility (McGregor, 1966), who would be happier in their work, and perhaps 'self-actualised' (Maslow, 1943). However, such practices have resulted in employees articulating ambivalence towards bureaucracy, as they experience its enabling as well as constraining effects. Indeed Adler (2012) argued that the demise of bureaucracy is a fallacy. Indeed, my daily experience of employees following step-by-step instructions from their computer screens illustrates that departmental hierarchies have been replaced by electronic or e-bureaucracy. Later, corporate entrepreneurship (or intrapreneurship) emerged in the UK, paralleling the growth of marketing, with the product or brand manager acting as a product advocate or product champion (Kotler, 1984: 722; Peters and Waterman, 1982: 9) and getting 'things done by influencing others' (Kotler, 1984: 740). However, neither the term 'entrepreneur' nor 'intrapreneur' tends to denote a social orientation (Cornwall and Naughton, 2003), unlike the terms 'social entrepreneur' or 'public entrepreneur'. These distinctions are made explicit below.

The social entrepreneur is regarded as having the vision and drive associated with the 'regular' entrepreneur. Moreover, societal transformation (Alvord, Brown and Letts, 2003) can take two forms. The first constitutes

the provision of public services in new and innovative ways and generally takes place under the auspices of established social services; the second is a broader activity within which individuals set up new approaches to specific problems, within the social economy (Hibbert, Hogg and Quinn, 2002: 289).

The first refers to public entrepreneurship: 'Through entrepreneurial risk-taking, public entrepreneurs generate creative policy solutions, redesign governmental programs, and implement new management approaches to revitalize the public sector' (King and Roberts, 1992: 173). The second form of social transformation refers to 'social enterprise'. This is an evolutionary mode of social entrepreneurship which has traditionally been associated with the voluntary sector (Thompson, 2002) and more recently refers to 'caring capitalism', with its reliance on market forces generating profit to be redirected towards social problems (Hibbert, Hogg and Quinn, 2002: 289). Hence social entrepreneurship has developed to include for-profit in addition to not-for-profit enterprise (Social Enterprise Magazine Online, 2003) – for example schemes to help the unemployed into work. (See Chapter 1 above, where governmental and business drivers for such initiatives were discussed.)

However, the term 'social entrepreneurship' has not generally been applied to those individuals who drive social responsibility within the private sector firm, even though Thompson acknowledged that 'social entrepreneurship is in evidence in many profit-seeking businesses' (Thompson, 2002: 413) and corporate philanthropy has existed since the Industrial Revolution (Murray-Rust, 1995). Moreover, it is worth noting that due to increasing levels of corporate interest in CSR, the potential for a blurring of the boundaries between a social enterprise and a firm that has embraced CSR in the multifiduciary way (as described in the introduction to this book) becomes ever greater. How much investment is required to differentiate the social enterprise from the socially responsible corporation? How much net profit is 'enough' (Hemingway, 2005: 237)? But even though the majority of corporations nowadays claim to be fully committed to CSR, it is pushing the boundaries to describe even the most hybrid of companies (such as those dedicated to the growth of fair trade, or environmentally sustainable production) as social enterprises staffed by social entrepreneurs. This is because the remit of the organisation, defined as a corporation in its articles of association, requires employees to deliver returns to shareholders, through their job roles. As a consequence the CSE is unlikely to have the time or other resources to commit full-scale towards progressing a socially responsible agenda, because the corporation imparts constraints (Hemingway, 2013). Indeed, in Part III below we see how corporate social entrepreneurship is characterised by its informality, in terms of its being added on to the job and performed in an ad hoc way, and this results in its tremendous variability. This also parallels the contested nature of CSR that was described in the introduction.

It is also confusing that public entrepreneurship and/or social enterprise is often referred to synonymously with policy entrepreneurship. For example, in her European study on health provision, De Leeuw identified that 'policy change is dependent on the presence and actions of social entrepreneurs' (De Leeuw, 1999: 268). Therefore, whilst 'Policy is the expressed intention of an institution (government, corporation, volunteer group, etc.) to act strategically towards the attainment of specified goals' (De Leeuw, 1999: 264), policy entrepreneurship can be regarded as a formalised agenda for the pursuit of social initiative, such as health care reform (Newhouse, 1995) or income support reform (Howard, 2001).

It may be that the difference between social and policy entrepreneurship is an issue of the levels of power held by these two types of entrepreneur. The social entrepreneur is likely to be the driving force that follows through once the policy has been agreed, such as the

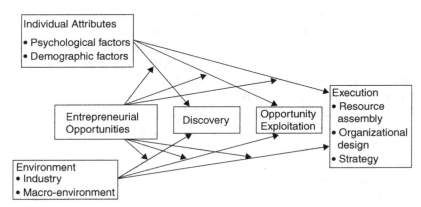

Figure 5.1 Shane's (2003) model of the entrepreneurial process (courtesy of Edward Elgar Publishing Ltd)

youth workers involved in increasing the participation of thirteen- to nineteen-year-olds in education and training as a result of the UK government's White Paper in 1999 (Ainley, Barnes and Momen, 2002: 381). Conversely, King and Roberts differentiated the policy entrepreneur (from the public entrepreneur) as someone who 'worked outside the formal boundaries of the governmental system (King and Roberts, 1992: 173). However, power was also pinpointed as a differentiator between the two types of entrepreneur – not in terms of the levels of power, but with regard to how that power was expressed, such as in a collaborative manner, 'working with others, rather than employing coercive tactics to overpower them' (King and Roberts, 1992: 185).

Furthermore, policy entrepreneurship may apply in any sector: public, private or voluntary. For example, Drumwright's policy entrepreneurs, who were almost evangelical in their pursuit of socially responsible buying, were described as 'working to put issues on the corporate agenda' (Drumwright, 1994: 4). However, whilst it is 'personality characteristics and abilities' (Huefner and Hunt, 1994: 63) that may differentiate any type of entrepreneur from a manager, administrator or bureaucrat, Shane (2003: 96) warned against defining an entrepreneur solely by personality characteristics, emphasising that entrepreneurial *activity* has to be the most obvious differentiator. This was shown in his model of the entrepreneurial process (Figure 5.1), which illustrated the antecedents of entrepreneurial activity, including both structural and agential forces as influencers.

My contention, however, is that it is the deployment of the individual's dominant personal values, a component of these psychological factors, which differentiates the choices made between the regular or the public entrepreneur and the social or policy entrepreneur: 'Psychological profile indicates that policy entrepreneurs are well integrated, cognitively complex, achievement-oriented change agents who espouse and adhere to core values while seeking to serve the public interest and make a lasting contribution to society' (King and Roberts, 1992: 173). Indeed, King and Roberts (1992: 185) described the 'deeply held beliefs' of policy entrepreneurs. This was supported empirically by Drumwright (1994) in her study of environmental champions who were described as 'propagating [their] values through buying initiatives' (Drumwright, 1994: 5). Hence, my presupposition (Hemingway, 2002) was that the championing of CSR would depend upon a *salient* sense of personal responsibility or a collectivistic sense of duty to society that is valued by the individual, as opposed to an individualistic orientation. As a consequence, I have coined the term 'corporate social entrepreneur' (Hemingway, 2004; Hemingway, 2005) in order to identify the individual who operates within the corporation in a socially entrepreneurial manner and whose personal values may be predominantly of a self-transcendent nature. Indeed, this idea was supported in the field of political economics: 'A social entrepreneur carries strategic CSR beyond profit maximization and market value maximization' (Baron and Diermeier, 2007a: 543; see also Baron, 2007).

Nevertheless, the question is still asked: is it the existence of an ethical or an unethical climate that predominates and influences behaviour, or do the presence or absence of a moral character and personal values have the greatest influence? And my argument throughout this book is that it is a mistake to pinpoint *either* the existence of an ethical or an unethical climate *or* the personal characteristics of the individual in terms of having the greatest influence on behaviour at work. This was supported in a study of abuse by Carnahan and McFarland (2007), who identified participant self-selection (as opposed to self-presentation) in a comparative study which replicated the Stanford prison experiment. The subjects' personality characteristics were measured prior to the study and the researchers concluded that

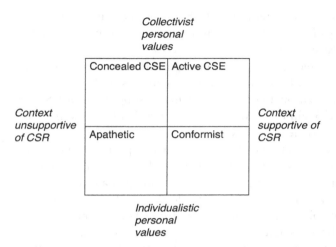

Figure 5.2 A typology of predispositions towards CSR (Hemingway, 2005)

person–situation interactionist approaches have greater predictive capability, providing a more nuanced picture of human behaviour than conflated situationist accounts. This concurs with my thesis regarding socially responsible or irresponsible behaviour at work. So my argument, back in 2002, was that scholars of business ethics cannot ignore the dual forces of structure and agency, which affect each other, as part of morphogenesis (Archer, 1995). Thus I proposed four predispositions towards CSR, based on the variable nature of both perceived organisational context and dominantly expressed personal values (Hemingway, 2005). These four extreme cases were theoretically proposed as 'Active' and 'Concealed' corporate social entrepreneurs, 'Conformist' and 'Apathetic'. The last two subgroups were conceptualised to represent the majority of employees in the corporate context who are not corporate social entrepreneurs, with 'Active' and 'Concealed' CSEs in the minority.

Orientations towards CSR

Figure 5.2 represents the conceptual model from which the research questions for an exploratory empirical investigation into social responsibility as a subjective state were derived. It was produced on the basis of the multidisciplinary literature which has been discussed through-out this book so far. The two dimensions of this two-by-two matrix represent a predisposition towards CSR according to the individual's dominantly espoused values as self-enhancement or self-transcendence (individualistic or collectivistic) and the employee's perception of the employing organisational context, in terms of supportive of CSR or not. The four modalities of Active CSE, Concealed CSE, Conformist and Apathetic were described as follows.

The 'Active' corporate social entrepreneur was posited to be driven by their collectivistic, self-transcendent values. I stated that the individual might be in a very senior position in the company, a *leader*, able to inspire a socially responsible culture (Agle, Mitchell and Sonnenfeld, 1999: 507; Lincoln, Pressey and Little, 1982; Posner and Schmidt, 1992: 86) on the basis that 'the management specifies the nature of the relationships which prevail and, thus, the norms which are applied' (Iribarne, 2003: 1300). A fictional example of an 'Active' CSE would be George Bailey, the community-spirited bank manager portrayed by James Stewart in the film *It's a Wonderful Life* (Capra, 1946). However, my thesis was that *any employee* could progress a CSR agenda in an organisational culture that is predisposed towards CSR, regardless of their formally appointed role. Seniority would not be a prerequisite for corporate social entrepreneurship.

The 'Concealed' CSE would also exhibit self-transcendent personal values, but these would not be as saliently expressed as those of the 'Active' CSE. Due to the perceived culture of the organisation, the 'Concealed' CSE would place emphasis on the economic benefits of CSR to the firm. Examples are the policy entrepreneurs identified in a large UK retail chain (Crane, 2000), or the retail manager who claimed to argue the case for equal opportunity and diversity policies (Watson, 2003), or perhaps those managers who indicated in surveys that they would like to see their companies involved in socially responsible activity (Collins and Ganotis, 1973: 83; Lincoln, Pressey and Little, 1982: 484). Corporate social entrepreneurs in this mode might express a desire to be involved in CSR but remain mute and do nothing. Or they might develop opportunities for CSR but reframe them into more commercially acceptable terms (Bird and Waters, 1989; Catasus, Lundgren and Rynnel, 1997; Fineman, 1996: 488; Gabriel, Fineman and Sims, 2000; Lovell, 2002a; Lovell, 2002b). They might be nonconformists,[2] even operating covertly 'under the radar'. In this latter case, the 'Concealed' CSE might be regarded as a maverick acting subversively (Friedman, 1970) against a corporate climate that is averse to CSR. Moreover, these employees would perceive their activities as win–win – good for the corporation as well as for the CSR cause – such as the 'tempered radicals' who worked as change agents within their companies on issues such as race or gender (Meyerson, 2001). Or they may enjoy getting one over on the corporation. Again, the 'Concealed' CSE was conceptualised as occupying any position in the corporate hierarchy, from senior manager or director to shop floor worker. I also presupposed that regardless of their formal job role, the 'Concealed' CSE would have the greatest potential as a whistleblower, as a result of feeling unable to operate at work in a manner fully congruent with their dominant personal values.

A third mode, the 'Conformist', would not be regarded as a corporate social entrepreneur, because dominant personal values would not have driven them to initiate CSR of their own volition. The 'Conformist' might even be complicit in corporate wrongdoing and morally disengage in order to survive within the firm, perhaps to progress in their career or just to keep their job. Included within this modality would be the CSR professional with dominantly expressed individualistic values, such as the pragmatic environmental managers who claimed that they would not be in their role if they were 'idealists' (Catasus, Lundgren and Rynnel, 1997: 202). Even if they were particularly good at their job and demonstrated entrepreneurial characteristics, I conceptualised the 'Conformist' as a foot soldier, complying with requests to co-operate or even develop CSR initiatives as a result of formal sanction by top management. Hence my presupposition was that the 'Conformist' subgroup of people would represent the largest empirically derived mode of moral commitment to CSR in the majority of corporate cases, not least because of the difficulties inherent in taking a stakeholder approach (see the introduction to this book). This connects with the prevailing view in business ethics regarding

---

[2] It should be noted that the notion of nonconformity when applied to the CSE refers to a tendency to disregard organisational constraints, as opposed to nonconformity to societal norms. As whistleblowers are protected by laws, such as the UK's Public Interest Disclosure Act, this indicates that the whistleblower may be regarded as a conformist with regard to society's norms.

organisational constraints upon the employee which may produce moral muteness, or even corporate misdemeanour, in an amoral work context (see above, Chapter 3, and a discussion of cognitive moral development in Chapter 2).

My fourth mode was hypothesised as the 'Apathetic', who, along with the 'Conformist', would not be a corporate social entrepreneur. Moreover, the 'Apathetic' would not show any real interest in CSR and dismiss its value. This individual would perceive their company to be antagonistic towards CSR, or be hostile towards the notion him- or herself, even blocking initiatives, due to the perceived non-economic focus of CSR (Fineman, 1996; Harris and Crane, 2002: 220). Saboteurs of CSR could also emerge in a supportive culture. Nonetheless, bearing in mind contemporary values theory (see the previous chapter) and the capacity for individuals to reprioritise their values and change their attitudes and behaviour (see, for example, Drumwright's 'converts' and the literature on culture change (Drumwright, 1994: 6; Leiberman, 1956)), the potential exists for all employees to become corporate social entrepreneurs. Important and central to my assertions, however, was the necessity for some exploratory empirical research, in order to determine the conditions under which this might be possible. Even so, a nomothetic study of the personal values of corporate social entrepreneurs compared with other types of entrepreneur, including the social entrepreneur, is an unexplored area which requires investigation and was not the subject of my own tentative empirical study. Regardless, my contention was that it is the collectivistic, or self-transcendent, values that characterise corporate social entrepreneurship, despite the moral context (Hemingway, 2004; Hemingway, 2005).

Potential subjects were not anticipated to be consistently classified into one particular quadrant. Moreover, the two dimensions of Figure 5.2 were not intended to represent bipolar opposites. As described in the last chapter, whilst our personal values remain relatively stable, they can also be reordered in different contexts. Importantly, values theory states that an individual possesses personal values within the domains of the *four* bipolar dimensions – openness to change, conservation, self-enhancement and self-transcendence – and not on the basis of individualism or collectivism alone (Schwartz, 2006). Thus Figure 5.2 represented a hypothetical construct deduced from the literature, as a foundational device, to be used as an analytical tool for comparison with empirically derived insight and subject to change: 'We are dealing with empirical phenomena, and the world has an uncomfortable way of not permitting itself to be fitted into clean classifications' (March and Simon, 1958: 1).

So I return to my key, and as yet unanswered, question. Is it the existence of an ethical or an unethical climate that predominates and influences behaviour, or is it that the presence or absence of a moral character and personal values has the greatest influence? Hence in the next chapter I explore the notion of a moral character. And I begin by examining the relevance of virtue ethics to the idea of a corporate social entrepreneur, followed by a more contemporary interpretation by Foucault, in terms of the 'care of the self'. Here, ideas regarding a sense of social duty, which were first introduced above in Chapter 2 with the theory of the cognitive moral development of the individual, recur and resonate with notions of integrity. Nonetheless, the notion of a hierarchy of personal values remains central to this discussion.

6 | *Integrity and the moral character*

So far, I have argued that an employee's behaviour is in part determined by their personal values, manifesting in a range of behaviours from corporate misdemeanour at one end of the spectrum of moral agency to corporate social entrepreneurship. We might also anticipate differing levels of involvement in CSR: with passionate champions, or CSEs, with or without formal authority, and others who may be involved in CSR but who do not act in a socially entrepreneurial manner whilst carrying out their job function. Indeed, the *discretionary* element of CSR has been highlighted as an important facet, as well as the notion of a personal sense of duty and moral obligation to society. Moreover, these ideas were illustrated in the last chapter as theoretical predispositions towards CSR.

However, the question remains: what is the nature of the corporate social entrepreneur? The distinction between personality and character suggests that a psychological perspective alone would be inadequate to address this question, where morality emerges as a distinguishing feature between 'character' and 'personality':

Personality: (1) the combination of characteristics or qualities that form an individual's distinctive character; (2) the qualities that make someone interesting or popular.

Character: (1) the mental and moral qualities distinctive to an individual, strength and originality in a person's nature, a person's good reputation; (2) the distinctive nature of something.

Notably, Ciulla detected a shift from character to personality in the study of leadership, which she described as a move away from morality under the guise of value-free social science (Ciulla, 2002: 338). Hence this chapter synthesises ideas from both moral philosophy and psychology in a discussion about integrity and moral character, beginning with the connections between virtue and value. This leads into a discussion regarding the care of the self. Here, notions of power and control, freedom and autonomy (introduced in Part I above) are posited as antecedents of corporate social entrepreneurship, activated through the mechanism of reflective judgement. Indeed, Foucault (2000) argued that it is our capacity for reflection that generates the conscience, but reflection requires a level of maturation and self-mastery. Contemporary scholars of psychology also agree that integrity derives from the conscience, connecting with self-actualisation and happiness. Hence the notions of self-actualisation and self-transcendence are unpacked in this chapter, within the context of their contribution to the idea of a moral character. It may be seen that not only are the notions of integrity, self-actualisation and self-transcendence conceptually very close, they may also be key towards an understanding of corporate social entrepreneurship.

The relationship between virtue and value

Human motivation and notions of excellence unite the very close distinction between virtue and value. The philosophical tradition of virtue ethics was created from Aristotelian and Platonist ideas about the development of a good character in living 'the good life' (Pence, 1991: 255; Rescher, 1969; Zagzebski, 1996), indicated by this definition of virtue: 'An acquired disposition that is *valued* as part of the character of a morally good human being and that is exhibited in the person's habitual behaviour' (Velasquez, 2006: 110, my emphasis). A virtue was the mean between two vices (see Fisher and Lovell, 2003: 73) and the four main classical virtues were courage, justice, temperance (self-control) and wisdom (encompassing ambition), all of which were included in the Rokeach values survey (Rokeach, 1979). Compare also with Schwartz and Bilsky's definition of value, cited earlier in Chapter 4: 'values are (a) concepts or beliefs, (b) *about desirable end states or behaviours*, (c) that transcend specific situations, (d) guide selection or evaluation of behaviour or events, and (e) are ordered by relative importance' (Schwartz and Bilsky, 1987: 551, my emphasis).

So, considering that the term 'moral character' is part of our everyday parlance, it is very surprising that its empirical investigation has been largely ignored by scholars of organisation, particularly when values and beliefs 'are the subatomic particles that make up our ethical

DNA. How we behave, according to the ancient Greeks, expresses our character' (Darcy, 2002: 401). This gap in behavioural ethics theory is particularly notable in recent times, after the global financial crisis and amidst the reform of our financial institutions.

A relatively more contemporary (than ancient philosophy) emphasis on the importance of moral character was expressed by the management theorist Peter Drucker, with his statement that 'the public good must always rest on private virtue' (Drucker, 1968: 465). This indicates that any potentially negative effects of capitalism can be policed via the practice of moderation and the application of self-control, which was also advocated by the economic historian Richard H. Tawney: 'The will to economic power, if it is sufficiently single-minded, brings riches. But if it is single-minded it destroys the moral restraints which ought to condition the pursuit of riches, and therefore also makes the pursuit of riches meaningless' (Tawney, 1926: 36).

However, the actions of the corporate social entrepreneur are dynamic and proactive and not restricted to corporate governance measures. Indeed, my argument is that a moral character can manifest via the initiation or championing of a social agenda at work, in conjunction with the profit-driven one. This relates to definitions of CSR as activity which goes beyond the law (see the introduction to this book). But I have already highlighted the subjectivity of the word 'morality', particularly in relation to the contested and controversial nature of CSR. Indeed, many have argued that a purely profit-driven motive is virtuous, even though this may be unconventional from the perspective of philosophical virtue ethics. Therefore, whilst a virtue might be described as being a value, whether or not a value can be described as a virtue is subjective and in the eye of the beholder. So my point is this: how the virtue is applied, and to what ends, can be variable and subject to what is valued.

By way of example, *ambition* is a value (Rokeach 1979), but the context for the ambition can be scrutinised. Ambition in the sense of aspirations towards advancing a career is the obvious interpretation. But we can be ambitious for others, e.g. our children, or ambitious in planning to achieve something such as climbing a mountain or executing a bank heist. Clearly the latter could not be regarded as virtuous. But is ambition for the acquisition of wealth virtuous? In the classical sense it was not, but the pursuit of wealth, nowadays, is clearly regarded by very many as virtuous, if not the ultimate virtue and more important, for some, than integrity. So what has changed? Archer's (1995) morphogenetic theory helps to illustrate the shift.

Morphogenetic theory was applied in Archer's (2012) analysis of postmodern society. She described the transition from morphostasis, habitus and contextual continuity (which, she argued, characterised pre modernity and the end of traditionalism) to the *contextual discontinuity* of modernity, itself characterised by population shift and the rise of market fundamentalism. Archer argued that we are now in a period of nascent morphogenesis again, post-global economic crisis, where 'socialisation isn't what it used to be' and 'young people are increasingly thrown back upon reflexively assessing how to realise their personal concerns in order to make their way through the world' (Archer, 2012: 97). And so our personal concerns, or our personal values, have shifted in line with cultural change and what we regard as virtuous behaviour has shifted over time. The classical example of this is often used to illustrate the original context of virtue ethical theory: 'all the great ancient philosophers thought slavery was natural and correct' (Pence, 1991: 254).

Now, the incommensurability of value can also be illustrated by such titles as *The Virtue of Selfishness* (Rand and Branden, 1964) and *The Virtue of War* (Webster and Cole, 2004). These examples suggest the need for the 'practical usefulness' of virtue and remind us that 'the rational pursuit of excellence' (Hosmer, 2003: 93) was an instrumental *political* philosophy of the ancient Greek classes to maintain the social order. So the value of a virtue may be assessed in terms of its social, or apparently altruistic, benefits, but, as Hosmer points out, someone who exhibits many of the traditionally cited virtues may well be self-interested (Hosmer, 2003: 95). Moreover, this political function of the traditional virtues indicates a consequentialist quality to virtue, even though virtue ethics represents normative ethical theory, as distinct from deontological and teleological ethical theory. Further complications arise if we consider whether a virtue makes a 'good person', or whether the virtue is 'good for' (beneficial to) the holder. Consequently, Zagzebski referred to the many notions of virtue:

different lists of virtues in different cultures and in different eras of history . . . John Locke stresses the diverse conceptions of virtue in different times and places but claims that everywhere what is called a virtue is what is judged to be praiseworthy and what is called a vice is what is judged to be blameworthy. (Zagzebski, 1996: 86–90)

Indeed, scholars have debated the notion of 'a core of virtues' (Pence, 1991: 255): a universal list of one-size-fits-all meta-virtues. Therefore virtue ethics alone is unhelpful for an understanding of corporate social entrepreneurship in practice, because it is an intellectual framework for analysing issues of morality. However, if virtue is connected with notions of integrity as part of the moral character, as advocated in Islam (Qur'an, 13:11) and in the Judaeo-Christian, Buddhist and Confucian perspectives (Koehn, 2005), then the development of a neo-virtue ethical theory is crucially relevant to today. And a good starting point brings us back to ancient Greek and Roman philosophy with Foucault's analysis (2000) of the notion of 'care of the self'. Again, Foucault reminded his readers of the historical and cultural context of ancient Greek and Roman philosophy, with slavery as part of the normal fabric of society. In this sense, *freedom*, in the form of the autonomy of the individual, was key to the notion of a moral character.

The importance of reflective judgement and methodological implications for behavioural ethics research

Acknowledging Habermas, Foucault identified four main types of technology: (1) technologies of production, (2) technologies of sign systems, (3) technologies of domination and power, and (4) technologies of the self. It is the technologies of the self which are of specific interest here. These

permit individuals to effect by their own means, or with the help of others, a certain number of operations on their own bodies and souls, thoughts, conduct and way of being, so as to transform themselves in order to attain a certain state of happiness, purity, wisdom, perfection, or immortality. (Foucault, 2000: 225)

According to Foucault, a component of the technologies of the self was the care of the self: an ethos or 'a way of being and of behaviour' (Foucault, 2000: 286) and a key principle of cities, of personal conduct and of social cohesion:

in all of ancient philosophy the care of the self was considered as both a duty and a technique, a basic obligation and a set of carefully worked-out procedures . . . a form of living . . . the conversion to oneself . . . [or] soul service. (Foucault, 2000: 95–9)

The care of the self was a concern to make oneself a better person. Foucault cited Socrates (469–399 BC) in Plato, who told the judges that they need to be concerned with 'wisdom, truth and the perfection of the soul' rather than 'wealth and reputation and honors' (Foucault, 2000: 226): an idea central to Christianity and replayed in the Gospels where Jesus upturns the tables of the moneylenders in the temple. Even earlier than this: wisdom; knowledge and truth were also taught by Confucius (551–479 BC) in the honing of a superior character and for personal and social harmony (Zhang, 2002). So in the context of Greek and Roman cultures, with their clearly defined class system, slaves were the lowest and least important class. And the principles that were intrinsic to the philosophy of care of the self entailed displaying your superiority as a non-slave – a free person – by – 'not being a slave to oneself and one's appetites' (Foucault, 2000: 284). This point was made relevant to today's context by Lent (2012), who argued that our contemporary notion of freedom has transformed into a prevailing individualism and 'getting what I want'.

Governmentality of the self was described by Foucault (Foucault, 2000) as a necessary component of preventing our abuse of power and offsetting the power relations which, he argued, are intrinsic to our human relations. He described governmentality thus:

the range of practices that constitute, define, organize and instrumentalize the strategies which individuals in their freedom can use in dealing with each other. I believe that the concept of governmentality makes it possible to bring out the freedom of the subject and its relationship to others – which constitutes the very stuff [*matière*] of ethics. (Foucault, 2000: xvii)

Indeed, self-mastery has been a theme in philosophy, social theory and psychology, for example in Frankfurt, who argued that our strongest urge does not always prevail (Frankfurt, 1988); in Archer's (2003; 2007) findings on the internal conversation; and in Bandura's (1986) social cognitive theory regarding our mechanisms of control. Importantly, though, care of the self was about self-cultivation and not about altruistic behaviour and putting others first, which came later, with the spread of Christianity. What has survived to the present day, and is encompassed within the ethos of the care of the self (and was adopted by Christianity), is the notion of reflection. This is the edict to 'know thyself', which, since Descartes, Locke and Husserl (Archer, 2003: 21), is now more commonly remembered than care of the self (Foucault, 2000: xxv). So governmentality is a function of knowing oneself, being concerned with reflective and reflexive judgement, which entails 'an examination of the *conscience*' (Foucault, 2000: 237, my emphasis) in order to be of good character: 'Care of the self is a practice of our freedom: ethics is the considered form that freedom takes when it is informed by reflection' (Foucault, 2000: 284). This is an argument for the power of agency and moral character as determined by self-reflection and personal conscience and it links directly with my thesis regarding discretion (or autonomy) at work and corporate social responsibility as a subjective state: 'Foucault understands thought as the exercise of freedom' (Rabinow, 2000: xvii).

However, Archer's (2003; 2007) investigation revealed that not everyone can be empowered by self-reflection. Indeed, she found 'passive agents' in the form of a subgroup that she called the 'fractured reflexives': 'people to whom things happened, rather than active agents who could make things happen, by assuming some governance in their own lives' (Archer 2003: 164). Accordingly, care of the self entails a greater sophistication in one's character, a maturity, or strength of character derived through our experience in a process of ongoing moral growth (Rosenthal and Buchholz, 2002): 'The care of the self always aims for the well-being of others; it aims to manage the space of power that exists in all relationships, but to manage it in a non-authoritarian manner' (Foucault, 2000: 287). This point also connects with the psychological studies of human development referred to in Chapter 2 above. Indeed, Habermas, who 'links morality with respect for autonomous agency', acknowledged the influence both of Piaget, with regard to human development, and of Kant's ideas of our conscience and sense of duty to others (Bohman and Rehg, 2007). There is a further connection, too, with psychological notions of autonomy, such as an internal locus of control and field independence which were identified by Treviño (1986) as moderators of ethical behaviour and also, in the previous chapter, as characteristics of the entrepreneur. This is not to suggest, of course, that all entrepreneurs have a moral character (in the classical sense). Nevertheless, if the ownership of a mature character is generally associated with experience, then this implies that empirical studies into CSR and personal values using students in their early business life is likely to affect the validity of such research. This methodological issue was previously raised in Chapter 4, as was the proposal that in vivo research such as ethnography is a more appropriate research method for the exploratory investigation of corporate social entrepreneurship than the controlled laboratory style study, where the latter is conducted away from the organisational context.

For example, Hitlin described volunteering in the student community as

a relevant identity for analyzing a student population because it is becoming an official requirement for high school graduation and an unofficial criterion for acceptance into college. Although 'volunteer' ultimately might be low in an individual's salience hierarchy, many college students have volunteer experience and develop some degree of this identity. (Hitlin, 2003: 124)

Yet volunteering is not a requirement for institutions of further and higher education in the UK. This illustrates the national differences which give rise to the implicit and explicit model of CSR (Matten and Moon, 2004). But Hitlin found an emphasis on 'self-oriented desires' amongst his student sample and he described the student self-identity as not 'solidified' compared with older students (Hitlin, 2003: 128, 133). However, I made the point in Chapter 5 above that corporate social entrepreneurship entails particular characteristics and behaviours, exhibited in particular situations, regardless of whether or not these are permanent features of the agents' character. So whilst virtue ethics defines moral character as habitual behaviour, my own empirical investigation was concerned with the individual's relationship with CSR, which is likely to be variable. But the idea of the (honed) moral character – of ingrained ethical behaviour – is encapsulated in the notion of *integrity* (Horowitz, 2002; Solomon, 1992) and it is this quality which was found to distinguish the 'Active' and 'Concealed' corporate social entrepreneurs from other employees who were also engaged in some form of CSR, in the findings of the empirical study (see Part III below). Thus in the following section the concept of integrity is clarified and I have connected it with the notion of self-transcendent personal values, in order to provide further insight into the antecedents of corporate social entrepreneurship.

Integrity

Integrity is another multifaceted notion. The *Concise Oxford English Dictionary* defines integrity as: '1. the quality of having strong moral principles. 2. the state of being whole'. It is a personal characteristic which is associated with being true and consistent with one's personal standards, thereby indicating a wholeness of character (Archer, 2000: 249; Brown, 2005; Crane and Matten, 2004; Horowitz, 2002: 558). Indeed, consistency as a key feature of integrity is also used in other fields, such as art and architecture – for example to indicate features that are congruent with the existing design of a building.

Integrity was described as 'a complex and thick virtue term' (Cox, La Caze and Levine, 2003: 41). Whilst it was not one of the classical Greek virtues, it was important in Eastern philosophy and in the West it was adopted as part of the Judaeo-Christian tradition. Indeed, along with wisdom, integrity is a higher-order or meta-virtue (Zagzebski, 1996: 137). Zhang (2002) described wisdom, bravery and benevolence as the highest moral principles in Confucianism, with benevolence as 'the root cause of virtue', and also as 'respectfulness, tolerance, trustworthiness in word, quickness and generosity',[1] acquired and continually practised in the honing of a moral character, or 'self-cultivation' (Zhang, 2002: 218–20). This echoes the notion of the care of the self and reflective judgement that was introduced in the previous section. So the idea that a principled individual *consistently* demonstrates these virtues appears to be key to the attribution of the label of integrity.

However, and putting aside the difficulties in establishing motive, can we describe someone who *consistently* acts in their own self-interest as acting with integrity? The literature suggests that having integrity is tied up with having sympathy for others, an 'other'-focus, and is not solely confined to an adherence to what one believes is the right thing to do, whatever that may be. Thus a salient compassion for others and human sympathy are important elements which link this discussion to the psychological processes associated with prosocial behaviour and with the notion of benevolence from values theory, described in Chapter 4 above. Certainly, Confucius defined benevolence to his disciples as 'to love people' (Zhang, 2002: 187).

---

[1] The reference to 'quickness' seems to refer to quickness in thought and Confucius's instruction to his disciples 'to be quick and eager to learn...' (Zhang, 2002: 215).

And in the context of morality, integrity is often used to describe the courage (a classical Western virtue) to act or speak out in the instance of a moral dilemma. Thus the individual's conscience gives them the impetus to 'do the right thing' by sticking to their principles or personal values, which may be challenged during their employment. This prompted the sentiment that it is 'hard to find a manager who does not feel the pressures of careerism or suffer some contradiction between obligations to the company and his or her sense of personal integrity' (Solomon 1992: 5). Indeed, a greater potential for moral conflict in contemporary corporate working life was attributed to technological development:

> There is a strong risk of techniques and practices leading to infringement of the personal integrity of almost anybody coming into contact with the modern corporation... The faster the pace of change in that world, the weaker the moral agreement. (Gustafsson, 2002: 298)

Nevertheless, in Chapter 1, I acknowledged the possibility of congruence between the values of the organisation and those of the employee and indeed empirically derived examples of this are described in Part III of this book.

Referring to psychoanalytic theory, Horowitz explained the development of character identity and integrity during the life cycle. He explained how people with *higher* levels of integrity have greater sophistication, described as the 'self–other schematization' of beliefs. This involves 'an empathetic quality for cherishing the unique individuality of others' (Horowitz, 2002: 565, 561) and the ability to behave more flexibly. Hence the notion of the developed or developing moral character re-emerges. Moreover, it is these ideas regarding higher levels of self-consciousness and the development of a conscience, achieved through introspection and what Koehn (2005) referred to as 'the true self', contrasting with the ego, that appear to distinguish integrity. Interestingly, Julie, from the exploratory empirical study described in Part III below, spontaneously referred to the voluntary work that reflected her 'true self', in contrast to her identity as a factory operative at work (see Chapter 9).

This 'other' orientation, attached to notions of integrity, also links with the (again, Judaeo-Christian) virtue of humility, which has also been associated with self-awareness. According to Tangney, humility involves a realistic assessment of one's own strengths and weaknesses in relation to those of others, and not false modesty or a lack of self-esteem, as is often commonly assumed. Tangney cited Means et al. (1990) in her article on humility: 'humility is an increase in the valuation of others and not a decrease in the valuation of oneself'. Thus 'a person who has gained a sense of humility is no longer phenomenologically at the center of his or her world. His or her focus is on the larger community, of which he or she is a part' (Tangney, 2000: 73, 72). Further, humility was found to be a characteristic of the corporate social entrepreneurs in the empirical study, with one case, Eric, a senior manager, referring to a significant event in his own life which had caused him to realise that 'the world is bigger than you' (see Chapter 8). Moreover, a more sophisticated or cultivated self might be, in part, the product of so-called 'character-building' life crises, evolving the self to higher levels of integrity. At the very least, crises may cause us to rethink our values, to *re-evaluate* (Pence, 1991; Sull and Houldner, 2005: 90). Notably, the majority of respondents who were identified as corporate social entrepreneurs described in Part III (nine out of thirteen) reported such an incident.

A further feature of high character integrity is an internal locus of control, whereby negative moods are owned as 'of the self' and guilt and blame is not inappropriately misattributed to others (Horowitz, 2002: 561; Logsdon and Young, 2005: 116). Again, this is an aspect of taking responsibility for one's actions and echoes a key theme in this book regarding autonomy and a mature, more developed personality and moral character. Further, the empirical research described in the following chapters revealed examples of corporate social entrepreneurs who expressed their integrity and demonstrated this personal sense of responsibility. Thus, whilst the employee with integrity is mindful of others, this is coupled with a degree of autonomy whereby the individual *thinks for themself*,[2] as opposed to morally disengaging and perhaps succumbing to the social pressure of 'group-think'.

---

[2] Using a limited literature, I have indicated how ancient Eastern and Western philosophy encouraged reflection in the lifelong search for wisdom, truth and knowledge. But over time there were pedagogic differences, for example the Socratic emphasis on encouraging students to work things out for themselves, as opposed to the Stoic or Epicurean model of the student having to listen to the teacher (Foucault, 2000: 101). With the exception of Confucius' instruction to 'be seated and I shall tell you' (Zhang, 2002: 209), I did not find any reference to an anecdotally derived idea of a Confucian emphasis on listening to the teacher. Instead, I found emphasis on the student being encouraged 'to think

Once more, this equates to notions of free will and the development of moral character in the 'care of the self' and self-cultivation (Foucault, 2000; Zhang, 2002); along with Kant's ideas about purposive freedom; Lyotard's reflective judgement and Ingram's ideas about 'self-mastery ... a maturation of critical and reflective powers in the moral subject' (Curtis, 2001: 6, 12). But how can these ideas apply in business and management? Here, we return to the key theme of this thesis, regarding personal autonomy and agency in the workplace.

In Chapter 3 above, agency was acknowledged as a tenet of the neo-human relations school, whose scholars advocated greater levels of autonomy and responsibility in the workplace to promote job satisfaction and efficiency. Thus the idea of social responsibility linked with a more sophisticated mature character continues with Argyris, who advocated job enlargement on the basis that the child is self-centred and dependent upon adults to control him or her, whilst the mature adult has learned to act more autonomously. Job enrichment was promoted by Herzberg, claiming that man is capable of rising above 'environmental limitations, of self-realization' (Pugh, Hickson and Hinings, 1971: 141). Moreover, having autonomy was advocated by the 'positive psychologists' as conducive to a sense of well-being, thereby concurring with ideas in management regarding job satisfaction (Seligman, Rashid and Parks, 2006). Conversely and also more crucially, a recent medical study found that fifteen per cent of 473 participants in a European meta-analysis reported job strain. The study correlated job stress, including *low control at work*, with heart disease (Kivimäki et al., 2012).[3]

independently and enhance their ability of reasoning and judgement' and a reference to Confucius's 'diversity in teaching method' (Zhang, 2002: 129). Furthermore, as moral agency is such a central topic in moral philosophy, this section was not intended to provide a comprehensive discussion from this perspective. See Painter-Morland (2008) for a good exposition of moral agency. My aim was simply to make some insight into the topic of a moral character, in order to highlight its connections to business ethics and corporate social entrepreneurship.

[3] The abstract to the study reports that the researchers 'used individual records from 13 European cohort studies (1985–2006) of men and women without coronary heart disease who were employed at the time of baseline assessment. We measured job strain with questions from validated job-content and demand-control questionnaires. We extracted data in two stages such that acquisition and harmonisation of job strain measure and covariables occurred before linkage to records for coronary heart disease. We defined incident

We might also note that the word 'integrity' comes from the Latin *integer*, meaning whole, or complete: denoting the character as 'the finished article', i.e. that the character has been honed and developed through life's experiences (Darcy, 2002: 403). And the notion of the more sophisticated personality was also described by the psychologist Maslow in his theory of motivation, where self-actualisation is the driver of an individual who has satisfied lesser physiological, safety, belongingness and love and esteem needs (Maslow, 1943). Maslow argued that work alone cannot lead to ultimate fulfilment and happiness. Therefore, in the last section of this chapter, Maslow's ideas regarding self-actualisation and self-transcendence are unpacked. I also posit that self-transcenders are differentiated from self-actualisers in terms of their dominant self-enhancement personal values, and that this distinction may provide us with further pointers towards the character of the corporate social entrepreneur.

Self-actualisation and self-transcendence

The concept of self-actualisation, or reaching one's full potential, is commonly attributed to Maslow, but was conceived by Goldstein (1939) 'as a morally neutral reference to the development of an organism's potential, irrespective of content' (Maclagan, 1998: 77). Moreover, Maclagan acknowledged that the term is used interchangeably with 'self-fulfilment' and 'self-realisation' by some scholars (Maclagan, 2003: 334). This is pertinent to the previous discussion of character development and its potential connection with CSR.

Maslow referred to self-actualisation as 'the desire to become more and more what one is, to become everything that one is capable of becoming' (Maslow, 1943). But Maclagan posed this question: 'A self-actualising person will constantly *experience* "restlessness" ... and a desire to do something. But what might this "something" be?' This higher drive was identified as 'commitment to an important job and to worthwhile work' (Maclagan, 2003: 335, original emphasis, 336). This introduces two issues: first, the question whether the constantly restless individual can ever achieve lasting fulfilment, and second, the risk that value judgement is once again apparent if we consider what constitutes

coronary heart disease as the first non-fatal myocardial infarction or coronary death' (Kivimäki et al., 2012).

'worthwhile' activity. Clarification on these issues was offered via the notion of peaking and non-peaking individuals:

> Wilson... noted that just before his death Maslow was following up on his speculation that there are peaking and non-peaking self-actualizing people. Peakers, he found, are likely to be involved in aesthetics and religion, while non-peakers tended to be influential social workers and 'world betterers'. (Thornton, Privette and Bundrick, 1999: 262)

Furthermore, Maclagan argued that an organisation is morally obligated to help the development of the employee in terms of 'the realisation of personal moral ideals, entailing participation in socially useful and ethically acceptable work', thereby connecting these two issues of lasting fulfilment and worthwhile activity: 'taking responsibility for the improvement of the world, and for the elimination of human misery in so far as this affects both oneself and others, might constitute the context for self-realisation or self-actualisation' (Maclagan, 2003: 340, 335). These ideas are very relevant to CSR. But the idea that self-actualisers have not yet peaked in realising their potential implies another level in the hierarchy of needs. Hence it is necessary to highlight an important distinction which was made between the self-actualisation and self-transcendence constructs and any confusion between the two.

Koltko-Rivera (2006) described how Maslow refined his understanding of self-actualisation over time. Initially, Maslow's ideas of self-transcendence were conflated with his original concept of self-actualisation (Maslow, 1943; Maslow, 1959). But in the 1960s, Maslow began to discuss self-transcendence as a separate, higher motive above self-actualisation, reporting that 'self-actualization is not enough'. Hence an individual who is at the level of self-actualisation may be described as seeking 'fulfilment of personal potential' (for example as a mother, or as an artist, or an athlete). But the self-transcender seeks 'to further a cause beyond the self and to experience a communion beyond the boundaries of the self through *peak experience*' (Koltko-Rivera, 2006: 303, 304, my emphasis). Going beyond the self

> may involve service to others, devotion to an ideal (e.g., truth, art) or a cause (e.g., social justice, environmentalism, the pursuit of science, a religious faith), and/or a desire to be united with what is perceived as transcendent or divine. (Koltko-Rivera, 2006: 303)

Moreover, peak experience 'may involve mystical experiences and certain experiences with nature, aesthetic experiences, sexual experiences,
and/or other *transpersonal experiences,* in which the person experiences a sense of identity that transcends or extends beyond the personal
self' (Koltko-Rivera, 2006: 303, my emphasis).

Maslow came to believe that the cognitive activity (what he referred
to as 'B'-cognitions: 'for the Being of the other person or object'
(Maslow, 2011: 62)) effected by peak experience produces self-
transcendence. Such 'acute identity experiences' (ibid., 85) enable the
appreciation of a world view. Whereas self-actualisation is linked with
a reinforcement of one's personal identity through peak performance
(he used the examples of a mother, artist or athlete; but one might
include business person, tradesperson or any job or activity), self-
transcendence involves moving beyond personal identity 'in favor of
service to others and to some higher force or cause conceived as being
outside the personal self' (Koltko-Rivera, 2006: 307). As a consequence, Maslow argued, peak experience through self-transcendence
allows the individual to feel at one, or to 'fuse', with the world,
thereby experiencing the 'real self' (Koltko-Rivera, 2006: 304). Thus
peak performance entails doing something well, whereas peak experience is about fulfilment and is more spiritual. Significantly, examples
of peak experiences were spontaneously described by the corporate
social entrepreneurs who were interviewed as part of the exploratory
empirical study (see Chapters 8 and 9 below).

The implication here is a connection between service to others and
job satisfaction, or *well-being* (see also Gurney and Humphreys (2006:
90) for apparent declarations of happiness from employees working
for a socially responsible organisation). Moreover, the positive effects
of altruistic love on the immune system were described by McClelland
(1986). Furthermore, contemporary research conducted by neurosci-
entists and 'positive psychologists'[4] using brain scans and self-report

---

[4] Positive psychology has emerged from the work of Seligman, who developed
the concept of 'learned helplessness', whereby human beings are said to have
been genetically programmed as pessimists in order to cope with their early
hostile environment on Earth. Thus, in depression, we learn to become helpless
and we give up, even when the situation confronting us is probably not
presenting a truly insurmountable problem. The argument is that the human
brain has not caught up with civilisation and that we are, generally and
naturally, negative thinkers who need to make a conscious effort not to be. The
positive psychology school believes that we can train ourselves to be happier.

measures have found that people who meditate appear to be happier than those who do not (Fredrickson et al., 2008; Wade, 2005). And whilst there may be a difference between meditation and reflexivity, I am proposing that they are linked through the process of active, conscious thought. Indeed, the clue is in the prefix 'trans–' (defined in the *Concise Oxford English Dictionary* as 'across or beyond'). This connects with those ancient ideas from moral philosophy and religion with regard to transforming oneself (Foucault, 2000: 225), for example: 'Allah will not change the condition of people, unless and until they change themselves' (Qur'an 13:11).

In his final years, Maslow regarded self-transcendence as so important that in 1969 he founded the *Journal of Transpersonal Psychology*. It is also interesting to note that Maslow's interest in idealism or spirituality is evidenced by his chairmanship of a multidisciplinary conference on the subject (1959) (Koltko-Rivera, 2006). However, misconceptions regarding the hierarchy of needs have persisted, with introductory textbooks of both psychology and business/management continuing to publish the old pre-self-transcendence version of the hierarchy of needs, culminating in self-actualisation. It seems that 'there was little opportunity for Maslow to publicise his amended theory before his death'. But Koltko-Rivera speculated that the American Psychological Association may also have struggled to recognise the new theory:

the organized psychology of Maslow's day simply may not have been ready to incorporate Maslow's concept of self-transcendence into the quasi-official canon of acceptable theory . . . [and that there is] a tendency among psychologists to avoid issues that involve spirituality, presumably including mystical or peak experiences . . . (Koltko-Rivera, 2006: 308, 309)

Hence, whilst Maclagan did not overtly make reference to self-transcendence, he captured the spirit of Maslow's later work in his argument for employers to allow for employees' self-actualisation at work through service to others. Indeed, Maclagan's conflation of self-actualisation and self-transcendence is reflected in his criticism of the human relations school of management theorists whom he accused of 'hi-jacking' the concept of self-actualisation when they 'adopted' and 'adapted' it (Maclagan, 2003: 338). Maclagan argued

---

The inference, here, is the connection between job satisfaction/happiness and CSR. See the empirically derived examples of this in Part III.

that Maslow's work on achieving human potential was misinterpreted in an instrumental manner, job satisfaction being a cynical means of manipulating employees to be more productive, in order to achieve organisational ends. Nevertheless, enhancing the personal happiness and fulfilment of employees is a domain of CSR, although Maclagan's scepticism mirrors that which I described in the introduction to this book.

But the self-transcended 'world betterers' represent only a small minority: a rare type of person in comparison with the general population (Maslow, 2011). And if we extrapolate this to the corporate context, this implies that a CSR professional, for example, may well be self-actualised and very good at their job, but are they really self-transcending? Or, that they might be self-transcended due to the nature of CSR involving some kind of service to others (regardless of motive), but they may not be operating to their peak potential. Indeed, the findings of the exploratory study of corporate social responsibility as a subjective state found a smaller number of corporate social entrepreneurs compared with the rest of the sample (see Part III below). This tentatively supported Maslow's work and reflected the dominant economic argument or the argument of enlightened self-interest for CSR, in comparison to the multi-fiduciary argument (discussed in the introduction). Notably, Maslow observed that the rejection of the notion of self-transcendence by members of the American Psychological Association was attributable to what he believed was their own lack of B-cognitions (Koltko-Rivera, 2006: 309). Values theory (described in Chapter 4 above) provides a more nuanced perspective (Schwartz, 2010).

However, Maslow's ideas were developed by the school of positive psychologists, who described a self-transcender as someone who is 'able to see, appreciate, and empathize with the views of others' and have 'concerns and goals that are larger than their individual self-interests', or a 'worldview'. Such an individual has 'greater psychological complexity', having developed 'psychologically from greater to lesser degrees of egocentricism' (Logsdon and Young, 2005: 112–16). Indeed, self-transcendence as a cornerstone of happiness and fulfilment is part of cognitive therapy, giving meaning in life, whereby sadness and depression are said to be reversed through techniques such as goal setting and self-affirmation (Seligman, Rashid and Parks, 2006; Seligman and Csikszentmihalyi, 2000).

Further, an individuals' sense of *autonomy*, or perceived freedom, was cited as a facilitator of creative thinking and a key driver in achievement (Csikszentmihalyi and Csikszentmihalyi, 2006: 1; Thornton, Privette and Bundrick, 1999). Other significant factors are the ability to concentrate and 'flow', i.e. a 'full focus on object and on self' (Thornton, Privette and Bundrick, 1999: 254), or 'mindfulness' (Langer, 1989), a state of 'optimum efficiency' where the activity is enjoyed 'for itself and not for external rewards' (Logsdon and Young, 2005: 113). Additional psychological processes that have been identified with peak performance (self-actualisation) are the sense of joy which is experienced as a result of the flow of activity, said to produce feelings of power and self-worth in the individual (Thornton, Privette and Bundrick, 1999). Therefore meaningful work such as that provided by helping others through CSR can be anticipated to provide job satisfaction, at the very least. And my argument connects back to the discussion in Chapter 4 regarding the structure and function of values, where personal values were described as innate mechanisms that are designed to help us to achieve our goals and our ultimate happiness: 'Value is rooted in the fact that man is a goal-oriented organism seeking to achieve satisfactions and avoid dissatisfactions' (Rescher, 1969: 9).

Hence it is interesting to note the following. First, that there is an overlap between the psychological characteristics associated with peak performance and entrepreneurial values, such as creativity, need for autonomy, internal locus of control and sense of responsibility. Second, that these characteristics were displayed by corporate employees who were actively involved in CSR in the empirical study which is described in the following chapters. Last, that a concern for the *development* of both self and others, which was described as integral to the definition of a moral character, was also a key finding amongst corporate social entrepreneurs in my study. Therefore Figure 6.1 conceptualises these ideas regarding the psychological processes of self-actualisation and self-transcendence as a virtuous process, in our human drive for our own self-esteem and true fulfilment. I have also posited CSR as the resulting behaviour at the end point of either self-actualisation or self-transcendence, mediated by either individualistic (self-enhancement) or collectivistic (self-transcendent) values.

Consequently we can regard CSR as sometimes championed by people with integrity or by self-transcending corporate social

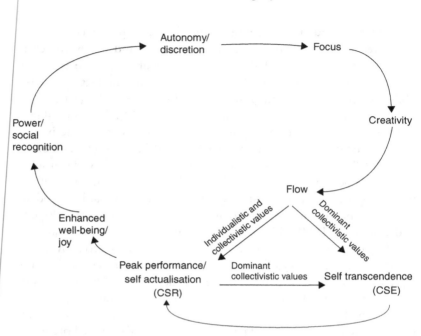

Figure 6.1 Theoretical model of the role of personal values as a mediating force in CSR and corporate social entrepreneurship

entrepreneurs realising their innate human drive, or as driven by others who are motivated by their self-enhancement personal values. And in line with the moral philosophy described above, Tawney seems to have anticipated the empirical findings of the psychologists: 'unless they can persuade themselves that to be rich is in itself meritorious, they may bask in social admiration, but they are unable to esteem themselves' (Tawney, 1926: 39).

Summary

At the beginning of this chapter I posed a question: what is the nature of a corporate social entrepreneur? And as part of a discussion about virtue and moral character I explained how value and virtue may be linked in their relationship with motivation, but that they can also be differentiated. So whilst much has been written about the incommensurability of values, I argued that this description may be more suited to ideas of virtue. We might value different 'things' but there is nevertheless consistency regarding the meaning of the objects of value, whereas ideas of what is virtuous are variable and thus unhelpful in our understanding of corporate social entrepreneurship. However, the notion of integrity is most relevant. And whilst making reference to ancient Eastern and Western moral philosophy, the question of moral agency was discussed in terms of the necessity of autonomous thinking and self-reflection in order to cultivate reflective judgement or conscience. Here, values were connected with the innate human drive for self-transcendence. I also proposed a link between corporate social entrepreneurship and a drive towards self-transcendence in some people.

Are CSEs deontologists or teleologists? They may be both. They may well think through the consequences of their actions, in terms of an action being 'for the good of the environment' or 'to make a difference to society'. But my thesis is that CSE or not, we act instinctively according to our personal value system, which dictates what is the 'right' course of action at the time, regardless of the influence of others. Our personal values operate as a system of rules that we feel duty-bound to live by. Nevertheless, Bowie acknowledged that ascertaining motives is notoriously difficult and, furthermore, that a pure Kantian would not accept that acting on one's inclination would be sufficient reason to qualify socially responsible activity as a genuine moral action. The Kantian would say that the motive has to be in accordance with respect for the person's principles and act in line with the categorical imperative: a universal law (Bowie, 1999: 4). However, the plurality of values that produce moral dilemmas in the world has already been noted, thereby making the idea of a categorical imperative impractical. Indeed, the pragmatist might simply argue, who cares about the motive? As long as CSR happens.

This is not to deny the existence of moral disengagement, which was discussed in Chapter 3 above. What I am suggesting, however, is that the levering of the dominant personal values of employees may contribute, in a practical sense, to the development of socially responsible corporate culture. And whilst the immense methodological difficulties in gathering data concerned with morality was noted, the case for a qualitative investigation into the relationship between personal values and CSR was mooted, on the basis that individuals' values 'frame the appropriate means and ends for social action, provide motivational impetus for such actions, and are vital for self-definition' (Hitlin and Piliavin, 2004: 383). Furthermore, the notion of lasting or true fulfilment as the vital difference between self-actualisation and self-transcendence that was described in the last section of this chapter brings to mind an analogy with business strategy, regarding the distinction between competitive advantage and sustainable competitive advantage. Indeed, if involvement in CSR enables individuals to achieve authenticity and true fulfilment through their work, then this may enable the realisation of a sustainable competitive advantage through the activities of the organisation's committed employees. Indeed, the connection between individuals' perceived congruency of values and job satisfaction was identified in Chapter 3. This implies that if the values of an organisation connect – in the multifiduciary sense – with CSR, then that organisation might expect greater longevity and sustainability as a result of the integrity of its processes and practices and the integrity of the employees who work there.

Thus the purpose of Parts I and II was to lay the theoretical foundations for the exploratory field research which was designed to investigate how personal values may or may not impact on the socially responsible activity demonstrated by corporate employees. This study will be described in Part III below. It comprised a form of ethnography which was conducted within the headquarters of the division of Brayford Health International, a leading UK-based multinational. Data gathering was geared to address the following questions: might CSR be driven, in part, by personal values and the possibility of a personal agenda? What do employees perceive as the main facilitators and barriers to particular CSR activities at work? These represented unexplored areas of investigation and were important to the development of organisational, ethical theory. Indeed, there has been mixed support for behavioural ethics theory (O'Fallon and Butterfield, 2005; Tenbrunsel and Smith-Crowe, 2008), with Maclagan describing management theory as 'conceptually deficient' with regard to 'responsibility as a subjective state felt by employees' (Maclagan, 1998: 77). Therefore the following chapters are devoted to a discussion of this empirical study. Chapter 7 describes the methodological approach that was taken and Chapters 8–11 comprise a discussion of the results and findings regarding four modes of moral commitment to CSR which included corporate social entrepreneurs. These are described using data from the study, in terms of the verbatim quotations which illustrated the subjects' sense of autonomy and self-governance, their prosocial behaviour at work, their declared levels of self-reflection and their integrity. Other subjects, whilst still involved in CSR, could not be described as corporate social entrepreneurs. These comparisons and distinctions will be made explicit.

PART III

Modes of moral commitment to CSR

7 | *Investigating corporate social entrepreneurship*

At the beginning of this book, the burgeoning interest in CSR was described in terms of the attention it has continued to attract across the range of scholarly fields of management and other disciplines, such as law and politics. In addition, the CSR industry has developed significantly, in parallel with interest from corporations themselves, with most displaying some kind of CSR or sustainability report on their websites. This interest has intensified since the onset of a global financial crisis, which has refocused a renewed interest from all quarters in some of the issues surrounding business ethics and CSR. However, despite the multidisciplinary nature of academic research into CSR, it remains a relatively new area, particularly with regard to an absence of field data and an understanding of the subject at the micro and meso levels, compared with the other, more established, fields of business and management.

Hence the previous chapters have examined the rationale for an exploratory, empirical study into the largely unexamined proposition that an employee, at any level in the organisational hierarchy, can be a moral agent. I have argued that agents are driven by their personal values, and in some cases use their discretion to champion what might be regarded as a socially responsible outcome – excluding the obvious socially responsible outcome of doing their jobs properly and contributing to the company's achieving its profit targets. This is despite a body of evidence which suggests that personal values may be sacrificed at work and compromised in deference to commercial or political pressures. Thus, using various literatures, the interface between CSR and personal values was discussed and I introduced the notion of a corporate social entrepreneur (CSE).

However, whilst Dyer and Wilkins (1991) stated that the aim of researchers is to get as close as possible to the subjects of the investigation, empirical study in business and management is characterised by the difficulties encountered in obtaining the co-operation of willing respondents. This might be with respect to obtaining access to organisations to begin with, or in terms of busy employees' being loath to 'waste' their time in assisting an academic researcher, manifesting in terms of refusal to participate and/or low response rates. Arguably, the CSR researcher is faced with even greater hurdles than other business and management subjects, due to the controversial nature of this subject. In particular, if moral disengagement is the prevalent modus operandi, as the business ethics literature suggests (see Chapter 3 above), then the methodological implications of such an empirical study were always going to be a tricky issue, not least before any methodological constraints associated with the collection of valid and reliable data regarding questions of personal values might be realised. Due to these specific considerations, a single exploratory case study was my chosen method of research.

Nonetheless, despite these potential difficulties, my own status as an ex-employee of the selected firm, albeit eighteen years previously, facilitated the necessary trust in me as a researcher to conduct this study, and I was granted open access to the company. Indeed, I was made to feel welcome by the majority of the subjects who kindly agreed to be interviewed. As a result, the planned exploratory case study turned into a form of ethnography (Burawoy, 2009).[1] However, making such claims to good access within the company can also invite criticism regarding researcher bias, an issue that I have discussed as part of the limitations section at the end of this chapter. In what follows, then, I will describe the aims of the study, the research context and the methodology in greater detail.

Research aims, objectives and questions

The aim of the field study was to provide insights into the moral psychology of employees and social responsibility as a subjective state. More specifically, the presupposition was of a causal connection between personal values and CSR. The research design was thus developed in order to investigate how personal values might influence CSR: how might people account for their behaviour using their espoused personal values? Accordingly, my objective was to evaluate

---

[1] Personal email correspondence with Michael Burawoy, 18 June 2011.

both conceptual frameworks at Figures 3.1 and 5.2 in the context of the empirical data. The following five research questions were posed:

1. How are personal values articulated within the organisation?
2. Within the organisation, what is the meaning attached to particular values and how important are they?
3. How do espoused personal values impact upon discretion in the exercise of CSR within the organisation?
4. What is the nature of the socially responsible actor and, as part of this, what role does integrity play?
5. What are the conditions under which these impacts may be attempted and realised? For example, how do people experience the constraining and enabling effects of corporate values within the organisation with regard to CSR?

These questions denote the entirely exploratory nature of this study, necessitated in response to deficiencies in our understanding of the role that personal values play in the context of CSR.

The research context

The headquarters of Brayford Health International, a UK-based multinational corporation, was purposely selected in which to conduct a single case study. This was done for two key reasons. First, the company operates as a significant player in the global health care industry,[2] which assists the firm's reputation as a socially responsible company. This is in part due to its Victorian philanthropic heritage, its business of supplying products to hospitals and a long history of 'staff welfare'. Indeed, the employee profile contained a large proportion of employees who had very long records of service, of between twenty and forty

---

[2] The 'health care' industry comprises a number of different market segments, each supplying a wide range of manufactured products or services, with diverse competitive structures and customer profiles. In fact, the nature of the business of the case company is distinct from the pharmaceutical and care homes industries, for example. Hence one of the presuppositions of this study was a connection between CSR and industry type, on the basis of employee self-selection. In fact this notion emerged from the informants as a distinct facet of the espoused organisational culture. For the purposes of confidentiality, the identity of the case organisation and the participating employees cannot be disclosed.

years, including some at the very top of the corporate hierarchy. Brayford Health International's reputation had also been bolstered by its listing on the FTSE4Good index and it was also cited as one of the world's top hundred sustainable companies (Corporate Knights, 2005). At the time of data collection there were no formal positions within the company with CSR or ethics in the job title, although the company's sustainability report was compiled by the company's 'health and safety and environment director' and communicated via the company's corporate communications personnel, along with the company's citizenship activity.

However, this organisation's traditional, paternalistic reputation had been challenged and arguably eroded, due to rationalisation and considerable reorganisation since the 1980s. Significantly, the number of employees had been reduced due to consecutive rounds of redundancies over the previous three years, and this process was still ongoing throughout the data collection and analysis phases of the study. The majority of these job losses were from the factory and support services, due to increased automation of manufacturing processes. Therefore, at the time of data collection, this had produced an uncertain context for many of BHI's employees and was reflected in the research data, particularly from manufacturing operations and technical support personnel, who were all anticipating a new battery of psychometric testing and assessment. Equally significantly for this study, I was unaware that, prior to data collection, the corporate context had also been affected by the introduction of the 'Brand Ambassador' scheme.

The Brand Ambassador scheme had been launched two years previously as a part of the repositioning and relaunch (Kotler, 2000) of the corporate brand, as part of a transformation process. The new corporate brand vision had been communicated as *Healing people*. In addition to changes to the corporate graphics and livery, the relaunched corporate brand encompassed three new espoused 'brand values' of *achievement, creativity* and *integrity*, which were communicated internally throughout the company. Approximately twenty-five brand ambassadors, plus assistants, were employees who were selected from factory operatives through to middle management, to aid the 'new brand' relaunch. Notably, the brand ambassadors were employees (both volunteers and nominated) who were regarded by the company as embodying the new 'brand personalities' (again, internally communicated) of *positive, active, truthful* and *team-playing*.

Thus the intention was that the brand ambassadors would act as influential role models from within, to embed the brand values and aid the transformation process. The installation of the brand ambassadors is reminiscent of Treviño's recommendation that 'if organizations are interested in influencing the ethical behavior of their members, they should focus on identifying appropriate referent others, perhaps through the organization's choice of heroes and heroines' (Treviño, 1986: 612). The role of the brand ambassadors was thus a dual one: to facilitate improvement/cost-saving projects and also to implement projects associated with helping the local community. This CSR aspect to the company's relaunch was regarded as entirely congruent with the company's corporate culture and socially responsible reputation and was an aspect of the corporate brand that the company wished to lever (Keller, 1993; 1998). Examples of local community projects were the decorating of a local hospice by employees, the digging out of an overgrown play area in the city and the organisation of a Christmas party for the company's pensioners. All employees, including directors, were encouraged to embody the brand personalities (*positive*, *active*, *truthful* and *team-playing*) in order to help the company achieve its goals. The Brand Ambassador programme was co-ordinated by the communications adviser, Sally Bennett, and her manager, the president's PA. They reported directly to George Carr, the president of the division. George, a marketing man, had been the initiator of the company's rebranding, which had been designed by a firm of consultants. Furthermore, George reported to the chief executive officer of the company. When he was interviewed, George acknowledged the support of his boss with regard to the development of CSR within the company. At that point I was already aware, through my own local priest, that the CEO of the corporation was a practising Roman Catholic.[3] Indeed, the connection between religion and CSR was highlighted in Chapter 2 above (see also Angelidis and Ibrahim, 2004; Rice, 1999). Thus the company's management of its corporate culture is significant, providing the context for this study and thereby affecting its results.

My second reason for the purposeful selection of this case organisation was my knowledge of it as an ex-employee, having worked

---

[3] I did not use this very tenuous connection to the CEO of the company. Instead I wrote an unsolicited letter to the president of the company, describing the proposed research study and asking his permission to conduct it.

and been promoted there, albeit eighteen years previously. Indeed, I had retained contacts within the organisation and the president of the company knew me, as we had both worked in the same marketing department when I joined the company as a graduate trainee. Hence I was trusted to conduct the research study, not least because I was regarded as someone who understood the business. This confidence in me as a researcher was reflected through George Carr's full support and enthusiasm for the study and he expressed his interest in the further development of the company's CSR. Thus open access was granted to the company for data collection and follow-up purposes. This privileged access afforded a deep level of immersion into the case organisation.

At the time of data collection, this company employed approximately 900 people and was divided into two distinct centres: operations, or 'site' (manufacturing) and the global business unit (GBU). The site comprised all operations and services to do with manufacture of the product (such as engineering, facilities management, packaging, production planning, manufacturing accounting, quality assurance and the factory itself). The GBU comprised the functions responsible for marketing and distribution of the product worldwide, such as procurement, human resources, innovation (i.e. product development) and the commercial department. This organisational split, which was attributed to management consultants by the subjects who were interviewed, was not found to be wholly conducive to a coherent organisational culture.

Data collection

My simple brief to the company was that I was looking for employees, at any level, who had a reputation for prosocial behaviour (see Chapter 2) at work: individuals who might be regarded as corporate social entrepreneurs. Thus the initial selection of potential subjects was driven by the typology of Figure 5.2 and the top half of the matrix was targeted. So it was that during the initial research setup meeting between George Carr, Sally Bennett and myself, twelve potential informants were identified by George and Sally who could be approached for interview (Gummesson, 2000: 33). The twelve names comprised a mix of employees from different functions and at different levels of seniority, including five brand ambassadors and five board directors. Permission was also granted for me to make contact with further potential subjects, in order to boost the initial group of people who had been identified. These additional names would be employees who were recommended to me by those who had already been interviewed; that is, via snowball sampling (Moriarty, 1983). Thus, at the end each interview, every respondent was asked the following question: 'Can you think of anyone else in the company who you think might have personal convictions to "do the right thing" in terms of social responsibility, even though they might not articulate it as such?'

This exploratory ethnographic study was conducted over a three-year period, between 2005 and 2008. It comprised just twenty-nine personal, semi-structured interviews which lasted between half an hour and over two hours, with an average duration of seventy-five minutes. These semi-structured interviews were conducted face to face as personal meetings which took place either in each subject's private office or in a meeting room which had been pre-booked. The interviews included a second, follow-up face-to-face interview which was conducted with one of the directors who was identified after first interview as an 'Active' corporate social entrepreneur. Ten out of the twelve pre-identified subjects were interviewed (with two from the initial list unavailable for interview). All the interviews were digitally recorded and a further six follow-up telephone interviews were conducted in order to verify aspects from the face-to-face interviews. Further to this, there were additional informal meetings with subjects, which took place either immediately prior to or after the interview. The extra contact with these employees was useful, as the extra time spent with them facilitated understanding of the context and processes under investigation. All in all, over thirty-three hours of data were recorded, plus additional file notes were produced throughout the data collection, analysis and interpretation stages. Other written materials were also collected from the company, such as strategy documents and in-house staff brochures.

Data collection in the interpretivist tradition was adopted, which is acceptable to a critical-realist approach to research (Archer, 2012; Johnson and Duberley, 2000: 154). Thus each research subject told his or her own 'story' of their socially responsible activity, if any, and of the personal values acting as the antecedents to their behaviour. These

Table 7.1 *The position of subjects within the corporate hierarchy*

Status	Number of subjects
Directors	6
Snr. managers	5
Middle managers	6
Lower managers/ administrators/support	8
Factory operatives	3
n = 28	

interviews followed the same basic structure, but there was considerable 'flexibility in questioning to allow each informant some control over deciding what aspects of the phenomenon are most important from their experiences' (Shah and Corley, 2006: 1833). Tables 7.1 and 7.2 show the profile of the exploratory sample, in terms of the status and functional spread of the people who were interviewed.

All the subjects were asked their job title, and to briefly summarise their role. They were then told that the study was concerned with the company as a socially responsible organisation and how the company impacts on the welfare of others, through its employees. Subjects were then asked if they could think why they might have been recommended 'as someone who has personal convictions to make a difference in life, in addition to helping the company achieve its profit targets', to describe the sorts of things they do that might have given them this reputation, and to describe how they had become involved. Following each individual's explanation, a CSR prompt sheet was then introduced in order to further probe CSR. This incorporated a list of CSR definitions and domains, compiled from a variety of CSR literature sources (see Table 7.3). Thus CSR was primarily defined by the subjects themselves.

It is important to note that the subject of personal values was not introduced at this point, in order that the relationship between the subjects' unprompted personal values and CSR could be addressed indirectly, by capturing any insights that might be revealed through the subjects' display of their sense of self (Hitlin, 2003; Wickham and

Table 7.2 *Profile of subjects by function within the company*

Function	Number of subjects interviewed
President	1
Operations	6
Innovation (product development)	3
Health and safety	3
Technical and engineering	3
Quality assurance	2
Packaging	2
Marketing	2
Finance	2
Human resources	1
Toxicology	1
Global supply chain	1
Occupational health	1
n = 28	

Table 7.3 *Interview prompt sheet: 'some descriptions of CSR'*

- The 'three pillars of CSR': the balance between people, the planet and profit, or,
- The 'triple bottom line': the environment, society and economics
- Contributing to a better quality of life
- <u>Going *beyond* the requirements of the law in a wide variety of areas:</u>
  - Corporate citizenship – the company/its employees behaving as a responsible citizen
  - Helping the community (local or worldwide)
  - Environmental issues – waste management, emissions, renewable and non-renewable resources
  - Sustainability – however defined
  - Managing relationships with all stakeholders (employees, suppliers, customers, community, unions, local and national governments, NGOs)
  - Employee welfare and human rights
  - Integrity in your dealings at work

Parker, 2007; Williams, 1997). So it was not until at least the second half of the interview that the subject of personal values was overtly introduced. To minimise researcher bias, the informants' personal values were prompted using Form G of the Rokeach Values Survey (RVS) (Rokeach 1973), comprising a list of terminal values and a list of instrumental values. Now, in contrast to the traditional positivistic studies which investigate specific behaviour as the dependent variable and values as the independent variable, this exploratory qualitative study was designed to examine behaviour as 'the independent variable',[4] on the basis of a literature which shows that values and behaviour can be linked in systematic and predictable ways (see Chapter 4 above). This original research design represented an innovative use of the RVS (see Feather, 1986 for a conventional example of its application), considering that the purpose of this investigation was not to determine the value hierarchies of these subjects. Hence the instrument was used in an ideographic sense, as a discussion tool, to force the subjects to think about the subject matter and to help them articulate the meaning and importance of their personal values.

Data analysis

The research design allowed for a comparison of data within the controlled environment of this small ethnography. The data analysis phase was thus driven by a simultaneous deductive and inductive approach, using thematic analysis (Braun and Clarke, 2006; Brown and Locke, 2008; Goulding, 2002; Miles and Huberman, 1994). It consisted of the production of transcripts, the assigning of descriptive coding and the production of cognitive maps. Interpretive themes using multiple coding were assigned, which formed a second level of coding. After the interpretive codes were assigned, each respondent was evaluated against the framework of Figure 5.2, followed by random data-checking and, often, a reworking of codes. Moreover, the technique of constant comparisons was employed to identify patterns, particularly with the borderline cases, for example, between an 'Active'

---

[4] The terms 'dependent variable' and 'independent variable' are used loosely in this qualitative research context, in order to communicate the design of this research study.

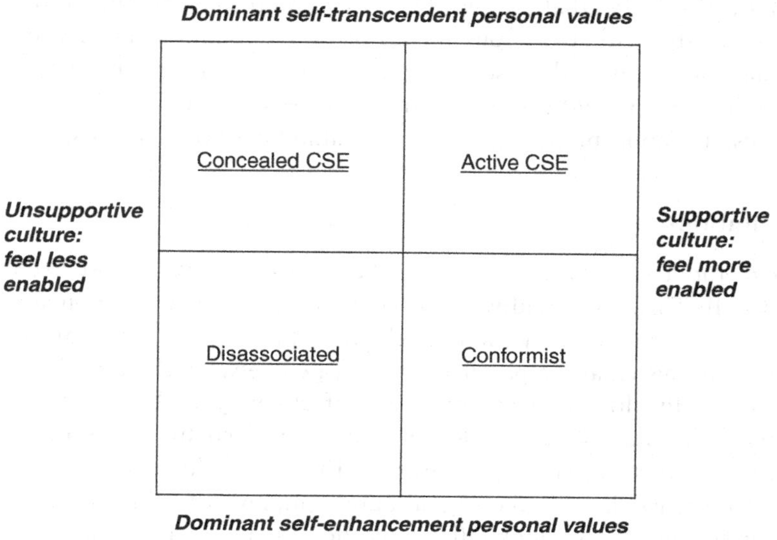

Dominant self-transcendent personal values

Concealed CSE	Active CSE
Disassociated	Conformist

Unsupportive culture: feel less enabled

Supportive culture: feel more enabled

Dominant self-enhancement personal values

Figure 7.1 Results of the exploratory study: modes of moral commitment to CSR

or 'Concealed' CSE (Shah and Corley, 2006). As a consequence, the theoretical framework was revised in the light of the empirical results and the 'Apathetic' case now represented a revised modality, referred to as 'Disassociated' (see Figure 7.1). Furthermore, teaching cases were produced for postgraduate students on the University of Nottingham MBA and also the British Councils' Chevening Programme.[5] Interim results were also presented to senior colleagues at the University of Nottingham and to two of the subjects who were identified as 'Active' CSEs. In the final stage of analysis, a meta-level of coding was applied whereby the relationships 'between and across incidents' (Goulding, 2002: 69) were pulled together to produce six coherent 'patterns of meaning' (Braun and Clarke, 2006: 86), or meta-themes: background, values, personality, beliefs about CSR, beliefs about the company and outcomes.

[5] A group of senior international scholar–practitioners who were attending the University of Nottingham. They were sponsored by the British Council and described by it as the 'potential leaders of tomorrow'.

In the discussion that follows, I will focus on the key finding of this empirical study: that the four modes of moral commitment to CSR mediate organisational constraints and enablements in quite distinctive ways. These represent entirely different stances towards CSR. Before I do this, it is appropriate to reiterate the fallibility of these results.

Limitations

The methodological minefield that is the study of values was discussed in Part II. This, combined with the contentious nature of CSR, made for a challenging investigation which was ripe with the potential for insight. In this regard, a parallel can be drawn between these methodological difficulties and the problems of claiming to be a socially responsible organisation while not being perceived by stakeholders to be entirely successful. So once again I return to the theme of personal responsibility, as the organisation, employee or (in this case) researcher needs to adopt reflexivity and systems of governance in the quest to achieve high standards, or even leadership. Hence this study was characterised by an experimental approach that employed perpetual analysis, perpetual questioning and a perpetual search for 'Why?' 'What can this possibly mean?' These are weapons which may be used to defend against making value judgements: 'the interpreter does not take the data on face value but considers them as a field of inferences in which hypothetical patterns can be identified and their validity tested' (Goulding, 2002: 28). And even though Bhaskar noted that 'social science is non-neutral' (Bhaskar, 1998: 409), I acknowledge the potential for researcher bias. As a consequence, much attention was paid throughout the collection and interpretation of the data set and to the potential for inaccuracy and misrepresentation during this investigation. Indeed, the validity of this particular sampling procedure (targeting individuals with a reputation for CSR) is evidenced through the finding that *most turned out not to be CSEs.*

Moreover, we might argue that the endorsement of this project by the company's top management, along with its selection of particular individuals to take part in the study, exacerbated the potential for social responsibility bias, particularly if the company was fielding its most impressive employees. However, the snowballing technique of identifying subjects with a sense of duty to others, in addition to a duty to their own families, was consistent throughout the project.

This left the interpretation of 'CSR' and 'socially responsible' open for the sponsors to define, and thus the meaning of SR and its degree of implementation, if any, was defined by each subject. Furthermore, a degree of triangulation was achieved when an individual's name was recommended more than once, providing the opportunity to obtain another opinion regarding experiences of the named individual.[6]

As a corollary to this, my methodology does not prevent research subjects talking to other research subjects and priming them prior to their interview, thereby reducing the potential for spontaneous, 'top-of-mind' answers and increasing the chances of a rehearsed interview, although the latter effect can also happen when the researcher sends each respondent a list of questions prior to the interview (which was not a practice adopted here), or even a survey questionnaire. As part of this study, these research subjects agreed to the mutual confidentiality, which was necessary for the gathering of spontaneous data in this exploratory investigation. But social desirability bias is always a hazard in social science, the more so considering the CSR context of this research, where subjects might have accentuated – or conversely played down – their role in CSR. But the function of values in displaying our sense of self and protecting self-esteem was contended in Chapter 4 and so ethnographic study was the most appropriate method for the task, enabling a greater depth of understanding of the research problem by asking the subjects to reveal 'who they really are' (Hitlin, 2003: 132).

Nevertheless, this research project was entirely exploratory and the tentative results presented here need to be tested as part of a further, much larger-scale, investigation. Much deeper refinement is required. For example, the emotional responses such as anxiety, empathy or passion which were noted as findings of this study were themed under 'personality'. Yet psychologists still debate how to categorise emotion: 'The degree to which empathy is viewed as a cognitive response, as

[6] The company uses this technique in employee appraisals and refers to it as either 'customer feedback' (to reflect the service nature of some departmental functions) or '360 degree performance review'. In preparation for an employee's annual appraisal, the line manager consults three or four colleagues regarding the appraisee's performance at work. The colleagues are not selected randomly: this is purposive sampling (Silverman, 2001: 251), whereby the line manager approaches 'internal customers' – people whom he/she is aware have been working with the appraisee – and asks for their opinions. However, there is no guarantee, of course, that the information obtained is any more reliable (Miles and Huberman, 1994: 287).

an affective response, or as having elements of both, is controversial' (Zahn-Waxler 1991: 313). But on the strength of the enduring nature of personal values and the integrity of this methodology, I have confidence that similar findings would have been replicated by another researcher, despite the reorganisation of the division that occurred during the phase of data collection. This confidence would be extended if the project were to be replicated, despite the installation of a second president since George Carr retired. Indeed, despite the 'double-dip' economic recession, there is the possibility of a continued commitment to CSR, due to the installation of the new president (2009) with over twenty years' experience within this organisation. However, I would expect to find some shifts, with an even greater proportion of 'Active CSEs' within this particular company, due to CSR's anticipated development over time in the mainstream (Archer, 1995). This is discussed further in Chapter 13 below. Whether the same findings would be replicated using a different organisation is rather more tricky. Even trickier is the question whether these findings can be generalised across the health care industry, or even across different industries. Certainly, the whole sample comprised only British nationals and no others. These more difficult issues can be addressed using a mixed methodology and a far more robust sample of subjects for investigation.

As a consequence of this research, my findings tentatively supported the conceptual model of Figure 5.2 and produced a much richer vein of insight. Thus each of the following four chapters constitutes a hypothesis in its own right (Archer, 2003: 165): Chapters 8, 9 and 10 suggest that there are such different modes of moral commitment to CSR as to warrant distinguishing between 'Active CSEs', 'Concealed CSEs' and 'Conformists'. In Chapter 11 the dominant mode of commitment was represented by the 'Disassociated' subject, who rejected CSR as an inappropriate and irrelevant strategic direction for Brayford Health International. The implications of these findings will be taken up in Part IV.

8 | *The active corporate social entrepreneur*

The purposive sampling method was geared towards interviewing known CSEs in the company, within the usual constraints of an exploratory and unfunded research project. However, the study revealed that only three subjects could be described as 'Active' CSEs, out of the ten individuals who had been initially proposed for interview. But after bolstering the sample using the snowballing technique, the final results revealed eight 'Active' CSEs, out of a total of twenty-eight subjects who were interviewed for the study. In what follows, then, I have set out the actions and characteristics of the 'Active' CSEs, described in this chapter as people who had enlarged their jobs in order to initiate and progress an SR agenda at work.

This subgroup espoused their belief in the social moral duty of both individuals and corporations, conformed to descriptions of moral character, and confounded the business ethics notions of the amoral or morally disengaged employee that was described in Part I. Indeed, this modality displayed moral imagination; conforming to Moberg and Seabright's description of 'moral exemplars' (Moberg and Seabright, 2000: 874). However, even though the members of this group might be reminiscent of the 'Good Samaritan' described in the New Testament, it would be naive to claim that the 'Active' CSE is a paragon of virtue. Furthermore, in Part I, we saw how the Friedmanite perspective on CSR ('the business of business is business') may be interpreted as a modern-day idea of virtue. Nonetheless, the background, espoused values, personal qualities and beliefs of the CSE accorded with ideas regarding integrity and moral character. Moreover, the majority of this subgroup described the organisational culture as supportive of CSR, with three spontaneously mentioning a supportive boss who had inspired them with regard to their drive to progress CSR at some time in their career.

The involvement in CSR by the 'Active' CSEs encompassed a wide range of CSR domains, both societal and environmental. Table 8.1

135

Table 8.1 *Characteristics of the Active*
CSE: SR outcomes

CSR outcomes	Number of subjects
Community work	5
Development of self/others	5
SR leadership	4
Fairness/equality	4
Environmentalism	3
Health and safety	2
Ethical marketing	1
n = 8	

Note: in this and subsequent tables the discrep-
ancy between the total number of subjects and
the actual subgroup size reflects subjects' participation in more than one domain of CSR.

shows which areas were most clearly identified from this study, reveal-
ing some areas of overlap. By way of explanation, examples of these
CSR outcomes are provided throughout Part III.

A key feature of the 'Active' CSE was their apparent internal locus
of control (Rotter, 1986; Treviño, 1986). Indeed, each member of
this subgroup had, voluntarily, self-selected for the activities in which
they were involved and these were, in most cases, not the original
requirements of their formal job role. In fact, each of these people had
taken personal responsibility for building into their jobs one or more
of the domains identified in Table 8.1. A second key point was that
their involvement in CSR was not a short-term, temporary response.
These individuals were personally responsible for having *adapted* their
job role to encompass CSR. Moreover, members of this subgroup
espoused helpful or caring values, both in terms of their descriptions
of what concerned them and in their responses to the Rokeach Values
Survey. Their ability to take the CSR initiative was summarised by one
'Active' about another, who described her colleague as 'a good example
of someone who just takes on and does things'. Another example
was Francesca, a board director, whose views were representative of
the rest of the subgroup, in terms of her personal concern to behave
with integrity. Indeed, all of the 'Actives' expressed highly principled

views, such as Francesca's declaration that she felt 'strongly' about maintaining 'ethical standards' in a number of areas.

Francesca described sustained commercial pressure exerted by sales staff to conduct product testing on animals, in order to expedite the production of sales aids and advertisements. Clinical trials using humans take much longer. This pressure was resisted:

we'll only do that if we can't do it in humans in any way [pause] and sometimes that does get challenged: 'Why *can't* we do that?' Just to get a piece of data that might produce one graph in a promotional piece. You see the argument is: 'Well, to be honest a nurse doesn't know whether that graph has come from a clinical study or from animals, so why don't we do an animal study? – And if we can get that in three months...' That's the challenge.

She also described a meticulous approach with regard to the fair treatment of her subordinates. Moreover, five of the subgroup espoused equality as a personal value, which translated into a drive to treat others fairly – for example, a strongly espoused belief in 'doing things on the basis of knowledge' – and this encompassed a diligent approach to regular performance appraisals in order to protect staff and to facilitate their promotion. There had been situations

where people get labelled and it's hard for them to shake it off. You can have someone really exceptional but they can't perform because they've been labelled for something that might have happened a long while ago. Everyone should be given a fair opportunity to try and achieve...

Francesca described how, once or twice a year, she had found it necessary in board meetings to speak out against proposals to begin disciplinary proceedings against subordinates whom she regarded as being judged unfairly:

there may have been a view or a situation about an individual where this has to happen. So, 'Hang on a moment, that's just not – I don't think that's the way we should deal with it.' I think that's led to where I would be [pause] I don't want to be viewed as being difficult, but when it comes to those sort of situations [pause] I would consciously say, 'Well, I'm sorry, I'm not going to do that'.

And:

if I was told to go and tell someone about a performance issue and I fundamentally disagreed with it, again, I wouldn't do it and I wouldn't worry if it
had an impact on my career: I don't *care* about that in that sense . . .

This indicates Francesca's personal sense of autonomy and field independence. Indeed, she described how her sense of fairness was more
important to her than playing organisational politics, echoing the theory of dissonance reduction (Festinger, 1957; Leidtka, 1989), referred
to in Part I: 'I feel quite comfortable with doing things that might
not be best for my long-term career [pause] the inner conflict would
really be huge in me if I took a compromise'. But Francesca had the
confidence to speak out, because she perceived the corporate culture
to be supportive of her views on fairness to individuals. This was theoretically proposed in Chapter 5 and substantiated by all of the eight
'Active' CSEs. Indeed, the whole of this subgroup described how the
company encouraged its employees to support the local community, in
terms of mentoring disadvantaged children at school, or they described
how the company had a strong, historical reputation for staff welfare.
Nevertheless, Francesca's senior position in the company, with its formal authority, engendered the respect which enabled her to have the
confidence to be seen to be upholding socially responsible standards.
Notably, though, Francesca's name was not on the original list of
names provided by the company. She was selected for interview as
a result of recommendation by her colleagues, who regarded her as
someone with 'personal convictions to "do the right thing", in terms
of social responsibility (even though they might not articulate it as
such)'.

Francesca also believed that she had a reputation as someone who
is honest, as well as principled:

So yeah. That's always been part of who I am. I think it's something as
well, that [pause] when I get feedback from my peers when we're doing
performance review – 360 degrees – people say [pause] what people say
is that they think I'm honest! So I take that as quite a [pause] challenge,
because that means that if people think you're honest you'd better hell be
certain that you are *always* being honest, because you can destroy that very
very quickly, I think.

But it is also noteworthy that this subgroup were pragmatic individuals
who articulated both a concern for the success of the company and that

they were driven by a sense of accomplishment.[1] Indeed, Francesca's senior position in the company is indicative that she did not lack capability and ambition. Francesca also described how she believed that having ethical standards makes for a sustainable business:

what I feel is why don't they think, well, we've been in this business for a hundred years, we want to be in it for another hundred years and not, you know [pause] we're not going to jeopardise a product like AGO for a short-term [pause] so that some person can make an impact in the organisation, can get a nice advert out?

These responses typify this group of individuals, who described using their discretion to progress CSR and taking personal responsibility for it, over and above the expectations of their role. Certainly, these employees could not be described as morally mute, being actively engaged in socially responsible issues at work. Moreover, they displayed moral imagination: a reasoning process, comprising the four decision processes identified by Rest (1986), i.e., moral sensitivity, moral judgement, moral intention and moral behavior. But in this particular case study, the context of moral imagination was prosocial behaviour as well as the prevention of antisocial behaviour, with the moral imagination of these informants acting 'as a kind of creative force' (Moberg and Seabright, 2000: 845), enabling Francesca to imagine the company as a sustainable business into the next century, due to its ethical ethos.

Indeed, moral imagination was demonstrated by another informant, Eric, a senior manager, who expressed 'a desire to make a difference where I can'. Eric described a 'a wider social agenda', articulating a collectivistic sentiment that he wanted 'to make a difference [pause] life isn't about yourself. The world is bigger than this'. He also quoted the president of the division (another 'Active' CSE): 'with privilege comes responsibility', and Eric expressed his frustration with consumerism, citing his children's desire for flat-screen televisions, as opposed to a focus on helping people in need. Eric's sense of social responsibility was expressed as follows:

---

[1] Five out of the eight 'Active' CSEs expressed a sense of accomplishment and self-respect as key drivers. These espoused personal values were also indicated as key concerns on the RVS.

and usually we get – the company gets a number of requests every month, you know, 'Can you support this, can you help that?' [pause] I suppose I'm fairly vociferous in saying [pause] 'Yes'. And when they're asking for, you know, can we have someone to actually sit on this panel or to come along and [pause] help here, or whatever, then [pause] a lot of the others'll sit there and [pause] and mumble and go quiet. And I'll say – there's two of us – who'll say 'Yes'.

Through the company, Eric was active in Common Purpose,[2] a not-for-profit organisation which promotes social entrepreneurship across the private, public and voluntary sectors. In addition to this, his commitment to 'wider social issues' was a proactive involvement via his church. For example, Eric took paid leave to work in India for the week immediately following the Indian tsunami of 2004: 'I will be asking the company for some funding', he said. He also described putting his own money behind the sponsorship of a midwife friend who was going to help the needy in Bogotá. 'Money follows vision', he declared. Indeed, the views expressed by the 'Active' subgroup accord with the idea of the moral character, described in Chapter 6.

For example, a sense of moral duty was articulated clearly by another senior executive, Helena, who described her personal agenda at work in terms of being able to 'hold our heads up high'. Helena spoke quietly when she recalled a story regarding recruitment practices she had recently experienced abroad:

H: . . . but you still do have some things which [pause] a g-good example would be [pause] [whispers] you know, recruiting people, like, somebody said to me: 'Well, you know, you shouldn't recruit that person because, well, ahm, she hasn't had a baby yet and she'll probably want to have a baby [pause] 'Well', I said 'Look, I didn't hear that. And I said [pause] 'No. Certainly, I didn't hear that, that will not be – that was not a factor in this – in this discussion.' You know and you have to be quite firm about things!

C: It would be easy for you to slip into the 'as in Rome' mentality.

H: Oh yeah! Yeah. And people will sort of say well, age [pause] and you know, all of – all of those things, and it's actually [pause] but – but I think the issue [coughs] you know [pause] whether or not, er, I'm doing it right or not, I think [softly] the issue is, well, it's what do you do, do you actually change your moral compass, or your [pause] whatever your guiding – you know,

2 See www.commonpurpose.org.uk.

Table 8.2 *Characteristics of the Active CSE: seniority*

Status	Number of subjects
Directors (including president)	3
Senior managers	2
Middle managers	0
Lower manager/administrator	2
Factory operative	1
n = 8	

your guiding principles. Do you change them because of the environment in which you find yourself, or, do you actually say, 'Well these things are actually worth having'? They're of value and hence, you're not going to change things. You know, my view is that the Nuremberg defence didn't work at Nuremberg! [Laughs] And so it's the obligation on all of us is that we actually have to be driven by our own sense of right and wrong.

This very personal conviction regarding the social moral duty of individuals within corporations was a key theme amongst the 'Active' subgroup. And it is interesting that Helena used the term 'moral compass', a phrase that I had not used. Nevertheless these extracts from my conversations with Francesca, Eric and Helena support the prevailing notion that having the integrity, or moral courage, to speak out at work is likely to be the domain of the senior executive.

Yet, in Brayford Health International, seniority was not found to be a prerequisite for corporate social entrepreneurship (see Table 8.2). For example, Andy, a junior manager, had initiated of his own volition a recycling project across the site, which was not part of his job remit. Indeed, Andy conveyed an entrepreneurial attitude that it was better to go ahead – without obtaining agreement from superiors – in order to lessen the probability of the initiative being vetoed: 'because I know I'm doing it right and I'm just gonna do it, anyway. Regardless of...' This view was also expressed by Helena (in a different departmental function): 'it's better to beg for forgiveness than to ask permission'. But, compared with Helena, the courage expressed by Andy was more tempered. Andy was uncertain as to whether or not he could be a whistleblower, if he discovered that his line manager (in a key technical function) was cutting corners:

That's the thing, what impact would it have on *me*, would it make my [pause] if it was making my life *harder* [pause] ahhhhm, yes, I'd – mmm God! That's such a good question! I'm more yes than no, but it's not a firm yes, that's the thing.

Thus Andy's difficulty here demonstrated the possibility for moral muteness, which I connected earlier in Chapter 3 with power and deference to authority (Bird and Waters, 1989; Lovell, 2002a). Even so, despite findings in the literature regarding perceived futility by lower and middle management regarding their ability to influence top management on matters of CSR, it is an important finding from this tentative study that the moral courage to speak out was not exclusively confined to the senior executive (see Table 8.2 which shows that the 'Active' CSEs in this study polarised at the top and bottom of the organisational hierarchy). This contrasts with Drumwright's policy entrepreneurs, who were most prevalent amongst middle management (Drumwright, 1994: 17). It is also worth noting here that job insecurities were also expressed by two of the 'Active' CSEs, from the very top and bottom of the organisational hierarchy (see Chapter 7 regarding successive rounds of redundancies that formed part of this organisational context).

So might middle managers be the least likely group in the organisational hierarchy to use their discretion at work to champion CSR, where 'technical responsibilities tend to displace wider moral concerns' (Gabriel, Fineman and Sims, 2000: 69)? Or because middle managers maybe feel more vulnerable to organisational change? Certainly, the muteness described in Chapter 3 has previously been attributed by some scholars to the powerlessness felt by management (Collins and Ganotis, 1973; Lovell, 2002a; Lovell, 2002b). Notably, all four 'Concealed' CSEs (see the next chapter) were volunteers in the community. And whilst they may be regarded as corporate social entrepreneurs because of their involvement with other SR activities, *all* of the community work was conducted by the 'Concealeds' out of official working hours. Moreover, none of the 'Concealed' CSEs were directors of the company and three out of the four subjects in this subgroup were managers who expressed job security issues. The key point here is that the sense of personal moral duty articulated by the 'Actives' was actively and visibly channelled into CSR. Moreover, having a reputation as a CSR champion (not a term used in this company) was, in some cases, domain-specific. Some aspects of CSR were easier to progress than others. Nevertheless, the combination of the personal concerns of the 'Actives', plus their perception of a supportive context, enabled this subgroup to progress a CSR agenda at work.

Typical of the 'Actives' was Diane, an administrator, who had also volunteered to be one of BHI's brand ambassadors (see Chapter 7). Diane had started working at the company as a secretary, but she had developed her own job through the initiation and organisation of charity events within the company. Diane described how she had become a highly successful fundraiser, managing to galvanise staff into raising £33,700 for different charities over a four-year period. These donations were over and above the company's official charity budget of £2,000 per annum. Importantly, she had exerted her influence over colleagues in order to garner their support and part of her influence involved leveraging the company's internal PR system to generate publicity for her activities.[3] In fact, Diane was so successful that she was the most salient and commonly cited person by her colleagues. And whilst one cynic implied that Diane was a self-publicist, assuming that the cynic was right to suspect Diane's motives (who openly described herself as an ambitious person during the interview) this does not detract from her commitment to CSR and the scale of her fundraising activities. Indeed, the likelihood of mixed individualistic as well as collectivistic motives has already been mooted in Chapters 2 and 3 above, where it was also emphasised that the purpose of this study was not to empirically establish the existence or otherwise of 'pure' altruism. Regardless, Diane clearly demonstrated prosocial behaviour.

The case of Diane illustrates how some SR activities were easier than others with which to build a reputation as a CSE. Organising charity events was considered by the company to be fully congruent with the corporate brand (see Chapter 7 regarding the company's culture). But Eric used his discretion to act in a socially responsible manner, by employing an individual as a consultant who was known to him through his church and who had a history of drug addiction. Eric paid for the consultant from his departmental budget in order to bypass the

---

[3] See Anderson, Spataro and Flynn (2008) and Shane (2003) regarding the importance of personality in the ability to influence at work.

company's human resources recruitment procedures. Similarly, Helena admitted to using money from her departmental budget towards the private health care of a sick employee, in order for the employee to return to work faster. Of course, these two actions would not be publicised in the company newsletter, in the same way as Diane's activities were. Nevertheless, the common ground between these three cases were the descriptions of how these subjects had regularly stepped beyond their formal job role in order to help others and to act in a socially responsible manner, regardless of any authorisation by the company. These individuals were driven by their dominant self-transcendent values. In Kohlberg's terms, they appeared to have moved beyond the conventional stage in their cognitive moral development. But how can this happen? What are the triggers?

Socialisation as a result of parental influence and other factors was cited in Chapter 4 above. And whilst the scope of this tentative research project (and the president's stipulation that the interviews should, ideally, be confined to less than one hour) did not permit the time to dwell on the respondents' biographies: half of the 'Active' subgroup spontaneously referred to their family upbringing as a source of their values, when probed. One graduate environmentalist, Andy, reported that his mother had been a member of Friends of the Earth.[4] This compares with Helena, who described herself as having 'a strong sense of humanistic values [pause] I was brought up having a strong sense of social values and with a sense of, you know, always trying to help somebody who needs help: help the underdog, or whatever'. In the second interview I conducted with Helena, two years after our first meeting, she criticised the indigenous population of a developing country where she was employed by BHI, for prioritising the accumulation of wealth above all else. Helena lowered her voice to a whisper as she said, 'In the UK, you don't look up to people just because they've made money, you're more likely to look up to somebody [pause] who has done – like Bob Geldof, who's you know, actually done [pause] actually [pause] changed something; done something'.

And to illustrate her collectivistic values:

you know, we grew up in a liberal [pause] social democracy [pause] you know, I mean, lots of us, you know, had problems with Thatcher because

---

[4] An environmental pressure group. See www.foe.co.uk.

we didn't think she was part of that. And, you know, and as much as anything, that fashions [pause] how you grow up; how you feel about things and um, but if you – if you grew up – you know, some of the attitudes I come across [pause]. You know!

My point is that there was no company pressure being exerted on these individuals to take responsibility for CSR in these ways, to take their CSR activity so personally and articulate their personal beliefs so passionately. But the question remains, how could these values inform SR behaviour in this manner? Are they stimulated in certain situations?

An unanticipated finding from this study was the six out of eight 'Active' CSEs who related a 'necessary turning point' (Erikson, 1950) which had either changed their outlook on life from being self-centred to more concerned with the welfare of other people or acted as their conscience and reminded them how they ought to behave (Foucault, 2000; Maclagan, 1998).[5] The incidents can be related to the peak experiences described by Maslow, that I referred to at the end of Chapter 6, because they were stories of salient and deeply embedded memorable events that were reported to have changed the informants' behaviour and shaped their moral character. Eric described his own turning point:

OK [pause] the reason I sort of get involved in sort of wider sort of social issues is really [pause] because of my [pause] Christian conviction and Christian beliefs [pause]. When I was at university I had a sort of quite a life-changing sort of series of events, really. Prior to that I was fundamentally very self-focused and what I wanted, very career-minded and all that sort of stuff and, you know, the agenda revolved around me. And while I was at university I became a Christian and [pause] really recognised that the world is a little bit bigger than that. Um [pause] and a lot of that got turned on its head and so really since then [pause] I've had much more [pause] of a desire to [pause] you know [pause] make a make a difference where I can [pause] and sort of and *what I can sort of contribute to and change, really* [my emphasis].

Eric's declaration was that this experience had turned his life around. His main goal, now, was to make a difference in life. It's about 'knowing that the world is bigger than you' and that 'there's more to life than

---

[5] Four of these subjects spontaneously related a turning point without being prompted.

Table 8.3 *Characteristics of the Active CSE: necessary turning points*

Type of turning point	Number of subjects
Family member trauma: accident/serious illness/death	3
Christian conversion	1
Intense training course about personal goal setting and taking responsibility for improving one's life (RWG)	1
Closing a factory	1
n = 6	

flat-screen TVs'. Significantly, this religious conversion was one of six dramatic accounts of a conscious turning point which was reported by the 'Active' CSEs and cited by them as the source of their personal values (see Table 8.3). Three of the subjects reported serious incidents involving family members that had acted as a turning point.

Indeed, Diane movingly described how she had been profoundly affected by the unexpected death of her sister, who died of a heart condition at an early age:

Going back about three years ago, I was asked if I would [pause] run [pause] a big employee event, which was the fun day and I agreed. I said, 'Yeah alright', then I was given a low-down of what we needed to do, so I arranged it. And the same year I was asked 'well do you think you could organise the Christmas party this year' – as a favour, really – so I said, 'Yes alright, then I'll do the Christmas party as well.' And then it's just escalated from there. But [pause] going back [pause] four years [pause] what really kicked all this off, was [pause] I lost my sister – she died – she was only thirty-three [pause] and [pause] and I was only like thirty-one at the time [pause] and [pause] you know, it makes you take stock, doesn't it? Do you know? [pause] and [pause] I thought, Right [two-second pause], well at mine what will they say about me? You know, I [pause] I don't know whether it's twisted, or what [pause] but I just thought [pause] how do *I* make a difference? What do *I* do [pause] for anybody else? You know? And it just gets you thinking about [pause] what you actually do [pause] and I thought [pause] what will they say about me at mine. So, that's where it sort of all came from, really. And I thought, well, how do *I* make a difference? What do *I* do to actually [pause] make a difference to anybody? Other than [pause] like [pause] you know [pause] my mum, my dad, my daughter, do you know what I mean?

Diane described how her sister's very early death, at thirty-three years old, had spurred her into making a conscious decision to change her own life for the better: not only in order to 'improve herself', but also so that she would be remembered as someone who had really contributed to the lives of others, to

get off your arse and go and do something, to make a difference to somebody. And you think, you start thinking [pause] about your own [pause] path in life really, don't you? So, Bridget died in the April [two-second pause] and then [pause] in the September I signed up for an HNC [Higher National Certificate] [pause]. My boss at the time encouraged me and said, 'You know, I really think you're capable of more and with what you've done, with the organising and the charity stuff, I really think, you know that you should go and do this HNC.' So it all happened really within the month because [pause] not only did I buy a house, I'd started this HNC and I thought, Right! You know, this is, this is going to be [pause] I'm going to make good this year and do something that is going to change my life . . .

These stories of life-changing events did not always occur in the work situation, as suggested by Maclagan, who acknowledged the importance of 'significant personal experiences . . . triggers which awaken a moral sensitivity' (Maclagan, 1998: 20). And regardless of the context of the event, they accord with notions of the developmental crisis identified by psychologists and the formation of character integrity (Erikson, 1950; Horowitz 2002; Maslow, 2011; Rokeach, 1979).

Another such trigger was the training course on personal goal setting, which was conducted by the Results Worldwide Group (RWG), a firm of consultants. Surprisingly, every employee in this very large organisation had attended the course, which was reported to have had a profound effect on employees. Indeed it was spontaneously mentioned by eight out of twelve of the CSEs,[6] despite having been conducted nine years prior to this study. One keen advocate of the RWG course was Brian, another senior manager, who echoed the

---

[6] The RWG course was spontaneously mentioned by six out of the eight 'Active' CSEs and again spontaneously by two of the four 'Concealed' CSEs (see the next chapter). This particular finding in CSR regarding turning points is currently the subject of another article.

words of Diane, above, regarding the importance of taking personal responsibility:

You make a path through life yourself. There was a fantastic training course a few years ago called RWG [pause] goal setting and choices [pause] opportunities when they arise [pause] taking responsibility for your own destiny; firmly realise that you're in control of your life rather than other people are [pause] be comfortable with the choices you're making as well.

And also:

I struggle with people who aren't independent, who won't do things for themselves. It's going back to this RWG-type course that we did. I struggle with people believing that the world and life owes them something. And I guess that's because I'm very independent [pause]. I used to work with some shop floor people and they were hard work because they – and I found it really difficult – the ones that wanted everything just handing on a plate [pause] because I don't like being told what to do . . .

Now in Chapter 4 I described the sources of our values as varied. But regardless of the source of our personal values, examples of initiative in CSR and the role of some of the subjects in this study conveyed an internal locus of control (Rotter, 1986): qualities which were demonstrated by all eight of the 'Active' CSEs.

But it is important to point out that not all of the events listed in Table 8.3 could be described in terms of an epiphany of the 'road to Damascus' type which completely changed the lives of the sub-group. These crises differed in the degree of behavioural change which was generated. For example, in her second (follow-up) interview, I prompted Helena, who had not spontaneously referred to any kind of life-changing turning point during our first meeting. I referred to the RWG training course which had been conducted at the company before Helena had been recruited as head of her department. Helena's response was that whilst courses had affected how she perceived herself, they had not changed her behaviour in terms of the way she treated others:

but in terms of, did that give me, you know, a stronger [pause] motivation to be [pause] corporately responsible, then um [pause] I don't know, I don't think so. I think probably, the nearest thing in terms of work experience would probably be [pause] where I actually had to close a factory in Manchester and I think *that* kind of [pause] awakened me to a lot of the issues.

You know, that would probably be the nearest thing, I would say. Is that what made me think these things are important? It certainly reinforced it. But did I always think that people should be treated properly; should try and do your best, um, for your community – ah, I probably did raise it on my agenda . . .

The implication, here, combined with Helena's passionate belief in a personal obligation to society and in the individual's responsibility for making change, was that Helena was already practising the lessons taught by the RWG course, without having attended it:

I think there's probably an altruistic piece, which is about [pause] well, you know, if you see problems that are around about you and you can do something to help, well, why shouldn't you do it? You know, don't sit around and wait for somebody *else* to get involved, get involved yourself. And, I guess it's the classic: what Ghandhi said, was: 'Be the change you want to see in the world'. Yeah? Unless you're willing to be that change yourself then nobody else is going to be.

Her claim was that the event of having to close down a factory 'reinforced' Helena's existing belief regarding the need to treat people fairly. Thus the turning points related by these subjects seem to have acted as triggers that produced self-awareness regarding their value priorities, which in turn produced varying degrees of behaviour change. The inference is not a complete transformation of values from overtly individualistic to collectivistic; it is more: that the raw material of the collectivistic values was already dominant. And I have already pointed out that one would not expect an either–or situation in terms of an individual possessing solely self-enhancement or self-transcendent values. Indeed, I have emphasised that the CSE was not anticipated to be an entirely selfless individual.

This is illustrated by the charity fundraising administrator, Diane, who described her own motivation to develop herself and to 'do better' for her own family. Her entrepreneurial skills were demonstrated in a non-CSR example when she described how she approached her boss to volunteer to run an in-house computer training course for staff, in return for a £700 payment from the departmental budget for her to undertake a teaching certificate. She described the 'win–win' whereby the company saved thousands of pounds in external training as a result of her initiative, plus staff time saved from travelling, whilst she was successful in persuading her boss to pay her course fees. But

Diane's entrepreneurial discretion (Hemingway and Maclagan, 2004) was clearly applied to CSR as well. For example, she described how she made a proposal to the factory manager to close the production lines twenty minutes early before the end of a shift, so that all the factory personnel could 'Walk a Mile' around the site for charity, 'because I dared to ask'. She also described one occasion when she approached two colleagues who were training for a local half-marathon and used the opportunity to collect sponsor money in return for some company sponsorship and framed certificates. In this instance, Diane was able to manipulate the situation so that the beneficiary of the sponsorship was the same heart ward that had treated her sister (not a local hospital). Thus Diane used her discretion in two ways. First to initiate the sponsorship, and second to select the beneficiary.

Finally, the 'Active' CSEs conveyed their reflective nature, through their humility and self-awareness. This is consistent with the discussion in Chapter 6 above regarding a focus on the development of the self and others and the association with integrity. These features combined with a palpable sense of achievement and job satisfaction, even though the group also expressed some frustrations at work. Consider, for example, Brian, the senior manager who had been employed for seventeen years by the company:

I enjoy the comfort of working in this place and I'm happy with that choice. With my education and my experience I could be flitting off around all sorts of organisations probably earning much more than I do now and all the rest of it. I chose not to do that because I enjoy the comfortable lifestyle that I live at the moment.

Thus the idea of meaningful work in the form of CSR as a source of job satisfaction and general happiness links with my earlier discussion. Brian both had a strong belief in protecting the environment, which he had built into his job, and was 'heavily, heavily involved' in his local community, working on various committees and for his local school for the past thirteen years. Indeed, Brian described 'pushing' the environmental agenda at the company and recommended someone else to interview whom he described as both 'qualified in that way and believing in it as well'. What is more, Brian was also educated in CSR himself as part of a business qualification, having also personally elected CSR as the subject for his research module assessment. So Brian's sense of personal fulfilment was unequivocally expressed and his work–life

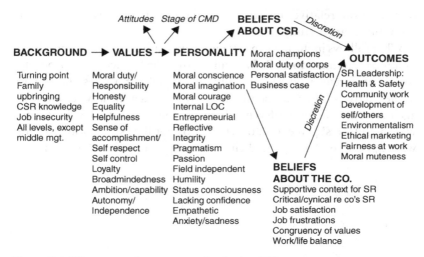

Figure 8.1 Diagrammatic summary: the Active CSE

balance was key to this. But there was no obvious demarcation to Brian's *activities*, with social responsibility as the unifying seam which produced his identity and sense of authenticity. This is how he differed from the 'Concealed' CSE subgroup (described in the next chapter): there was no visible split between the socially responsible activities associated with his home life and those of his working life.

In this chapter, then, we have seen how the research subjects articulated their personal concerns and where they placed their greatest emphasis. By way of summarising this, Figure 8.1, provides an illustration of the 'Active' CSE, using the meta-themes of background, values, personality, beliefs about CSR, beliefs about the company and outcomes.

By way of explanation, the order of the interpretive themes listed under each of the meta-themes in Figure 8.1 reflects the quantification of the number of subjects who exhibited each of the interpretive themes, in descending order. Also, the personal values represent the concerns of the subgroup and not every item that was indicated by the subjects on the RVS. Hence the order of listing gives some indication of the importance of these themes to the subgroup. However, as the number of cases within each subgroup is so small (no more than fifteen 'Conformists', for example), firm conclusions cannot be drawn regarding the relative importance of these themes. This must be left for a much larger study.

What follows in the next chapter is an exposition of a second mode of moral commitment to CSR. We will see that the 'Concealed' corporate social entrepreneur possessed many of the qualities, values and beliefs of the 'Active' CSE, and also that they progressed a socially responsible agenda at work. The difference between these two modes, however, was the subjects' perception of whether or not BHI's corporate culture was supportive of an agential championing of a prosocial agenda.

9 | The concealed corporate social entrepreneur

The 'Concealed' corporate social entrepreneurs displayed comparable characteristics to the 'Active' CSEs and articulated similar self-transcendent, collectivistic values. None of the 'Concealed' CSEs were directors of the company and three out of the four subjects in this subgroup were managers, all of whom expressed job security issues. Nonetheless, these individuals articulated their field independence and the indications of their moral courage support the statement made in the previous chapter that courage was not restricted to the upper echelons of senior management in this study. However, compared with the 'Active' CSEs, the moral courage of the 'Concealeds' was *tempered*, due to the subjects' perceptions of external constraints and limitations on particular SR activities. Importantly, though, there was no evidence of the moral disengagement that is prevalent in the business ethics, management and marketing literatures. This supports the notion of immutable, stable personal values (Schwartz, 2010) that, in some cases, can remain unaffected by organisational pressures. So I have proffered the notion of 'personal value contagion' in order to support the idea that personal values are brought into the workplace and, for certain people, morality cannot be bracketed. But the subjects' internal *and* external locus of control was demonstrated via a selective championing of particular CSR *domains*. This indicated rather more clearly that it is easier to build a reputation as a CSE with some SR activities than with others. In what follows, then, we see evidence of a belief in the social moral duty of individuals and corporations, along with the limitations to and perceived constraints upon CSR that the subjects experienced.

The 'Concealed' is also a corporate social entrepreneur. Amongst the sample of twenty-eight informants, though, only four people typified this mode. Each had dominantly expressed collectivistic values, comparable to the 'Active' CSE. Members of this subgroup also

Table 9.1 *Characteristics of the Concealed CSE: SR outcomes*

(C)SR outcomes	Number of subjects
Community work	4
Fairness/equality	3
Development of self/others	3
Ethical marketing	1
n = 4	

presented themselves as highly principled individuals and they artic-ulated strongly held beliefs about making a contribution towards the well-being of others. Their SR activity is listed in Table 9.1, which also shows the areas of overlap, in terms of involvement with more than one of the CSR domains. Notably, however, the 'Concealed' CSEs were differentiated from the 'Active' CSEs in their perception of a corporate culture that was not wholly supportive of CSR. Indeed, the distinguishing feature was their sense of constraint or limitation upon their SR activities, in terms of how far they felt they could champion CSR at work. In other words, their field independence was com-promised. In fact, all four 'Concealed' CSEs were volunteers in the community, but all of their community work was conducted out of official working hours. But it was their other SR activity at work, combined with their dominantly espoused collectivistic personal val-ues, which exposed them as corporate social entrepreneurs. This is not to acknowledge the SR activity conducted by the rest of the sample in their leisure time, but that the objectives of this investigation were con-cerned with the role and subjective interpretation of Brayford Health International's employees in corporate social responsibility.

I begin with Larry, a senior manager and an ex-volunteer, who had been heavily involved in the governorship of a failing school and latterly as chair of governors after the school had failed its OFSTED inspection. When I asked why he had become involved, Larry modestly described how the school was now out of 'special measures', under his successful leadership:

And my thinking was [pause] that [pause] I'd [pause] felt that I'd benefited from the education system, so [pause] I wanted to see if I could put some-thing back into it. Being married to [pause] to Wendy who *is* a teacher, I was [pause] aware of some of the *challenges* that [pause] that the teaching profession faces. And again, I was trying to [pause] to see what *I* could do [pause] to help and maybe [pause] apply some of the company's resources to er [pause] you know, to – to helping in the education setting. And I also thought, that [pause] with my connections within the company I could actually [pause] apply – or bring some *leverage*, I suppose, to – to the role. Er, and [pause] formally or informally, you know, use the company's resources to help [pause] the – the school.

But Larry's priorities had changed and he soon pointed out that he was stepping back from the governorship because 'I've put in enough . . . ' He also expressed disappointment in not managing to achieve what he had initially set out to do and some frustration about not obtaining financial support from the company to help the school, in the way that he had hoped:

in terms of the tour, there's a little bit of resistance to bringing [pause] school parties around, now because of the [pause] the complexity of getting into the factory and the – the factory environment and er [pause] So . . .

Also:

I suppose, in my mind, I had a picture of creating links with the school and maybe bringing [pause] some of the pupils through and perhaps into employment within the company. Ahhm, but the nature of the pupils that attend the school, doesn't really lend it – lend itself to that [pause] approach. They – they have severe [pause] learning difficulties, or moderate to severe. A lot of them have behavioural difficulties now and increasingly so. And [pause] the [pause] opportunities to [pause] to make the connection you know with them as as potential [pause] workers of the future is [pause] is limited.

At the end of our meeting, Larry told me that he was in the process of applying for another job within the company, as his role was being made redundant. In fact, a new role for Larry was not forthcoming and he left the business after twenty-five years' service. So we can understand why Larry indicated that his priorities had changed. Job insecurity was in fact expressed by three out of the four 'Concealed' CSEs as a key concern, along with four out of a total of fifteen people from the 'Conformists' (Chapter 10 below). It was also indicated by two of the 'Active' subgroup, but not expressed as a key concern. Table 9.2 shows the status of the 'Concealed' in the organisational hierarchy, with the lack of company directors in this subgroup.

Table 9.2 *Characteristics of the Concealed CSE: seniority*

Status	Number of subjects
Directors	0
Senior manager	1
Middle manager	1
Lower manager/administrator	1
Factory operative	1
n = 4	

Notably, two employees, Imelda and Julie, spontaneously referred to the RWG personal goal-setting training course early on in my meetings with them. This was described in the previous chapter within the context of catalytic events, or turning points, preceding the SR activity of some of the research subjects. Imelda, a manager, was a mentor with the Children's University.[1] She was also a member of the local hospital's paediatric family involvement group – 'but it's not really work related, it's just on a personal level'. Imelda expressed her concern to help others, as a result of her own experiences, describing how her son had nearly died in hospital of meningitis twelve months previously: 'your life changes and you think of all the things that you could do better...' Nevertheless, Imelda's SR activity was not confined to outside working hours, expressing her passion for staff welfare, in a similar way to Francesca from the 'Active' subgroup. Imelda notably described her intense dislike of racism, which prompted her to speak out and urge her colleagues to 'think for yourself' when she overheard racist comments about immigrant employees. This demonstrated her field independence and internal locus of control, described in Chapter 5 above as entrepreneurial character traits.

In fact, entrepreneurial skills applied to SR activity were shown by three of the subjects from this subgroup, including Kate, a middle manager, involved in running the Juniors Club, a group for small children. The club teaches young children citizenship and social skills,

---

[1] An English trust which provides out of hours schooling in disadvantaged areas, in the service of social mobility. See www.childrensuniversity.co.uk/about-us.

and motivates them to achieve. Kate explained how she had stepped in with a friend to save the club from folding up, spotting the opportunity to lever her management skills: 'we just took it on and got started [pause]. I felt I could make a difference'. However, this activity was separate from her company role, and again it was conducted in her own time. Kate described how she had made an attempt to get support from the company, but it had been turned down:

When I asked if [pause] the Juniors Club could be linked to the company in some way, they just said, 'Well, it's not [pause] one of the things that we particularly support, so, you know, do it in your own time' kind of thing.

This illustrates Kate's perceived limits to her SR activity, articulated in terms of constraints with regard to CSR. Indeed, it was notable that Kate expressed her wish to be involved in the company's community activity, perceiving it 'as a good development opportunity for people', which would provide occasions to network within the company. But her attitude towards networking in the service of CSR was not entrepreneurial and Kate did not take the initative here. She needed more overt endorsement of CSR for it to be formally integrated into the job, because

people are too busy trying to impress people or trying to achieve something or deliver against their own set of mental objectives [pause]. It would be nice, though, if we had the blessing of the company to do it and they said, 'This is fantastic, how can we help?'

So despite the organisation's espoused CSR culture (see Chapter 7), departmental pressures or the anticipated vetoing by a line manager served to encourage or discourage CSR and thus impacted upon the perceptions of the 'Concealeds' of the supportive nature of the CSR context at BHI.

Certainly, Imelda spontaneously acknowledged her line manager's support when she asked to be exempted from giving 'customer feedback' about colleagues,[2] in her anticipation of a new round of job

---

[2] The company uses this technique in employee appraisals and refers to it as either 'customer feedback' (to reflect the service nature of some departmental functions) or '360 degree performance review'. In preparation for an employee's annual appraisal, the line manager consults three or four colleagues regarding the appraisee's performance at work. The colleagues are not selected randomly: this is purposive sampling (Silverman, 2001: 251), whereby the line

losses. She was proud of her good working relationships with staff and reported how she had taken this decision because she did not want to compromise those relationships. Now her decision may be viewed in terms of individualism (wanting to retain popularity and the quality of her contacts, for instrumental reasons). However, bearing in mind that 'customer feedback' was part of the company's appraisal procedures, this decision could also be seen as taking a stance: a decision based on principle and a sense of duty to colleagues and thus a courageous decision. Indeed, Imelda was arguably a borderline case between a 'Concealed' CSE and an 'Active' CSE. Certainly, her involvement with the children's hospital group was described, above, as a personal and not a corporate activity. But her collectivism was also evident via her espoused equality value and her sense of fairness was discernible in her acknowledgement of the company's commitment to CSR. Nonetheless, this credit was balanced with criticism of BHI, in terms of what she regarded as a widespread lack of recognition for the role played by the factory operatives in the company's success. More than this, Imelda was strongly critical of the company's human resources (HR) department, due to the treatment of particular employees during recent rounds of redundancies:

There's some very capable people been ousted, and then their job hasn't been made redundant, you see, they've just got new people in. And rather than maybe manage that situation [pause] by [pause] you know, training or just making people aware that you're failing on this criteria [pause] you've gotta improve, it's just like 'push off'. They've decided they wanted to get rid of certain people. The procedure for getting rid of them, it was all like, subjective, you know, your opinion on a person – or somebody else's opinion on you, rather than your ability to do the job. And, you know, gone [pause]. There was fifteen lost their jobs on this site. All but one of them were local people, who had spent *at least* ten years here. All very capable; nobody ever brought to question their ability to do the job; they were well respected [pause] but, they were local. And I think that [pause] because, we've had like a management *change* in the company over the last few years. Erm, not like a takeover, but for all intents and purposes it could've been. And so,

manager approaches 'internal customers', people whom he/she is aware have been working with the appraisee, and asks for their opinions. However, this is no guarantee, of course, that the information obtained is any more reliable (Miles and Huberman, 1994: 287).

you know, the top-level management has virtually all changed. And [pause] I think they wanted their own people . . .

This particular criticism of the company's HR department, which was perceived to be spoiling the company's traditional paternalistic 'welfare' culture, was a common theme and articulated by fifteen subjects out of the total of twenty-eight (including five of the 'Actives' and two of the 'Concealeds'), such as Brian, the senior manager, described in the last chapter as an 'Active' CSE: 'In my experience, you know, there's – we do some HR type things particularly terribly – the way we treat some people, sometimes, is awful. And we make some real cock-ups with people.' Such apparent frankness, combined with a principled nature and a sense of fairness to others, suggested the integrity of these corporate social entrepreneurs. Indeed, an awareness that BHI may not always be upholding its long-standing tradition as a socially responsible company was articulated by some of the subjects as a source of job dissatisfaction. In fact, Julie was the most vociferous in this regard, the last case from the 'Concealed' CSE subgroup.

Julie was a factory operative. And she was particularly frustrated by the absence of support for her voluntary work, in terms of a lack of recognition from the company and from her colleagues. Yet she had been on the initial list of twelve recommended people, indicating her recognised status as a CSE. And when I probed regarding her SR activity, Julie's response was: 'I come to work, I run a machine, I go home, basically [pause] the job I do is very straightforward.' However, outside work her story was very different.

Julie described how she had volunteered as a mentor at the Children's University (CU) five years previously and had continued ever since. Local disadvantaged children receive extra tuition and attend classes which are supervised by volunteers from the private and public sectors. The leader of the CU, a social entrepreneur, had initially approached the company and had asked if they would encourage employees to act as mentors. An email was subsequently sent to all company employees asking for volunteers to attend the CU for one hour, once or twice a week, at 3.30 p.m. Julie had started with the CU as a mentor, listening to a child reading, but very soon she had been asked by the leader if she would attend a training course and then write a taught module:

I actually teach the four-week module, all the ideas are mine. I've done it for five years now. I'm on my fifteenth module, now. I tutor on a Tuesday and mentor on a Thursday. I do two a week. I've got a lot of life-skills, it's just trying to point them in the right way, really.

Julie referred to teaching local disadvantaged children to respect their teachers at school and her most recent module was concerned with how to behave at a football match, to provide instruction on self-control: 'things won't always go right for you in life [pause] dealing with failure [pause] you will be angry and you will be frustrated, but you try and be self-controlled.' Julie's emphasis on self-control is significant and we can connect this with the earlier discussion (Chapter 6) on governmentality and self-mastery in ethical behaviour.

Even though Julie was a parent with children of her own, she talked about giving other children opportunities, helping them to get a start in life, because many parents do not show interest in their children: 'They just need someone to talk to and they just don't get it [pause] maybe some parents just don't give a monkeys.' Schooling was extremely important to Julie, who declared that she had not had educational opportunities herself and referred to her own family upbringing. So did Kate, who described herself as 'self-critical', having 'had quite a low self-esteem in the past'; 'I come from a very controlling family . . . ' The implication here is the source of the sense of limitations articulated by this subgroup, although this cannot be substantiated within the confines of this exploratory study. Nevertheless, Julie's work with the CU gave her tremendous personal satisfaction:

I just like working with kids. When I was at school I never 'ad no help, there was nothing like this. When I come away from a mentoring session I think, God, I've really made a difference to them.

She described her sense of pride in witnessing the childrens' progress:

I just look at the kids and look at the pupil who I do and I think – when I first did Lee at William Tell School and I saw his exam results when we'd finished and they'd improved. That's fantastic, you know what I mean? What a sense of achievement. And then Laura, last year, erm, she did fantastic – absolutely fantastic last year in her exam results. And she used to sit and I used to have to say to her sometimes, 'Laura, let me have a word in edgeways' [pause]. When I first met her, she wouldn't say boo to a goose. But within three or four months, we'd brought it out of her and I said,

'Come on, you can trust me, we can talk about what we want, anything...'
Sometimes I'll go and I'll talk – we'll sit and talk for forty-five minutes about
[pause] anything other than school. But it just gives that pupil [pause] an
opportunity to say stuff to other people who [pause] to somebody who they
don't know, but they trust. Obviously you have to build the trust up over a
time [pause] I just get the satisfaction and think, 'Great, I've done that for
them.'

In addition to her voluntary work with the CU, Julie also worked
voluntarily for the Education Action Zone (EAZ), an organisation
designed to boost the exam results of disadvantaged children who 'just
don't get enough help at school' and would otherwise 'go nowhere'.
At the time of the interview, Julie was also mentoring a sixteen-year-
old pupil with the EAZ. And Julie's enthusiasm and passion were
evangelical:

I'd say to anybody: if you like working with kids and you just want to put
a little bit back into somebody's life – at school – just go do it! Even if you
just do it the once [pause] but I guarantee it, you'll get bitten by the bug.

However, Julie's sense of the constraints upon her SR activities were
expressed bitterly when she described the company's lack of support
for the Children's University, despite the scheme having been promoted
throughout the company. Indeed, Julie expressed great frustration that
none of the other factory operatives knew of her out-of-work activities
with the CU and she blamed management for discriminating against
the factory workers. The CU project had been pitched to employees
as allowing them to attend in company time, leaving early in order
to be mentors. But this only enabled the office workers to attend,
because the CU's after-school start coincided with the factory shift.
Indeed, Julie reported having to rearrange her shift patterns so that
she avoided the 2 p.m.–10 p.m. shift in order to attend the CU in
her own time. Consequently, she blamed middle management in the
factory for blocking the good intentions of the senior management of
the company. Her comments also indicated a cultural division between
the factory site and the Global Business Unit, articulated by some
of the subjects in this study.[3] Notably, Julie also reported that the

---

[3] The division between the factory 'site' and the Global Business Unit was an
organisational structure attributed to management consultants in the interests
of efficiency (see Chapter 7 above).

lack of support for CSR in her department was changing as a result
of the appointment of a new head, who was identified during this
investigation as an 'Active' CSE.

Julie's frustrations were compounded by her lack of fulfilment at
work. She was not a brand ambassador and she complained about
what she saw as a lack of support for the factory workers to develop
themselves: 'We're held back, here, and I don't think we're given
enough to do at work. If they put more responsibility on us, we could
cope with that...' This contrasts directly with frequent comments
across the sample regarding the company's excellent training record
and widespread opportunities for development, such as that articulated
by Brian:

I believe in people and the company does in the ways it manages and develops
people, in their training [pause] a lot of opportunity if you want to take it.
The doors are there if you want to push them.

But Julie described how it was the Children's University and not her
job that gave her a tremendous sense of accomplishment and personal
satisfaction, which contrasted starkly with the dislike of her job and
the lack of social recognition attached to it:

When I've told people at work what I do, they go: 'I can't believe you do
all that, because, here, you just run a machine and go for a break and do
paperwork.' But sometimes you don't see the true self until – or the true
person until you get them out of their daily routine.

This reference to 'the true self' resonates directly with my earlier discussion about the nature of integrity (Chapter 6). But within this context,
Julie could not be described as self-actualised at work, knowing that
she was far more capable than her job 'allowed' her to be. Moreover,
these perceived constraints and limitations on the corporate social
entrepreneurship of this subgroup were expressions of an external
locus of control, as a result of their subjective experience. Julie's frustrations were articulated by someone who had worked for the company
as a factory machine operator for the last twenty years, despite the
company's staff development record. Why had she not taken advantage of the staff development opportunities that were available to her?
This case exemplifies a recurring theme of structure and agency, with
Julie fitting the profile of the family-oriented 'communicative reflexive', with her 'voluntary curtailment of ambition', or the vocationally

oriented 'meta-reflexive', whereby 'much of their inner conversation turns upon whether or not they are becoming the kind of person called for by their vocations' and 'blaming the social institutions that they encounter' (Archer, 2003: 208, 266, 270).

So the case of Julie and also the other 'Concealed' CSEs who separated some of their SR activity between work and home suggests the notion of compartmentalisation, from organisational role theory: 'By compartmentalizing, a person is able to separate role performance and obligations in both time and place' (Wiley, 1991: 499).[4] From a psychological perspective this is redolent of the business ethics notions of moral disengagement, or a moral bracketing, by managers, whereby personal morality is left at home. But it would be incorrect to conclude that these four individuals confined SR to their home life, or that they bracketed their morality. Their reality was much more nuanced than this. Whilst a *particular* SR activity may have been compartmentalised, these employees still practised CSR, despite their perception of the organisational limitations upon particular activities. And it is my contention that it was their personal values that prevented them from morally disengaging in the workplace. Indeed, in arguing the case against compartmentalisation, Wiley (1991) quoted Kanter's (1989) description of 'the myth of separate worlds', whereby an individual cannot completely separate off their home life from their working life and vice versa. Indeed, 'stress contagion' was mooted as a result of an employee having to move between multiple role identities.

The argument against compartmentalisation was also supported in a study of non-work roles that impacted upon the working life of 400 Tasmanians, employed full-time in a business context. The study described 'the multifaceted employee', where numerous family- and non-family-based roles were investigated. Of particular relevance, here, was the finding that amongst the list of thirty-five non-work roles which were identified, 51 per cent of the sample claimed to be

[4] Wiley (1991) attributed the concept of 'compartmentalisation' to Long and Porter (1984) with regard to women and role theory. In business ethics, Lovell (2002a; 2002b) cited Jackall (1988) with regard to managerial bracketing in the context of moral disengagement (see Chapter 3 above). Compartmentalisation was also observed in the marketing and organisational behaviour literatures by Drumwright and Murphy (2004) with regard to the personal morality of advertising executives, and in Wickham and Parker's (2007) study of the non-work roles of business people.

volunteers and 32 per cent reported their work on external committees. The following result connects with Julie's frustrations:

Where respondents indicated that their organisation restricted their ability to enact their charity-based roles in favour of enacting their workplace roles, higher levels of dissatisfaction were reported. Conversely, respondents also indicated that where their organisation failed to recognise the specialist skills developed in their charity-based roles, increased levels of dissatisfaction were reported. (Wickham and Parker, 2007: 451)

But Kate (the middle manager described above) did not report dissatisfaction at having to compartmentalise her SR activity with the Juniors Club. In contrast, she had initiated and negotiated a six-month career break with the company, in order to spend more time with her young family. Nevertheless, this had generated considerable personal anxiety about the effect it would have on her career:

but it's taken me a long time to get to where I feel I am now in this organisation. And the ironic thing is that, now having got to the point where, you know, I am [pause] *appear* to senior managers – I can go to meetings that other people couldn't always go to. I'm taking six months off and I'm, effectively, sort of giving all that away, because I don't know what I'm going to come back to. So, I *may not* come back to the same level that I leave at. And – and that's a bit ironic, really, it's – it's sort of quite funny, because, it's been a *real* bug bear of mine, that I've worked really hard and I've done everything that I can possibly *do* to achieve and to [pause] make a success of every role that I've ever been given [pause] and yet, getting a promotion was nigh-on impossible [pause] and I couldn't get to the nub of what I was missing; what I was doing wrong [pause] there was something in my personality that didn't fit. And then all of a sudden it happened. And [pause] you know, now *I'm* making a conscious choice to leave it all behind.

In summary, the 'Concealed' CSEs articulated the limitations and constraints upon their socially responsible activities at work, which sometimes compromised their moral courage. Nonetheless, their prosocial behaviour in the workplace refutes the business ethics notion of moral bracketing and indicates that we might fruitfully substitute this idea with the converse notion of 'personal value contagion'. This is akin to the notion of stress contagion, which was the product of multiple role identities producing stress 'spillover' into the home and work environment (Bolger et al., 1989; Wiley, 1991). And in the context of organisational morality at BHI, the personal values of these subjects

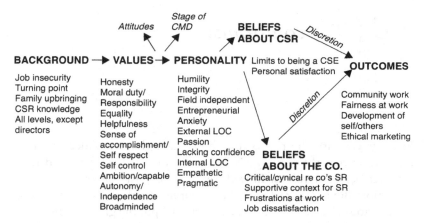

Figure 9.1 Diagrammatic summary: the Concealed CSE

leaked out of them, suggesting that, in some cases, dominant personal values will be effected, regardless of the context. And so we have some tentative evidence which indicates that, in the work situation, we may compartmentalise what we do, but not who we are. These results are summarised in Figure 9.1.

In the following chapter, the third mode of moral commitment to CSR, the 'Conformist', is distinguished from the previous two subgroups. Indeed, despite the company's espoused supportive context for CSR, CSR was not articulated as a personal concern of six of the employees from this subgroup, even though it was integral to their formal job role. Furthermore, their dominant personal values were individualistic in nature, compared with the dominantly expressed collectivistic (or self-transcendent) personal values of the corporate social entrepreneurs.

10 | *The conformist*

In common with the rest of this book, this chapter is dedicated to illustrating that the employee's behaviour at work is, in part, driven by their personal values. Indeed, the 'Conformist' subgroup was no exception. But in contrast with the corporate social entrepreneurs from the previous two chapters, the 'Conformists' put the greatest emphasis on their individualistic or self-enhancement values, in terms of their capability at work and also their home life.

The key theme articulated by this group was their pragmatic attitude towards CSR, which was expressed by way of corporate enlightened self-interest and, most commonly, in the context of CSR's effect on their career. Moreover, whilst *the majority of employees in this subgroup were involved in some kind of CSR* and expressed job satisfaction through their SR work, they did not discuss this with the passion and zeal articulated by the CSEs. There was no evidence of social entrepreneurial activity and they could not be described as CSR champions. Unlike the corporate social entrepreneurs, CSR was not a salient personal concern and it was not 'taken to heart'. Where this group did express their passion, it was in the context of their leisure time and home life, which was emphasised far more than in the previous two subgroups. Indeed, there was a suggestion of a compartmentalisation of differing social identities, particularly in the cases where company values and personal values were not regarded as congruent. The employees in this subgroup were thus identified as 'Conformist' because their pragmatism was highlighted as their dominant concern, both in terms of the business case for CSR and, particularly, in terms of its instrumental value to their career at Brayford Health International. Hence the data suggested that they would conform to the prevailing ethical climate, whatever that might be. This is not to make the ridiculous suggestion that the individuals described in the previous two subgroups did not possess individualistic values in terms of concern for their family and their social lives. More, that the moral duty of

Table 10.1 *Characteristics of the Conformist: SR outcomes*

CSR outcomes	Number of subjects
Community work	5
Health and safety	4
Environment	3
Fairness/equality	3
Development of self/others	1
No apparent CSR involvement	3
n = 15	

individuals to be socially responsible was not expressed as a personal concern of this subgroup, who also presented moral muteness. As the 'Conformists' represented the largest subgroup, this finding tentatively supported the business ethics perspective of a prevailing amorality in organisations.

The largest subgroup of employees were 'Conformist'. In many ways, these subjects were indistinct from the previous two subgroups who, on the whole, portrayed themselves as professional, responsible, corporate people, who conveyed ambition and a desire to be success-ful. The difference, though, was in the weight of importance attached by the Conformists to the pragmatic, business case for CSR, in terms of its benefits to the organisation and to their careers. This contrasts with the corporate social entrepreneurs, who advocated CSR as a per-sonal duty, more so than the business case. What was notable with the 'Conformists' was the relative unimportance to these subjects of the multi-fiduciary obligation of corporations and their employees. Hence these cases could not be described as corporate social entrepreneurs, despite the purposive sampling method whereby known champions of CSR had been targeted.

The scope of CSR amongst the 'Conformist' subgroup is displayed in Table 10.1. Whilst BHI did not employ any CSR or ethics officers, six people occupied a role that formally incorporated elements of CSR and four were brand ambassadors. (See Chapter 7 above for an expla-nation of the role of the brand ambassador within BHI, which included volunteering in the community and efficiency improvement projects.)

Table 10.2 *Characteristics of the Conformist: seniority*

Status	Number of subjects
Directors	2
Senior managers	2
Middle managers	5
Lower manager/administrators	5
Factory operative	1
n = 15	

Interestingly, three of the subjects did not articulate *any* involvement in CSR during their interview, indicating that it was not part of their job remit. Examples of the 'Conformist' group ranged across the corporate hierarchy, but the majority worked in middle or lower management roles (see Table 10.2).

The dominant values espoused by this subgroup were their ambition and capability as effective employees. And even though a capable employee (regardless of whether they are regarded as such by colleagues and/or formally recognised through the company's appraisal system) may not have ambitions for promotion (perhaps due to issues of job insecurity within the organisation): being seen to be capable could have been the difference between getting the next promotion or keeping their job. However, with the exception of an expressed internal locus of control, or a personal sense of responsibility, entrepreneurial leadership was not characteristic of this group. Indeed, there were just two examples of field independence: one exhibited by a director, Michael, and the other by Simon, a senior manager in a job role which was formally concerned with one of the CSR domains.

Simon's top priority was his next career move. He was proactively visiting job consultants and attending job interviews around the country. In fact Simon initiated our meeting, as he wanted to explore the possibility of postgraduate study in CSR, an option he was thinking about as part of his career development. Simon considered himself to be a late developer in his career and he was now driving hard towards directorship. But he did not portray any job security issues and appeared to be highly placed and highly regarded within the company. Yet Simon was impatient for his next move up the career ladder: 'I've written my next five-year plan and ten-year plan', he said. In fact Simon was typical of this subgroup in the emphasis he placed upon his family and his personal ambition as his main concerns:

So, I look at where I've come from and you know, what I've achieved and the position I've got myself into and sometimes I think: 'How the hell did I do it?' Because I haven't followed the classic path; I haven't worked hard to get where I am. But hopefully, you know, people respect what I do and how I do it. It's convincing the next people on . . .

This pragmatic emphasis on CSR as good for the career was a theme expressed by the majority of the brand ambassadors who were interviewed (four 'Conformists' and one 'Active' CSE), all of whom occupied lower management, administrative or factory-operative roles. Ulrich was an exception in this regard, although he had recently handed over his role as a brand ambassador to a more junior colleague. Ulrich was a middle manager with twenty years' service who was an advocate of continuous improvement and also of the integral role of the brand ambassador in the culture change of the company. Originally trained as a chemist, Ulrich was now particularly interested in developing his management skills and also in learning about innovative techniques in research methodology, in order to help him in his role.

The following three individuals exemplified the pragmatic stance of the brand ambassadors. The first was Anna, a young factory operative. Anna emphasised the value of volunteering as a brand ambassador, in terms of its effect on her image at work, enriching her job and enhancing her effectiveness at work. Indeed, these were all common themes expressed amongst the more junior of the brand ambassadors who were interviewed. Anna highlighted the instrumental value of being a brand ambassador to her job, not least due to the networking opportunities the role presented to her: 'It's brought me on [pause] I've been on that many courses and some of the courses only the managers and shift managers have been on and it's helped me a lot.' A second, William, was a junior manager who had been a brand ambassador for two years, having come forward after his boss had asked for volunteers. I asked William about his motives for volunteering:

From a *personal* point of view it's more of getting business knowledge for myself. Not just, you know, within this company but elsewhere, because it looks good on the CV, if you've got that cross-functional knowledge. So that's why I *personally* originally did it, because it'd broaden my experience. And also, to react with different people and get that [pause] cross-functional sort of view on things. And also, the things they do: the Walk for Life, and I've put my name down for some knockout challenge or something in August that – I don't really know what that involves, yet [laughs] but it's the community-type stuff as well that I get involved with.

The third was Xander, in a technical role, who described how he had volunteered four years previously in order to increase his visibility at work, explaining, 'I haven't got much self-confidence in myself . . . ' and that he had been approached to 'get yourself more out there'. Now, my purpose in highlighting the individualistic motives of the brand ambassadors is not to diminish their commitment to CSR. Certainly, Xander had nine years' experience helping disadvantaged children as part of the Children's University, which cannot be denigrated. He also described his 'sense of enjoyment' in 'helping the children progress'. This sense of personal satisfaction derived from CSR was illustrative of that expressed by over half of this subgroup. The key discriminators of the 'Conformist' (and also the 'Disassociated' – see next chapter), however, were their dominant individualistic motives coupled with an absence of entrepreneurial discretion in the development of a socially responsible agenda at work. This contrasted with the corporate social entrepreneurs, who initiated and championed particular CSR domains, driven by a collectivistic emphasis on CSR and their sense of social duty.

Another example of pragmatism within CSR was exemplified by a second senior manager, Quentin, who was involved in one of the company's environmental projects. Quentin emphasised his home life as his dominant concern, but he began our meeting by explaining how he valued working in the health care industry and how working within this relatively 'worthwhile' industry is a motivator for employees:

Q: [pause] It's not like making hand grenades. But people make hand grenades and rocket launchers and battleships.

C: Would you work for ZXT Technologies [a local weapons manufacturer], do you think?

Q: I don't know, now, having worked here and made that strapline that it's not like making hand grenades. So that would challenge my credibility, because I work for a weapons systems business or arms manufacturer, or distributor. Ultimately if they paid a big wodge of money [pause] the most important thing to me is the lifestyle.

C: So you wouldn't rule it out?

Q: No, not necessarily so, but I would challenge myself on it and say, is this something that fits with your core values, Quentin? But bearing in mind my biggest core value is having that family unit that's safe, secure: big kitchen for my wife, because she loves to have a big kitchen, nice garden and that sort of stuff, do you know what I mean?

Pragmatism, again, was demonstrated by Michael, a director, who argued that financial performance has to come first, above CSR: 'My focus on waste is for economic reasons.' Taken out of context, this response could be interpreted as an example of moral muteness or a reframing of the moral discourse (Crane, 2000). But Michael placed a heavy emphasis on his personal capability and skill as a leader and he could not describe any involvement in CSR. Nonetheless, the economic trade-offs associated with CSR were implicit in his comments, for example in the context of outsourcing and labour rates abroad, where Michael openly expressed his worries that CSR could negatively affect the company's corporate image:

... performance, financially, put to the city, carries a very high *dominance* in amongst what we do as a company. Now, you can argue whether that's right or wrong but it does. So I think the *dilemmas* we face, all the time, even if they're not explicit, is that there's always the pressure to achieve financial performance, versus doing what's right, maybe, in the social and the, um, in the environmental areas that you've talked about. I think there's an *inherent* pressure there, and it's not explicit in the org... it doesn't get talked about in the organisation such that it's a problem, but it has – it's dangerous territory.

Indeed such frankness was characteristic of the whole group of twenty-eight people that were interviewed. For example, in the case of Tony, another director who was clear about his stance towards CSR, 'its very hard to think of an area where we would go beyond compliance...' and 'meeting local legislation is as far as I would want to go, anyway'. Tony was also keen to stress the importance of the company not making SR claims that it could not uphold:

And that's [pause] I think that is *nicely* hand in hand, with [pause] driving *real* business benefit; covering our backsides and actually from a genuine desire to *want* to be better. And I'm [pause] *personally*, I'm *very* suspicious [pause] if you *don't* get that combination. You know, [speaking quickly] I'm not – I'm a very much [pause] as an issue for *here*, I'm very suspicious of any organisation that is currently doing it *purely* for the sake of doing it. Does that make any sense?

This illustrated an enlightened self-interest perspective on CSR, the business case, which was described in the introduction. Indeed, Tony's rational remarks included his view of corporate image as a driver of CSR and the necessity for BHI to publicise the ethical standards they adhere to:

For me, and I think for our organisation, really, the big driver is around [pause] perception. And how you want to portray yourself to the world at large. And for me, it's the notion that – particularly on the sustainable development, the broader sustainable development issue, it's *around* [pause] what you do [pause] if you're striving to become a first-class organisation. And that's what you concentrate on. So, one of our drivers and I'll make no secret of it, we actually subscribe to the [pause] Dow Jones [pause] Sustainability Index, we – we've taken part in that; we're actually taking part in [pause] FTSE4Good as well. And we *will be* [pause] guided and driven by some of those reports...

Now I am not suggesting that those individuals in the 'Conformist' mode of moral commitment to CSR were pragmatists and that the rest of the sample were not. More, that the employees in this subgroup placed their greatest *emphasis* on displaying their business pragmatism, in contrast with the previous two subgroups. Importantly, my intention is not to argue that the 'Conformists' completely lacked integrity either. Certainly Tony's approach to the honest communication of Brayford Health International's CSR performance was notable. However, integrity (as defined in Chapter 6) in terms of a compassion for others and human sympathy, in addition to being honest and true to one's principles, was not a concern of the 'Conformists', in comparison to their portrayal as competent achievers. Indeed, the organisational context of job insecurity will have influenced the widespread declarations of loyalty on the Rokeach Values Survey, across the total group of twenty-eight subjects who were interviewed.

Moreover, courage was notably absent as a concern of this sub-group, a finding that was also implied by the results of the RVS. On the other hand, moral muteness emerged as a characteristic theme. For example, Nigel, a junior manager said, 'I stand up for my beliefs to a certain amount, but, I think I kind of back down.' So too, Vincent, a young man in his mid-twenties in a technical role, expressed his belief in his own integrity and insisted that he would not back down in the event of pressure to cut corners. However:

V: If someone's fighting me and I accept it goes above my head, it comes down to a business decision in the end. But that wouldn't be my recommended way at the beginning, sort of thing.

C: So if it was somebody senior to you, then you would say 'Well, if that's what you really want...'?

V: Yes. 'This isn't the way we would support it for x, y and z reasons. But if the company had wanted to go that route, then it [pause] and that's out of my hands, I can't influence that any more than to say: 'This is the way you should be doing it.' I suppose there's a status and a hierarchy as well, because I report into my manager and obviously, it would go through him to say it.

This expression of obedience to authority and an external locus of control is not on the scale of the engineers in the Ford Pinto case of the 1970s, whereby the calculated launch of a new and defectively dangerous car took into account 'the cost of anticipated casualties, valued in actuarial terms ... outweighed by the benefit to the company' (Maclagan, 1998: 29). But it reflected Vincent's sense of limitations on his moral discretion at work. Indeed, a middle manager, Zach, who was in a job role which formally encompassed one of the domains of CSR, admitted to the circumstantial nature of his personal values:

If the mood's with me, I have to be honest [because of] [pause] stress, work, tiredness [pause] I'm aware of my own fallibilities. It's also circumstances. If my family were involved, there'd be no question. If the individual was somewhat remote to me, I'd feel as guilty as hell and curse myself for not having moral fibre, but not necessarily intervene.

This frank statement helps to illustrate the situational components of moral values and, more specifically, 'the object of the agent's behaviour' (Scott, 2000: 506). Thus the degree of closeness to the 'other' affects engagement with an issue. Indeed proximity, according to Scott, affects the perceived moral intensity of a moral dilemma:

'The proximity of the moral issue is the feeling of nearness (social, cultural, psychological, or physical) that the moral agent has for victims (beneficiaries) of the evil (beneficial) act in question.' As Jones notes, Milgram's experiments bear out this view by showing that people were less likely to harm people physically near to them . . . (Scott, 2000: 508)

Proximity also affects discretion in CSR, which was highlighted by Scott, who referred to the individual's 'degrees of voluntariness' (Scott, 2000: 503). But managerial discretion employed in the service of maximising profit, as opposed to CSR, was evident in a more recent report on BMW's management decision not to recall their defective Mini cars: 'BMW say that they're aware of an electrical issue which has the potential to affect the Electro Hydraulic Power Assisted Steering system fitted to more than 223,000 petrol-powered Minis sold between 2001 and 2007' (Unsworth, 2009). The company claimed that if the power steering failed, then the car would still be operable. Unfortunately, some consumers who experienced steering failure reported otherwise. One driver ended up mounting the pavement in an attempt to control her car, claiming that someone could have been killed (Unsworth, 2009). Further to this, when I suggested a hypothetical situation to Vincent that involved his boss cutting corners for commercial reasons, Vincent's faith in the regulations and in the company's reputation as a well-known organisation was undiminished: 'It all comes back to regulations [pause] certain guidelines that you have to follow [pause] [this] is seen as an ethical company and for such a large company I don't think that situation would happen.' This sentiment illustrated a lack of moral imagination on Vincent's part, which I have frequently found to be typical of the reaction of some undergraduate students during my own experience of teaching business ethics. Indeed, in spite of the regular cases of corporate misdemeanour hitting the news, many students cannot accept that major well-known corporations can be associated with unethical behaviour or corporate misdemeanour 'nowadays'.[1] But this demonstrates the blind trust that

---

[1] My view is that this phenomenon is exacerbated by using older case material in class. The age of the context should make no difference to the theory, but in my

can be engendered by brand awareness through marketing communications. For example, consumer surveys on trust have shown how
Heinz, Cadbury and Kelloggs were trusted by respondents as much as
their own family doctor and Boots the Chemist was trusted twice as
much as the UK government (Pringle and Gordon, 2001: 130).

A further finding relates to bracketing, or compartmentalising,
between the work and home identities of this subgroup (Leary and
Tagney, 2003; Wickham and Parker, 2007). Indeed, the 'Conformists'
and 'Disassociated' were the most vociferous in emphasising their
home lives as their primary concern. This compartmentalisation may
be differentiated from the 'Concealeds', who bracketed particular SR
activities. For example, Olivia, a middle manager, expressed some cyn-
icism regarding the espoused corporate values. Towards the end of our
meeting, she said, 'I come to work sixty percent [pause] probably sev-
enty percent for the money, to allow me to have what I have at home.'
In fact, over half of the people who were interviewed, including half
of the 'Conformist' subgroup, expressed their scepticism about BHI's
CSR. This also indicates one of the difficulties attached to making
claims about CSR and sustainability and was alluded to by Tony,
above. Espousing CSR can set high expectations, inviting the scrutiny
or unwanted attention of an organisation which, along with its employees, is fallible. Indeed, Vincent's interpretation of the company's values
as public relations hype generated his clear portrayal of a distinction
between his work and home identities and an insistence that his personal values and those of the company were 'mutually exclusive'.
Vincent could not see any connections between the company's
espoused corporate values and his own and he was resolute that his
most important concerns were his friends, reinforced by his selection
of social recognition on the RVS:

I don't think there's any [pause] I don't think there's a strong link between
me and my values and the company's values [pause] I probably just don't
look at it that deeply, just don't think that much about it. I don't think I'm
[pause] influenced that much – I agree with the company's values, but it's
not really the same as mine.

experience cases can be used more effectively if supported by visiting
practitioners, whose expert power produces credibility, thus enhancing the
learning experience. But recruiting practitioners who will talk about moral
dilemmas is not easy.

Even so, whilst Vincent was cognisant of corporate misdemeanour, he expressed his own confidence in BHI and his faith in the regulatory framework to protect the public. Notably, and despite his three and a half years' service, Vincent could not think of anyone in the company 'with personal convictions to operate in a socially responsible manner' who might be regarded as a moral champion. So despite the socially responsible nature of Vincent's technical role, he espoused some amorality and also dismissed the company's espoused values ('achievement, creativity and integrity') and brand personalities ('positive, active, truthful and team-playing'; see Chapter 7) as irrelevant to his own personal values. The suggestion here is of a compartmentalisation between home and working life, between social and personal identities, described by scholars as a psychological defense mechanism to avoid the cognitive dissonance where work and personal values may conflict (Leary and Tangney, 2003).

Moreover, some indications of Vincent's moral courage at work were driven by his desire for promotion and not by the social consequences of his actions. As he put it: *'but if I want to progress in this role* [my emphasis] I can't just back down to somebody saying, "Oh yeah, we don't need to do that," because we'll get a product on the market nine months earlier'. So whilst individualism in the form of 'enjoyment, achievement and self-direction values' (Schwartz and Bilsky, 1987: 554) was also expressed by the corporate social entrepreneurs, it was their dominant collectivistic values which defined them. In contrast, the individualistic personal values of the 'Conformist' subgroup emerged as their distinguishing characteristic.

Dominant individualistic values were also expressed by the three employees who did not report any SR activity in their job roles, even though they had been recommended for interview as SR individuals. These three subjects fitted Carroll's (1987: 11) descriptions of amorality in business, both in terms of the 'intentionally amoral' director, Michael ('they simply think that different rules of the game apply in business than in other realms of life') and in terms of those whom Carroll described as 'morally casual'. Notably, out of the total twenty-eight subjects in all, these three subjects appeared to be the most ignorant about CSR.

One was Yusuf, the middle manager with over forty years' service and retirement looming ahead. Yusuf was respected in the company as an honest, hard-working individual. He also depicted himself as a family man who works to live. Yusuf struggled to understand the concept of CSR:

[interrupts] No, tell me what you think of being socially responsible then and I'll – because – put words into my mouth, if you like, because, um, socially means to me, the way I live at home and the way I get on with my colleagues and things like that, but obviously it's wider than that, is it?

Yusuf reported that in his role, cost savings take precedence over environmental concerns and he demonstrated moral muteness. Also, he believed that SR change within the company was driven by legislation, such as ethylene oxide sterilisation and irradiation which the company contracted out rather than having to invest in new plant after legislation was introduced: 'we knew it was a carcinogenic gas and it was going into the atmosphere, but it wasn't illegal'. He stated that he would not speak out regarding such matters, because he was 'not involved'. Yusuf later said that he was 'not courageous' and he subsequently told a story about a previous boss who was over-controlling: 'he was a tyrant'. Sadly, a second informant in a different department, a middle manager with no apparent involvement in CSR, also reported some bullying some time before:

I think in the *past*, in marketing teams of old, there was quite a lot of aggression and it was the norm to put people down. And yes, if you were [long pause] caught as well-mannered. Yeah, OK, as far as the customer was concerned, but internally, it was like, dog eat dog.

Nevertheless, the pragmatic stance of these three subjects, who could not report any SR activity, suggested that they would engage with CSR if it was recommended to them as part of their role. Certainly, Michael declared some interest in learning about CSR, asking me to tell him what I had learned about the subject, stating that 'doing' CSR 'isn't easy' and that he was

conscious of it, in a big way [pause] but nobody's ever train – there's not a training course in this, there's not a [pause] there's nothing around, you know, if you want to be a finance manager or something. You can open a textbook. There would be an expectation that somebody in a managerial job would need to know financial management. So, that is something that you would naturally see on somebody's appraisal. I have not yet [pause] seen it saying, 'Well actually, social responsibility is very important. You'd better make sure that you've got this on your development agenda.' I haven't yet seen that.

Indeed, whilst some knowledge of CSR, sustainability issues or business ethics was expressed by over half of the total sample – derived via a formal education, such as a qualification in environmental science, or through personal interest – the lack of CSR knowledge was notable amongst the 'Conformist' subgroup. In contrast, Brian, the senior manager ('Active' CSE), was studying CSR as part of a part-time master's degree in business. Witness also Francesca ('Active' CSE), the board director who recommended a book that had influenced her about successful companies with an ethical corporate culture. Hence my point is to suggest a connection between prior knowledge of, or any sort of education in, CSR and moral courage. And also that this subgroup indicated the greatest likelihood of conforming to organisational pressures through the prevailing ethical climate, whatever that might be. But my contention remains that it is the subject's personal values, in conjunction with their perception of a supportive culture, which will moderate moral courage. Nonetheless, I am unclear regarding the importance of self-selection in CSR education. Would individuals with dominant self-transcendent values be more likely to select a course in CSR than those people with dominant self-enhancement values, and might a shift in values be discernible after completing an education in CSR?

Lastly, there were indications that personal moral courage may be affected by the subject's own level of seniority in the organisation. Certainly, the career-oriented brand ambassadors were in a junior position at Brayford Health International. Moreover, Kate, the middle manager, a 'Concealed' CSE, described personal autonomy (thereby reducing the scope for entrepreneurial discretion at work) as less likely to be met further down the organisational hierarchy. Kate described how she perceived a difference in terms of pressure at work between her current role within the organisation and a previous role nine years earlier:

here, the pressure is what I've made it, not what people have piled on me, d'you know what I mean? It's sort of self-inflicted pressure. Whereas down

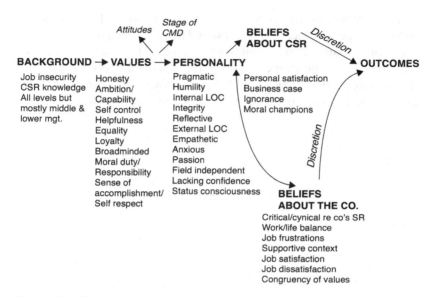

Figure 10.1 Diagrammatic summary: the Conformists

there [in a previous job] I felt – maybe it's because I was younger and doing more junior roles.

This perspective of reduced autonomy associated with the more junior employee is reminiscent of the discussion on maturity and moral character in Chapter 6. In this study, seven out of the eight 'Active' CSEs and three out of four 'Concealed' CSEs indicated courage as a key concern on the RVS. This contrasted with just three of the subjects from the fifteen 'Conformists'. A summary of these results is depicted in Figure 10.1.

Finally, on the basis of the business ethics notion of the ubiquity of amorality in management, it was my presupposition, reflected in these very tentative results, that the 'Conformist' mode of moral commitment to CSR would contain the highest number of subjects. A second presupposition related to BHI's relatively socially responsible reputation and its ethical culture, and thus my anticipation was for a fewer number of subjects in the 'Disassociated' mode. Indeed, only one subject, Bruce Clements, was found to be representative of the final subgroup. However, the data provided a more nuanced picture than the hypothesised version illustrated in Figure 7.1 (Chapter 7). Indeed, Bruce's distinctive mode resulted in a renaming of this extreme case from 'Apathetic' to the more appropriate 'Disassociated'. Consequently, in the following chapter, I have described Bruce through his dominant concerns, which enabled comparisons and contrasts to be made with the other modes of moral commitment to CSR.

11 | *The disassociated*

I reiterate that this investigation was not designed to discover the value hierarchies of a sample of employees from a UK-based multinational corporation. Moreover, I explained in Chapter 4 that an individual will possess a plurality of values, including self-enhancement and self-transcendent values. Indeed, the study was rather more complex in its quest to provide tentative insights with regard to social responsibility as a subjective state, via the connections between personal values and CSR. Hence over the last three chapters I have described the findings of this entirely exploratory study, using the theoretical framework of the four modes of moral commitment.

However, with reference to the fourth of these modes, I explained in Chapter 7 that only one case equated to the hypothetical 'Apathetic' mode of moral commitment to CSR, who was anticipated to articulate self-enhancement values:

My fourth mode was hypothesised as the 'Apathetic' who . . . would not be a corporate social entrepreneur. Moreover the 'Apathetic' would not show any real interest in CSR and dismiss its value. This individual would perceive their company to be antagonistic towards CSR, or be hostile towards the notion themselves, even blocking initiatives, due to the perceived non-economic focus of CSR (Fineman, 1996; Harris and Crane, 2002: 220). Saboteurs of CSR could also emerge in a supportive culture.

Interestingly, as opposed to being apathetic or neutral towards CSR, Bruce Clements felt rather more strongly than this, espousing beliefs comparable with the economic egoism described in other studies (e.g. Harris and Crane, 2002). Indeed, Bruce disliked the 'soft' SR culture at BHI and this needed changing through 'more aggressive performance management'. As a new president of the division had recently been appointed, such a change was anticipated. In what follows, then, the case of Bruce presents both comparisons and contrasts with the previously described modes of moral commitment to CSR: comparisons with the 'Conformist' in terms of amorality and contrasts with the dominant collectivistic values of the corporate social entrepreneurs.

Bruce Clements, one of BHI's directors, expressed a lack of interest in CSR and also dismissed its value. I was, in fact, surprised to find a dearth of such cases at this firm, considering the sampling procedure of targeting known CSEs and that BHI was selected as an organisation with a relatively socially responsible reputation. On the other hand, it ought not to have been surprising, bearing in mind the substantial business ethics literature on moral disengagement, which I described in Chapter 3. By way of background, Bruce was a fairly new appointment by the company's standards (five years' service) and he did not have a health care industry background.

Above all else, Bruce expressed both the Friedmanite view of economic egoism (Desmond and Crane, 2004; Gustafsson, 2002) and his own capability, and possibly ambition.[1] This was presented as extensive business knowledge, as a result of long and varied business experience, and also in terms of a perceived need to change the culture of the division. However, it was my observation that Bruce's repeated emphasis on his long career in business may have been in defence of a lack of formal business qualifications, but I did not substantiate this. This was mainly due to the sampling method and lack of time for the duration of each interview (the president's requested time limit), which prevented the compilation of an accurate demographic profile of this very small sample.

Nevertheless, Bruce was comparable to the three (non-CSR-practising) 'Conformists' who had displayed a lack of knowledge of CSR and did not perceive CSR to be relevant to their own roles. However, as depicted in the previous chapter, those three subjects had indicated that their attitude towards CSR might be shifted if they perceived any benefit to themselves in their role. But in Bruce's case, his attitude towards CSR was more entrenched regarding its ineffectuality as a strategic direction. Nevertheless, in contrast to my conceptual description of the 'Apathetic' mode in Chapter 5, Bruce's predisposition towards CSR was not open hostility, as has been found in other studies (Crane, 2001), it was a controlled, possibly arrogant, dismissal. In this case, Bruce accepted that the company's SR image had

---

[1] Bruce was later promoted as one of Brayford Health International's vice presidents.

historically played a useful part in recruitment at BHI, but this should not be the company's focus going forward. Hence he perceived it to be the wrong emphasis for what he regarded as the required shift in organisational culture.

Indeed, Bruce regarded himself as the protagonist of business performance, which he believed was in opposition to any non-economic values. Hence his mode of moral commitment to CSR could be described as either apathetic or disassociated, as defined by the *Concise Oxford English Dictionary*:

apathetic * adj. not interested or enthusiastic.
disassociated * v. another term for dissociate.
dissociate * v. 1. disconnect or separate

In this case, 'disassociated' is more accurate, on the basis that 'apathetic' may denote a degree of neutrality, which would be an appropriate description of the three 'non-practising' 'Conformists', but not of Bruce's political antagonism towards CSR. Moreover (and comparable with the 'Conformists', but in contrast to the corporate social entrepreneurs), Bruce did not articulate any belief in the moral obligation of corporations to engage in CSR and he expressed a personal detachment from it, reflecting the moral myopia (Solomon 1992) described in Chapter 3.

Bruce advocated that any focus on the local community was the production director's job, perhaps for the purposes of recruitment – a tactical reason for CSR. And at the close of our meeting, I asked him how he thought that the new president of the division would affect the corporate culture, in view of the departure of the outgoing president, George Carr, a man with a reputation in the company as an SR individual:

I think it will fundamentally change in the sense that it won't be Slough-centric. I think one of the issues you've had for this organisation is, is it's been Slough-centric. And, you know, my starter for ten is – my office just happens to be here – I could be anywhere on the M4 corridor. I could be anywhere. So, *my* view of corporate responsibility isn't Slough. I think, I think the company's corporate resp . . . social responsibility has been very Slough-centric. Would be a big criticism. I used to say this to George. 'George, I've – I've got – I've no more interest in Slough Chamber of Commerce than I have in the Le Mans Chamber of Commerce or the Melbourne Chamber of Commerce.' Whereas George did have. Alright?

C: Why?

B: Because he's a Slough guy.

C: I thought he was from the Midlands?

B: No, he's Slough. He's Slough. He's on the board of Slough United and and all that. He's a Slough guy. And [stammers] he had a strong passion for Slough. My *personal* view is [pause]? That was imbalanced. It was *too* Slough. And so my – my view of *corporate* responsibility is corporate. It's not just Slough. And my view – my view of the whole, the whole local relations, my view: that's Tom's [site director of operations] job.[2]

For Bruce, the corporate culture was synonymous with what was commonly referred to in the company as 'the brand'. This was described in Chapter 7:

The new corporate brand vision had been communicated as '*Healing People*'. In addition to changes to the corporate graphics and livery, the relaunched corporate brand encompassed three new espoused 'brand values' of *achievement*, *creativity* and *integrity*, which were communicated internally throughout the company . . . [along with the] new brand personalities . . . of *positive*, *active*, *truthful* and *team-playing*.

Indeed, George, the outgoing president, had been the architect of the transformation process, with its corporate rebranding and ethical repositioning, designed to build upon the existing SR culture at BHI. But, according to Bruce, there had been too much emphasis placed on these values, as opposed to 'business outputs'. What was really needed, argued Bruce, was 'an out-performance culture', which required 'doing things differently', such as facilitating staff turnover, an area that he was keen to advocate.

Bruce described how he believed BHI's low rate of staff turnover to be more of a weakness than it was a strength. People needed to be brought in from other companies, like himself, from the oil and banking industries (' . . . ten years in the oil business . . . ') who would bring with them new ideas:

One of our big weaknesses is we're such a nice company. We are! I mean, next year I'll be thirty years in business and it's the nicest company I've

---

[2] In fact, the outgoing president was not born and raised in Slough. He was born in Warwickshire and had joined the company from London, some twenty-five years previously.

worked in. By a country mile. But, the problem is we're a nice company. And that's a real challenge! And it *is* a challenge and it gets back to your value set issue. There's no point in having a *real* strong value set, unless it's got that commercial [pause] grit; commercial perspective to it! And that's all I try and bring. I try and say, 'Guys, look ...' you know, '... one of our problems, apart from perhaps *some* of our sales reps we have high turnover, but for a lot of our office environments we don't have *any* turnover!' If you go to *Australia* and places, or [pause] you know, we don't have any turnover! Now, you can argue on one hand that's *actually* brilliant: you get people stay because we're a value-based company and we're proud of what we do; we have a strong brand and da-de-da da-da. The downside is, over a business cycle you need new ideas. How do you get new ideas and new leadership when you never have any turnover? So it is a challenge. Um, and there isn't a right answer, but you *do* need turnover. I think the *trick* for any organisation is to keep enough of the [pause] right people and genuinely try and help people move on [pause] that aren't going to be the future of the organisation.

Bruce described a directors' meeting where he had advocated a necessity for the company

to try and create an out-performance culture [pause]. And one of the issues you've got is [pause] is a lot of companies, have a far more aggressive approach to performance management than we do. And then you get 'Ah, that's not our brand' and 'Oooh' and, you know and you think 'Well, guys, *why* isn't it part of our brand? Genuinely being open and honest with people about their performance, why isn't that part of our brand?' So, there's some challenges come with a *perspective* of us as a company which is not [pause] which is a little too brand-oriented.

Hence, on reading the prompt sheet regarding the domains of CSR, Bruce expressed the belief that CSR was in fact a by-product, or a side effect, of the company operating in the health care industry, which attracts 'vocational people' such as the ex-nursing staff in BHI's sales forces: 'and I think people still *join* us for those reasons [pause] and people who join us at a senior level, one of the things that comes across to them is that the [corporate] brand is really, really strong'. These were frank responses. But the new president of the division was now in place and George Carr had accepted a position as chairman of the board of trustees. Thus Bruce may have been encouraged by the changes at the top to advocate a greater emphasis on 'a more aggressive approach to performance management' and less emphasis on SR. So whilst I have already alluded to the strategic marketing management process of building upon an existing corporate culture (in this case, a health care company with a long history of employee welfare and philanthropy) in order to reposition and strengthen a corporate brand as part of organisational culture change (see Chapter 1), Bruce was not a marketing man and he did not demonstrate any knowledge of strategic brand management, or of the requirement for integrated marketing communications, such as the company's inclusion of employees to embody the brand values (Keller, 1998). This was clearly a disagreement over the strategic direction of the company, its positioning in the market place and Bruce's dismissal of a business case for CSR.

Despite my observation regarding Bruce's frankness, he did not specify 'honesty' as a key personal value on the RVS. And bearing in mind that truthfulness was one of the company's 'brand personalities' and one of the criteria that all staff were appraised against, this resonated with his assertions that the organisation was 'too nice' and needed a different emphasis from that propounded by 'the brand'. Being honest was not one of Bruce's concerns. Furthermore, he described joining the company five years previously and finding that the company's environmental and health and safety records had been 'way off the pace', particularly compared with his own experience in the oil industry. Thus, he argued, it would not be realistic for the company to make environmental claims. His belief was that the environmental projects were solely cost-saving measures:

So I think that some of the other tags that have come our way [pause] social responsibility I think being one of them: I think it's a ripple effect of that core issue, about – around the brand and what we make and fundamentally believing what we do is of value added to society. That's the heart of our – that's the heartbeat of our business. Not being a socially responsible employer. So our approach to things like the *environment* and stuff [pause] I don't think it's – I think it's [pause] I think it has come here because [pause] costs us a lot of money. I don't think we have a perspective about the environment at all!

Indeed, other subjects also reported that the company's environmental and health and safety records had, historically, been poor. But it was also reported by them that significant progress had been made and that the company was targeting specific areas for greater improvement. This was confirmed by the director in charge of these issues, another relatively recent appointment, who was gratified that the new policy document he had been tasked to create was regarded as strategic enough to be signed off by the CEO, when the executive board could not agree on 'the ethics of the organisation'.

Bruce's disregard for CSR was characteristic of our meeting. For example, I suggested that the new president, an American, might be predisposed towards CSR, due to the explicit American model of CSR (Matten and Moon, 2004), but Bruce dismissed this as a public relations activity (and the term 'corporate governance' was confused with philanthropy):

They *do* spend more money. I mean, I said, I've worked – I've always worked in multi – as I said, I've worked for a US business, so I feel – I feel as though I can say this: they – I *do* get the strong impression in the US, there's a semi-religious sort of ethic to some of this out there and it really [pause] I think it's one of those [pause] 'Do you go to church on a Sunday? Well of course I do!' You know, 'Are you big on corporate culture?' It's one of those things that [pause] that you've gotta do and been seen to do. Um, and [pause] there's a – it's very much a *giving* – the people have got money in the US, you know, that sort of corporate governance, *giving* element of society's really, really strong in the US.

Again, the idea of 'doing' corporate culture suggested either a denial that a socially responsible culture existed already or, more likely, a detachment from CSR as a strategic direction and a dismissal that the existing SR culture was a strategic strength. It was time for a change:

you need to be able to harness different people *as well*. You don't want just a regimented group of believers, because you need healthy tension as well. So, the dynamics of how a company operates are actually [pause] quite, I mean well, that's why I like working in business, because, in a sense you *do* want [pause] particularly over a business cycle, you know, you can set yourself out to – in a nought to two-year time frame, you can you can you can get most people saluting the flag and doing stuff, but when it's five years and then ten years – how y . . . companies need to reinvent themselves, to st . . . to exist in business, because the business [pause] changes. What do you reinvent? Do you just reinvent how you *deliver*, but your fundamental ethics and value set stays the same, or do you have to reinvent your value set as well, as you go around the business. And there's no answer to that, it's just – I think companies that understand those dynamics are in *play*, are actually the companies that sort of stay, stay in existence. Um, and understanding that those issues are as just as much a legitimate management agenda as [pause] what your last P3 results were, are the ones that properly, you know, are the ones that actually [pause] have corporate social responsibility or have a value set. I mean, corporate social responsibility is a bit of a mouthful. Um, I mean, I think, you know, [stutters] I mean in simple terms, it's is the *how* is as important as the what, for me, and if companies think about the *how*, then *broadly* I think that that will have a result in [pause] ahm some activities and some perspectives and some focus on some of the wider corporate social responsibility.

Bruce also displayed some entrepreneurial qualities, although these were directed towards non-CSR activities. These were portrayed as a pragmatic approach to bureaucracy and hierarchy, such as empower-ing staff to have a flexible approach to decision making, as opposed to an automatic response to the use of 'policy', or in terms of taking responsibility for the direction of one's career. For example, I pressed Bruce on why he thought that he had been recommended for inter-view as an SR individual. And he described how he was encouraging employees at the company to use their personal discretion to make decisions:

I fundament [pause] I *try* and set [stumbling] an ethic within the organisation from a [name of his department] point of view, is that we should always [pause] do the right thing, in the sense of [pause] policy is the start point of a conversation about a situation. I say to all my people, don't give me the policy answer, because that policy may have been written fifteen years ago and might not be valid, no. So virtually every decision is a new decision for me, based on the new evidence or whatever, so I – for me, it's doing the right thing at the moment we're talking about there. So for me: business is a real-time experience [pause] if you try to make sure [pause] that the answer is the right answer, then that has far more importance to the health of a business than um [pause] just repeating policy. Because repeat policy is just a recipe for going nowhere.

Similarly:

and giving people confidence to grasp that opportunity [pause] the people that *defer to hierarchy*, you know, on the belief that the person above them has [pause] more information, um [pause] is often flawed. And, one – slows it down, absolutely slows it down. And one of our *cultural* problems here, absolutely, is process. We defer to process in this company. Big time, compared to my experience. Compared with other [pause] it's hard work. Culturally, the biggest issue – challenge – frustration I have in this place, is the deference to process. 'Over the next steering meeting we'll sort it out.' 'And when's that?' 'Five weeks' time.' 'So between now and five weeks, we'll know the answer?' 'Oh, well, you know ...' I haven't got the time for all this meetings stuff.

Bruce gave examples from his career where he had used his discretion, for example, in closing down an oil refinery. It sounded very similar to Helena's story of factory closure. But Bruce was keen to point out that 'doing the right thing' was to go ahead without 'sign-off':

and I worked at Killingholme, the refinery in Ipswich. And we shut it down. That was 200 people; a thousand contractors and literally, I was the last one out of the refinery. And you learn a lot about [pause] having to do it yourself and [pause] do the right thing and try to make decisions and [pause] and [pause] it produces a self-reliance; a judgemental approach to that sort of stuff – *So*, I think there's always been stuff, to be honest, that I've done, policy-wise, that people haven't necessarily understood we're gonna, before we've done it – I mean I'd argue some of the stuff we've done on flexible benefits, I don't think [pause] people, particularly – I mean, I didn't [pause] we just did it. To be honest.

Also:

oh, I did a load of stuff when we, um, we were moving the head office of [oil company] from Holborn in London up to Derby, so we did a load of policy stuff there, just because it was the right thing to do, we didn't get sign-off for it. Um, I've often recruited people, just because I thought they were the best people to recruit. Didn't bother with sign-off, particularly. Yeah! It's not *abuse* of it, you just back your judgement! You back your judgement. Um, and and what you build up over the years is just that judgement, having been in these sort of situations before, you build up where you *do* need sign-off and you need people's *real* understanding, or where you just get on and do it.

These attitudes towards taking personal responsibility and personal control signified field independence and an internal locus of control, indicated via Bruce's proactive approach to personal career management:

I think [pause] erm, some of my approaches are a little bit different, particularly around independence. Ahm [pause] it's probably, it's probably not where we are at the moment, in terms of, you know: 'Guys', [pause] you know, 'What would *you* do; what do *you* wanna do' [pause], you know, 'Do what you think's right for *you*.' You know, trying to get more independence and individuality into the business, as opposed to [pause] the slightly more regimented; tenure-based [pause] because there are quite a lot of people around who joined the organisation and want to stay for a long time.

This was Bruce's social responsibility as a subjective state, but his morality was not CSR. Indeed, his dominant individualistic values were also espoused on the RVS and through his ardent emphasis on the importance of work–life balance and taking holidays. Bruce talked as he made his choices on the RVS:

B: Well the two that impact on my job and you can probably see the balance there, is that I've got four [pause] for me and my family and two which are orientated. Um, so balance is the important issue for me. Um ...

C: Work–life balance, you mean?

B: Yeah, absolutely. Really important issue. And I tend to always have – you know, I leave here whatever time and I very rarely hardly ever work in the evening or at weekends. I work at work, and then I'm at home. And that's kept me sane over the years. So I manage my life in the sense of what's important for me. And that's back to my fundamental point about [pause] organisations are fundamentally selfish beings. So rule number one and I say this in my in an induction programme, or [pause] you know, get in charge of your own destiny, guys. Do not ever believe that the organisation's going to look after you.

However, Bruce's concern for work–life balance can be interpreted in two ways, which are not mutually exclusive. For instance, Bruce was evangelical about the need for all employees to take their five weeks' holiday allocation. This included encouraging the Japanese 'who don't take their holidays', his efforts to increase the American allocation by a week to four weeks, and trying to influence the French to 'take less time off'. Arguably, this reflected his collectivistic prosocial value of equality, indicated via the RVS. Or it illustrated his attitude of enlightened self-interest for pragmatic, commercial reasons, because rested employees are going to be more productive employees.

So, in summary, the final case described here was a director who did not regard CSR as a useful way to run the business. In fact, CSR was actually *in opposition* to 'business outputs'. This brings us back to the contested and controversial nature of CSR that I described

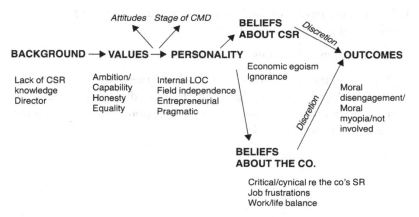

Figure 11.1 Diagrammatic summary: the Disassociated

in Part I of this book. Perhaps Bruce, and some of those in the 'Conformist' subgroup, possessed those deficient ('D') cognitions underlying their values, in contrast to the 'B' or 'being' ('at one with the universe') cognitions of the corporate social entrepreneurs (Maslow, 2011). This question is beyond the scope of my study and is a subject for further investigation. Nevertheless, this extreme case of the 'Disassociated' represented the fourth and final mode of moral commitment to CSR, summarised in Figure 11.1, and it completes Part III of this book. The three other modalities that emerged from this exploratory study were described in the previous chapters. In so doing, I have directly addressed the first two questions that were posed at the beginning of Part III:

1. How are personal values articulated within the organisation?
2. Within the organisation, what is the meaning attached to particular values and how important are they?

My intention in Part IV is to draw some conclusions and to proffer a way forward. So the next chapter begins by returning to the third, fourth and fifth questions that were posed initially, focusing upon moral agency:

3. How do espoused personal values impact upon discretion in the exercise of CSR within the organisation?

4. What is the nature of the socially responsible actor and as part of this, what role does integrity play?

And, addressing the organisational context for CSR:

5. What are the conditions under which these impacts may be attempted and realised? For example, how do people experience the constraining and enabling effects of corporate values within the organisation with regard to CSR?

PART IV

Developing a socially responsible organisational culture

12 | *Conclusion*

Ad hoc CSR cannot be sustainable

The first and second questions regarding how personal values are articulated and their meaning and importance to some of the employees from the case organisation were addressed in Part III. These modalities or extreme cases denote the interplay between the powers of structure and agency in terms of the constraints on and enablements for corporate social responsibility between the organisation and the employee. More specifically, I have shown examples of integrity in action at work and the nature of the agents of CSR, via the four modalities. What we are now left with is a picture of variability in both agency and structure, based on my 'partial and limited reading of the context' (Brown and Locke, 2008: 8). I will now deal with each of these forces in turn, beginning with the employee as agent.

It is now possible to build upon Treviño's (1986) conceptual model (Figure 12.1; Chapter 2 above) and to propose a new theoretical model of some antecedents and consequences not just for CSR, but encompassing moral agency. Hence Figure 12.1 consolidates the diagrammatic summaries of the four modalities described in Chapters 8–11, using the overarching meta-themes of *background, values, personality, beliefs about CSR, beliefs about the company* and *outcomes*. Here, the individual's background is regarded as a source of their personal values, which were described as 'intermediate phenomena' (Hitlin 2003: 123), influencing attitudes, the cognitive stage of moral development and personality, thereby producing beliefs regarding both the company and CSR in general. Importantly, discretion is shown to stem from both the agent's beliefs about CSR and the structural company context, to determine a *range* of behavioural outcomes. The complexity of Figure 12.1 reflects the critical-realist notion that causal mechanisms in social phenomena are contingent and relational (Sayer, 2004). And so in the interests of the development of behavioural ethics theory, I have concluded the following.

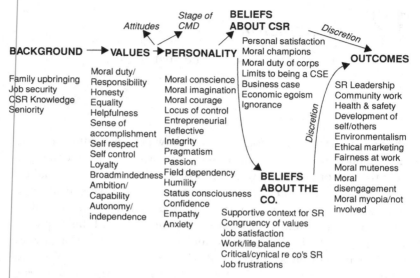

Figure 12.1 Pointers towards the antecedents and consequences of moral agency

First, the hypothesised relationship between moral judgement and moral action is now more developed than that which was initially proposed in Treviño's (1986) conceptual model of ethical decision making. This was achieved as a result of addressing the call for a study of morality at work to include employees' 'personal and biographical differences' (Maclagan, 1998: 11). Second, empirically derived examples of CSEs were found at Brayford Health International which supported the notion of CSR as a discretionary activity, with corporate social entrepreneurs as employees who would 'go the extra mile' at work for prosocial purposes. These tentative results illustrated the temporal and analytical distinction between the individual as agent and as role incumbent, with the CSE as social actor, 'work[ing] to change the structure of the system' (Archer, 1995: 187, 270). More specifically, where personal values moderated employee discretion this can be understood in terms of Bandura's (1999) finding regarding the engagement and disengagement of mechanisms of control in moral agency. These findings are therefore worth further investigation as part of a larger study, not least because they provide some nuance compared with extant management and business ethics theory.

Note, for example, the recent online discussion of the Academy of Management's Social Issues in Management (SIM) group, on whether companies would scale down their CSR due to the current recession: 'I suspect that since philanthropic contributions are a percentage of pre-tax profits... the amount contributed through charity will dwindle as profits dwindle' (Weber, 2009). This reflects the dominant and rational profit maximisation perspective of management. But the findings of this study suggest that certain individuals would find ways to continue their CSR (which was defined in the introduction as much wider than philanthropy). Nonetheless, I have also argued how discretion can occur in all sorts of ways: not simply with regard to antisocial behaviour at work, such as the so-called 'fat cats' of large organisations, paying themselves disproportionately high 'performance' bonuses under their stewardship of organisational failure. Indeed, a range of outcomes with regard to individuals' predisposition towards CSR was conceptualised in Chapter 5. And whilst unethical behaviour was not a specific focus of my investigation, I concur with Treviño's original (1986) propositions regarding those broad-brush moderators of the individual's (moral) decision-making behaviour at work, regardless of outcome. This leads to my third conclusion that whilst CSEs appeared to be in the minority, on the face of it their characteristics were by no means unique (although a study of 'Being' and 'Deficient' cognitions, as advocated by Maslow (2011), may provide further clarity). In other words, we would be mistaken to assume that the corporate social entrepreneur is a rarified and special 'saintly' type.

For example, the value of honesty was not the exclusive domain of those subjects with a social perspective. Illustrations of this were provided across each of the modes that were described in Part III, where subjects articulated their key concerns and what comprised 'doing the right thing' for themselves, their families and for the organisation. Similarly, pragmatism was not the exclusive domain of those who exhibited predominantly individualistic values; it was also demonstrated by the corporate social entrepreneurs.[1] Hence the majority of

---

[1] The word 'pragmatism' seems to be synonymous with business itself. It illustrates the elevation of business and making money as the ultimate virtue in late modernity. But it is the desired outcome – the object or the consequences of the pragmatism – that was my own concern here.

the attributes and characteristics shown in Figure 12.1 will be universal, in the same sense that the list of values in the RVS was described
as applicable to all, only with differences in both priorities and
emphasis,

and given the ubiquity of cultural discourses that serve to legitimate nearly
all the values included in the various surveys, we do not expect to find
many individuals who feel that a particular item is against their own set of
values. People merely value certain items less than they do others. (Hitlin
and Piliavin, 2004: 366)

So I am referring to matters of degree or scale, or levels of magnitude
which also moderate the discretion which is applied within the context of CSR: 'While the distinction in theory is between voluntary and
involuntary, in practice, people often judge degrees of voluntariness'
(Scott, 2000: 503). This connects with the idea of 'shades of green' with
regard to environmentalism, when Crane (2000) discussed deep and
shallow green perspectives in marketing. My point is that people cannot always be neatly categorised (I made this point earlier in Chapter 5)
and so the boundaries between the four modes can be blurred in practice. Indeed, the dominant mode of moral commitment to CSR for two
or three of the subjects was particularly difficult to establish during the
analysis.

An extreme case was Eric, the senior manager, who was so heavily
involved and passionate about his community activities both at home
and abroad that it was not a long stretch to imagine him as a full-time
voluntary worker. But when asked whether it might be possible for a
corporation to be a social enterprise, Eric's response was unequivocal. His view was that employees from the private and public
sectors cannot be as effective as those who are closer to the projects
and actually working *within* the voluntary sector. Yet Eric had also
expressed his own family as a key concern during our interview and
so this rational explanation regarding better efficiency in the voluntary sector may well have been a result of dissonance reduction, as
described in Chapter 3. Nevertheless, using Crane's (2000) analogy of
deep versus shallow green perspectives, Eric represented a 'deep Active'
CSE, due to the intensity of his personal convictions and the depths
of his immersion in CSR. Thus in practice discretion has emerged as
an important component of agency. Indeed, the subjects of this case
study demonstrated that they had a choice regarding their degrees of

Table 12.1 *Characteristics of the Active and Concealed CSEs: levels of seniority*

Status	Number of interviewees
Directors (including president)	3
Senior managers	3
Middle managers	1
Lower manager/administrators	3
Factory operatives	2
n = 12	

involvement with CSR. Moreover, 'values occupy an important place within individuals' social psychology and thus can help us understand links between antecedent social positions and the *individual choices* that serve to reproduce aspects of social structure' (Hitlin and Pili-avin, 2004: 384, my emphasis). But it is the 'Active' and 'Concealed' corporate social entrepreneurs who are of greatest interest, having reflectively deliberated their moral conscience and integrity, articulated their entrepreneurial discretion and demonstrated their leadership in CSR. And of particular significance was the presence of non-senior people operating as CSEs, notably the five CSEs who did *not* occupy management positions (see Table 12.1). This finding is worth high-lighting, because it contradicts the prevailing view of the CEO and top executives setting the moral tone of the corporation. It also refutes a significant literature which has suggested that those employees on lower incomes are 'less likely to act in ways that are conventionally agentic at work', due to factors such as lower self-efficacy and nega-tive affectivity (Leana, Mittal and Stiehl, 2012: 901). And whilst this study was not designed to empirically test particular attributes such as self-efficacy, the CSEs' high levels of self-belief were most apparent from this study (see Chapters 8 and 9).

So whilst seniority is commonly associated with leadership, this study tentatively supported research which has shown *personality* characteristics to be more important (e.g. Anderson, Spataro and Flynn, 2008). On the other hand, and reminiscent of the arguments in Chapter 6 above regarding a 'congealing' of values with age, only one subject out of the twelve from the combined 'Active' and 'Concealed' CSE subgroups was in their twenties: the ages of the rest of the sample were spread between thirty and fifty years old. Nevertheless, the presence of less senior employees who emerged as CSEs from this study suggests that age is not a prerequisite for integrity, although this particular conclusion cannot be drawn using this data set. But despite inconclusive findings regarding a demographic profile of the CSE, CSR leadership was clearly shown by the most senior of the employees in this study: the president of the division, George Carr.

I described George's enthusiasm and support for this investigation in Chapter 7 and how he was the instigator of the corporate brand vision: *'Healing People'*, supported by the espoused brand values of *achievement, creativity* and *integrity* and the four 'brand personalities' of *positive, active, truthful* and *team-playing*. Nevertheless, George's modality within the 'Active' group came as a surprise to me. I had known George from my days as a graduate marketing assistant, when he was a formidable marketing manager. But, due to the passage of time, I was unaware of his predisposition towards CSR, until he was interviewed:

Well I'm sorry, but I think you act through life with responsibility [pause] you see far less of that taking place, but it's actually what true CSR is all about. Actually using the decisions you have and sometimes the influence that you have to effect change in the social environment [pause] integrating the activities of the organisation to help develop the community. And that's what I've been doing.

Indeed, during the presentation of the preliminary findings to George, he was keen to be interpreted as an 'Active' CSE and the data suggested the congruity of this with his self-image. Other CSEs portrayed CSR as part of their personal identity.

For example, Diane, the charity fundraising administrator, described how her self-identity altered after the turning point of her sister's death: 'From a person that would be just carried along, to a person that wants to lead it. Do you know [pause] I want to make a difference.' And, 'So, to me, it's like [pause] I'd stopped being [pause] done to, if you like, do you know what I mean? I'd stopped sitting back and letting somebody change it for me or do it for me [pause] and I'm going out and I'm doing it.' Furthermore, a connection has emerged from this study between the shifts in self-identity as a result of the significant turning points that were characteristic of the CSEs, which were described in Part III:

the behaviours we enact as a result of our identities can cause us to reflect on our values and, over time, to find different values most compelling. When this happens, we experience shifts in our personal identity, our sense of 'who we are'... (Hitlin, 2003: 122)

Hence the findings of this study hint towards some intial support for Hitlin's (2003) perspective of 'values as the core of the self'. Equally importantly, George Carr acknowledged the support he had received for his activities from his own boss, the CEO. Therefore in drawing some conclusions about corporate social entrepreneurship, this study indicates that seniority is not necessary, but it helps. Certainly, the new 'how to do CSR' books acknowledge the social responsibility of all employees (Friedland, 2009; Grayson and Hodges, 2004; Kanter, 2009; Visser, 2011). Indeed, we might expect older and more experienced personnel, who may not be senior executives, to be more confident in progressing a CSR agenda, particularly if they are familiar with the company's systems and processes. On the other hand, the moral muteness of the 'Conformist' group was not confined to the junior personnel in this study.

However, George Carr's level of authority, by his own admission, had enabled him to impact on the division's culture so that it reflected his own personal values. Thus, in the case of the president of the division, the locus of responsibility for CSR is situated in the central point of the horizontal axis, reflecting a congruency between organisational and personal values (see Figure 12.2, reproduced again from Chapter 3). Other cases from the 'Conformist' and 'Disassociated' modes, who demonstrated moral muteness or indicated the compartmentalisation of their working and home identities, can be located on the lower half of the matrix nearer the corporate end of the locus of responsibility for CSR.

So far, then, I have addressed the role of personal values in discretion as part of the nature of the agent in CSR. In the following section I will deal with the fifth research question, regarding the organisational context for CSR. Similar conclusions are evident in terms of the variable nature of the ethical climate at Brayford Health International.

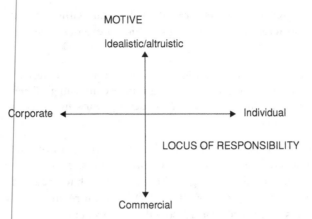

Figure 12.2 A framework for analysing CSR (Hemingway and Maclagan, 2004)

Structural variation: the ad hoc nature of the company's CSR

Research Question 5. What are the conditions under which these impacts may be attempted and realised? For example, how do people experience the constraining and enabling effects of corporate values within the organisation with regard to CSR?

In Chapter 7, I described the traditional, socially responsible culture of BHI as a health care company with a tradition of staff welfare. Indeed, at the time of data collection, the company was preparing for its hundred-years-in-business celebrations. Another notable feature of the corporate culture was the encouragement of intrapreneurship (Pinchot, 1985). This was reported by some informants and was also a memorable part of my own experience as an employee previously. Further to this, most of the subjects were at ease in discussing their CSR, despite the indications of moral muteness in some cases. Therefore, if amorality or moral disengagement was indicative of the modus operandi of this company, then the CSEs might have reported ethical dilemmas. As they did not, this contributes towards the indications of a relatively socially responsible climate at BHI, which was bolstered by the intrapreneurial personality of particular employees, enabling them to perceive opportunities for CSR, as opposed to difficulties. Moreover, I have also noted that the president of the division had acknowledged the support of his own boss, the CEO, with regard to his encouragement of CSR within the division. Thus, using the data that was discussed in Part III, there were suggestions of a congruency of values between the self-transcendent value orientations of the CSEs and the espoused socially responsible culture of the division, indicating a 'person–organisation' (P–O) fit in these cases. P–O fit was described by Anderson, Spataro and Flynn (2008) as 'the compatibility between an individual and a work environment that occurs when their characteristics are well matched' (Anderson, Spataro and Flynn, 2008: 703). Indeed, the researchers found P–O fit to be an important source of influence in organisations, which produces managerial implications for the further development of CSR at BHI.

Yet there were also indications of a socially responsible culture that was perceived to be in transition at BHI. Clearly, within the three-year period of data collection, the division had seen some changes. Most significantly, George Carr announced that he was taking early retirement, although staying on as chairman of the board of trustees. And perceptions were mixed amongst subjects regarding the company's support for CSR. This indicated its ad hoc nature within the division and an uncertainty regarding the company's commitment to CSR going forward. Some employees reported frustration that CSR was not enough of a corporate priority, and a perceived lack of support for CSR was a particular concern of the 'Concealed' CSEs, for example Julie, the factory operative described in Chapter 9, who blamed middle management for blocking what she saw as senior management's good intentions regarding CSR. Conversely, in the case of Bruce, the 'Disassociated' company director (who had dismissed the value of CSR and advocated that it had historically been too much of a priority in the division) revealed how he was hoping to effect culture change, away from CSR, under the leadership of the new president. All this illustrates in practice the contested nature of CSR that I described in the introduction to this book. And it also supports the assertion from the organisation performance literature that it is 'not clear that a single conception of purposes is shared among participants in an organization. It is not clear that purpose antedates activities' (March and Sutton, 1997: 698).

Thus the indications of the line managers' influence, or departmental influence, supports the perspective of scholars who disregard the notion of a homogeneous corporate culture, suggesting amendments to Figure 7.1 in order to reflect this nuance regarding perceptions of

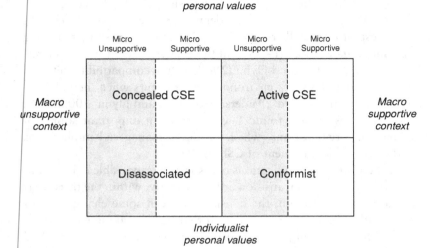

Figure 12.3 Modes of moral commitment to CSR, reflecting variability in employee perceptions of a supportive culture

a supportive culture. This suggestion of a micro-context, within the overall corporate context, is illustrated in Figure 12.3. Moreover, this finding provides an interesting parallel with extant theory regarding cross-national studies of cultural values, conforming with the notion of an 'overall pattern of cultural values' and, at the same time, cultural differences within individual countries (Kirkman and Shapiro, 2001: 611); it also supports Feather's observation regarding 'the fabric of variation within cultures' (Feather, 1986: 280). Indeed, these results make some exploratory headway towards an examination of within-culture variation in values (Hitlin and Piliavin, 2004: 377).

Within the current economic climate (and a double-dip recession in the UK), expectations that CSR and sustainability issues might have fallen down the corporate agenda, thereby curtailing the activities of corporate social entrepreneurs, was expressed by scholars of business ethics and relayed at the beginning of this chapter. But on the basis of these tentative results, the enduring nature of a socially responsible corporate context was evident, albeit under threat. Hence my prediction is to anticipate proportionally fewer CSEs, greater disassociation with CSR more prevalent amongst employees who do not wish to be perceived by employees as mavericks, and greater levels of conformism to the perceived ethical climate in an organisation with a less socially responsible culture than Brayford Health International. But the current economic crisis has highlighted the need for greater integrity amongst employees and thus the position of the 'Conformists' and 'Disassociated' is not sustainable.

Furthermore, and in addition to the growth of personal values literature in social psychology which demonstrates the connection between values and behaviour, the world has changed much since the onset of this study. Indeed, as part of these changes, CSR has developed as an academic discipline and business function, highlighted by the onset of a global recession, incited by financial irresponsibility and misdemeanour. This has increased the pressure on political leaders for greater market regulation and corporate governance. And those who eschewed the idea of a multi-fudiciary purpose of CSR are now more likely to be amenable to the business and society arguments. I also hope that there will be greater impetus in cross-disciplinary research in the creative pursuit of knowledge in this important area of social science. Normatively, do we just look after our own interests, or also look after the interests of others? In economic terms, giving self-interest free rein was referred to as market fundamentalism (Soros, 2008). And parallels can be drawn, here, between the Friedmanite perspective on CSR and the misinterpretations of Darwin's theory of natural selection and the 'the survival of the fittest' in the early twentieth century. Indeed, Marr (2009) described how Darwin's theory was misinterpreted for political ends with ghastly social consequences, such as compulsory sterilisation in the USA during the 1950s for those considered to be of 'feeble mind', and was also part of the rationale for the Holocaust:

> Hitler's generals quoted Darwin as they planned 'the final solution'. Darwin would have been appalled. He did not think all people were physically or mentally equal. But he also said that, no matter the effect on evolution, to neglect the weak 'would be an overwhelming evil' and that human sympathy was 'the noblest part of our nature'. (Marr, 2009)

Yet, for more than four decades, Friedmanites have argued that CSR has no place in business, that it detracts from the business of doing business because capitalism concerns the survival of the 'fittest' organisation in terms of its financial performance in the marketplace, that it is only proper that the free market allows the strongest and most

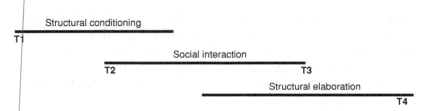

Figure 12.4 The morphogenetic sequence (Archer, 1995: 193)

profitable organisations to survive. But notwithstanding the arguments that CSR can contribute to the firm's profitability and longer-term sustainability (Orlitzky, Schmidt and Rynes, 2003), the argument for the development of social and spiritual capital in addition to sufficient economic capital is nowadays more generally widespread, along with acceptance by big business that CSR needs to be regarded as an investment (Handy, 1998; Zohar and Marshall, 2004). This hypothesised shift from self-interested to more widespread acceptance of CSR, and to an understanding of its multi-fiduciary orientation, can be illustrated using Archer's (1995) morphogenetic sequence from social theory (see Figure 12.4)

This sequence denotes 'the temporal interplay' between the structural and agential forces involved in the process of structural conditioning, social interaction and structural elaboration (Archer, 1995). As a consequence, the morphogenetic approach, through analytical dualism, helps us to understand the development of CSR. And my theoretical presupposition is of a shift at both the individual and organisational levels: first at the individual level, from the 'Disassociated' mode of moral commitment to CSR to the 'Conformist' mode and towards corporate social entrepreneurship. I have illustrated this presupposition in Figure 12.5, where the Z pattern shows movement from the 'Disassociated' at T2 through to the 'Active CSE' at T3. Second, Figure 12.5 also reflects the shift in the declarations of CSR by big business and the growth of the CSR industry, whereby the Friedmanite position that the purpose of business is business (largely articulated by undergraduate students of business rather than their practising counterparts) and the contemporary language of business *in practice* is more in line, nowadays, with the position of enlightened self-interest (see the introduction). My point is that CSR, in practice, has the potential to evolve

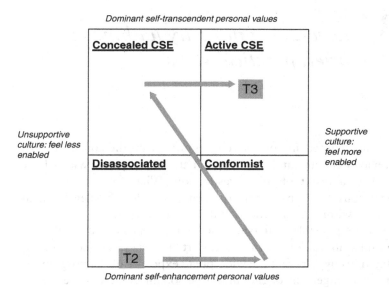

Figure 12.5 The structural conditioning of big business via CSR

further towards widespread corporate social entrepreneurship, based on a growing understanding of its multi-fiduciary duty.

So how might this be encouraged? The results of this study have provided some interesting take-outs, particularly with regard to the implications for socially responsible leadership and organisational culture. These will be addressed next.

13 | *Leveraging integrity within: some brief, practical steps*

In my final chapter, my objective is to infer from the conclusions of the previous chapter and elaborate on the implications which have emerged as a result of this investigation. What follows are some practical considerations and recommendations for the development of integrity within organisations and their employees.

Socially responsible leadership was formally promoted at BHI via the 'brand ambassador' programme. Certainly, the evidence from this investigation suggests that the widespread exposure of the programme and its encouragement of the 'brand personalities' across the corporation has had some success, in terms of its encouragement of SR behaviour amongst employees. Allied to this, there were indications of a synchronisation of values between some of the informants and the company (described as P–O fit in the last section). Whether these corresponding value sets had been cultivated within the company was beyond the scope of this study. Regardless, congruency between organisational and personal values has been associated in other studies with influential and motivated employees (e.g. Anderson et al., 2008), thereby facilitating team-working. Moreover, socially responsible behaviour was indicated, with more influential individuals acting as corporate social entrepreneurs. The results concur with Treviño's (1986) 'referent others', described as influencing ethical or unethical behaviour at work. Certainly, the corporate social entrepreneurs from this study clearly demonstrated their leadership with regard to CSR. And it is interesting that when the term 'moral fibre' was used by one of the 'Conformists' in the context of moral muteness, this sounded to me like a very old-fashioned term two years prior to the onset of the global financial crisis. Now, having employees with moral fibre is back on the corporate agenda.

So in addition to the need for vigilance in order to avoid the potential for corporate misdeeds, a normative perspective suggests that corporations have a duty to be looking out for opportunities for CSR – rather like the management cliché that there is no such thing as a problem, but an opportunity in disguise: ethical dilemma or opportunity for CSR? Furthermore, the personally fulfilling nature of CSR that was expressed by some of the case organisation's employees accords with the discussion of self-transcendence and happiness which was described in Chapter 6. And so I make no apologies for using the word 'leveraging' in the title of this chapter, where it is highly appropriate in the context of encouraging employees to fulfil their true potential as virtuous beings and developing their humanity as the authentic, true identity (Bandura, 1986; Maslow, 2011). Hence, if taking the initiative and pursuing opportunities are characteristics of leadership (Darcy, 2002: 402), and if the virtues of leadership can be taught, then the potential for all employees to be CSR leaders becomes apparent.[1]

However, the ad hoc and transitional nature of BHI's SR culture suggested that a renewed commitment to CSR needed to be demonstrated to employees if the company wished to retain its SR culture. Indeed, the company's origins and its background in the health care industry ensured that SR was an integral part of the corporate brand, even without the strategic marketing communications programme that was adopted by the company in more recent years. Thus SR associations already exist in the minds of this company's stakeholders, but if they are not renewed associations can deteriorate and change (Keller, 1993; Keller, 1998). And if we note the strategic benefits of CSR that were discussed in the introduction to this book, my key recommendation was that the organisation reinforce and continue to demonstrate its commitment to CSR. So, bearing in mind the congruency of CSR with this particular corporate brand, the recommendation to formalise CSR as a strategic direction, rather than leaving it to the volunteers, was logical on the basis of levering this inherent strength within the company.

This key recommendation included tackling the sporadic, voluntary aspect to CSR and the need to make it everyone's business. It applies to all employees within the organisation, because CSR is everyone's responsibility. Furthermore, through a widespread literature encompassing personal values theory, social cognitive theory and moral philosophy, I have shown that our humanity is central to our sense

[1] 'Confucius considered that all people could become a man of benevolence' (Zhang, 2002: 228).

of self, that social obligation lies at the heart of our self-concept. And I have shown some tentative, exploratory support for this through the corporate social entrepreneurs who emerged from this particular study. Engaging in CSR enabled these employees to become fulfilled at work. Thus my recommendations for the development of a more socially responsible organisation, in general, consist of wholesale adoption of CSR as a formal strategic orientation, headed up by a CSR director who embodies the company's moral conscience, with a seat on the executive board. Moreover, formalised CSR has to be supported via widespread employee training in CSR leadership, which can be managed by this formal CSR function. The CSR director should be a budget holder for all CSR-related projects, including philanthropy, community development and ongoing in-house CSR training, although the firm's public relations should remain part of a marketing communications budget.

Indeed, corporate communications, bolstered by education and training, can support adoption or reinforcement of CSR as an integral part of the corporate strategic plan. Certainly, the impact of the case company's goal-setting course ('RWG'),[2] described in Part III, was reported to have had a profound effect on the subjects of this particular study, thereby demonstrating its efficacy as a facilitator for personal agency. Even more specific to CSR was the success of the involvement in the Common Purpose programme by some of the 'Active' CSEs. Moreover, CSR training was available at the local university business school, where an executive training programme was used by the company for a number of years. This education in CSR was cited by an 'Active' as a key influencer. Indeed, Schwartz reported, 'Universalism values . . . are substantially higher among those who attend university. This may reflect both the broadening of horizons that university education provides and a tendency for those who give high priority to universalism values to seek higher education' (Schwartz, 2006: 10). Thus, on the basis of the results of this study, whereby CSEs felt enabled by their firm to progress a social agenda, the development of corporate social entrepreneurship within the organisation can be facilitated through increased knowledge and understanding of CSR via education. Subsequent to the current economic situation, however, the urgency for more overt moral-leadership courses, in the UK at least, is

---

[2] The name of this training firm has been disguised.

apparent. And whilst these have been available in the USA for a number of years, notably at the Harvard Business School, cynics may now question their efficacy. What is unknown to me, however, is the content of such courses, with respect to the development of moral character and integrity, incorporating lessons regarding reflexive judgement and the development of conscience, governmentality and self-control. Remembering one of the 'Concealed' CSEs, there is a certain irony that Julie, the frustrated factory operative, was teaching disadvantaged children lessons about self-control and the correct way to behave at a football match as part of her voluntary work. The competitive world of business needs more Julies. Further to this, BHI has manufacturing facilities in the Far East, where connections to Confucian teaching would have cultural resonance in local business training and could provide timely benefits.[3] Indeed, authoritarian regime aside, China has been reported to be keen to develop a sustainable market economy and does not wish to replicate the mistakes of the West (Zhang and Wen, 2008).

Moreover, a cognitive function whereby personal values are reordered was experienced by some of the subjects in this study. This, again, implies the potential for successful CSR leadership training. To recap, 'Though [personal] value systems have stability, they are not immutable' (Feather, 1986: 279). Indeed, Schwartz declared that 'activating values *causes* behavior' (Schwartz, 2006: 12, original emphasis). And the case for such training can be made by way of reference to some of the subjects of this study, who reported a connection between CSR and job satisfaction, thereby linking with the discussion in Chapter 6 above regarding the personal benefits of integrity. Hence personal agency, by being 'causally efficacious' (Archer, 2003: 16), benefits both organisation and individual. So the ancients' ideas regarding individual growth and self-realisation in pursuit of the development of character integrity and conducting oneself as a free and superior individual resonate with the CSEs described in this study.

In these cases, CSR had provided that sense of freedom from the often unfulfilling nature of work. For example, CSR provided Diane (Chapter 8) with the vehicle that gave her the freedom to escape an

---

[3] One subject from this study reported her experience of some poor ethical business practices in an eastern economy which were attributed to the race towards greater industrialisation (see Chapter 8).

unsatisfactory life, and gave Julie (Chapter 9) the freedom to escape the drudgery of a dull factory job with no job satisfaction. So if it is the subjective experience of freedom and autonomy and personal development that promotes the sense of satisfaction, then this can be further encouraged in the work environment. After all, the expression that we are 'slaves to the system' is common parlance in the work context. Importantly, this would be greatly facilitated through the streamlining of bureaucratic processes and the eradication of micro-management and 'tick-box' mentalities, where employee discretion in many spheres has been eroded over the last two decades, freeing employees to think for themselves. Back to Foucault: 'Freedom is the ontological condition of ethics. But ethics is the considered form that freedom takes when it is informed by reflection' (Foucault, 2000: 284).

My more controversial recommendation would be to adopt psychometric testing in the screening for self-transcendent personal values in search and recruitment, in order to provide a more proactive approach towards the development of a socially responsible organisational culture. And whilst some scholars would refute the validity and ethicality of psychometric testing, screening on the basis of personal values would support the existing battery of testing that is the modus operandi of contemporary corporate recruitment practice and is already comprehensively applied as part of BHI's recruitment and development processes. So rather than worrying about psychometric testing and the manipulation of corporate culture as a possible abuse of corporate power, even for socially responsible ends, my constructive approach is to focus on the power of moral agency, regulated by the inherent notion of governmentality or self-mastery.

Therefore, if, on the basis of these results, an ad hoc socially responsible corporate culture is typical, then this implies that the formalisation of CSR needs to be implemented via research-based interventions. This can be done through the attribution of personal responsibility and by the cultivation of a moral character amongst all the company's employees, as suggested above. Thus, in principle, the notion of 'the controlling mind' can also usefully be applied in CSR. This was the legal term, described in Chapter 3, used for allocating responsibility in cases of corporate misdemeanour. Thus the appointment of a CSR board director with an education in business ethics, responsible for the organisation's CSR in the organic sense and not confined to a public relations role, manifests the theoretical notion of corporate moral agency in practice. In this manner, Ranken's concerns about the term 'corporate moral agency' – 'Neither the corporation as an entity nor the organizational structure should be treated as having independent moral status' (Ranken, 1987: 633) – are addressed. In this way, CSR can be formally recognised and integrated throughout the firm via the CSR director's representation on the executive board, where all board members act as the organisation's formal, corporate moral agents, in conjunction with their empowered employees.

Therefore, whilst much practical guidance on the implementation of CSR itself has been published, particularly over the last few years, my recommendations in this final chapter have emerged as a consequence of the results of this study. It is my intention that these insights and recommendations may contribute towards enabling corporations to develop their more socially responsible organisational cultures and provide a platform for the development of a form of capitalism that is a vast improvement over what we have at the present time.

Appendix
Rokeach Values Survey

Which of these standards of conduct would you say are most important to you? (Please tick the ones you think apply most to you)

- **Ambitious** (hard-working, aspiring)
- **Broadminded** (open-minded)
- **Capable** (competent, effective)
- **Loyal** (firm, constant support)
- **Clean** (neat, tidy)
- **Courageous** (standing up for your beliefs)
- **Forgiving** (willing to pardon others)
- **Helpful** (working for the welfare of others)
- **Honest** (sincere, truthful)
- **Imaginative** (daring, creative)
- **Independent** (self-reliant, self-sufficient)
- **Intellectual** (intelligent, reflective)
- **Logical** (consistent, rational)
- **Loving** (affectionate, tender)
- **Obedient** (dutiful, respectful)
- **Polite** (courteous, well-mannered)
- **Responsible** (dependable, reliable)
- **Self-controlled** (restrained, self-disciplined)

Which of these would you say is closest to describing your goals in life/what means most to you in life? (Please tick the ones you think apply most to you)

- **A comfortable life** (a prosperous life)
- **An exciting life** (a stimulating, active life)
- **A sense of accomplishment** (a lasting contribution)
- **A world at peace** (free of war and conflict)

- **A world of beauty** (beauty of nature and the arts)
- **Equality** (brotherhood, equal opportunity for all)
- **Family security** (taking care of loved ones)
- **Freedom** (independence, free choice)
- **Health** (fit and well)
- **Inner harmony** (freedom from inner conflict)
- **Mature love** (sexual and spiritual intimacy)
- **National security** (protection from attack)
- **Pleasure** (an enjoyable, leisurely life)
- **Salvation** (saved, eternal life)
- **Self-respect** (self-esteem)
- **Social recognition** (respect, admiration)
- **True friendship** (close companionship)
- **Wisdom** (a mature understanding of life)

References

Achbar, M. and Abbott, J. (2004) *The Corporation*, film, Metrodome Distribution, Canada.

Adkins, S. (1999) *Cause Related Marketing: Who Cares Wins*. London: Heinemann Butterworth.

Adler, P.S. (2012) Perspective: The Sociological Ambivalence of Bureaucracy: From Weber via Gouldner to Marx. *Organization Science* 23 (1): 244–66.

Agle, B.R. and Caldwell, C.B. (1999) Understanding Research on Values in Business: A Level of Analysis Framework. *Business and Society* 38 (3): 326–87.

Agle, B.R., Mitchell, R.K. and Sonnenfeld, J.A. (1999) Who Matters to CEOs? An Investigation of Stakeholder Attributes and Salience, Corporate Performance, and CEO Values. *Academy of Management Journal* 42 (5): 507–25.

Ainley, P., Barnes, T. and Momen, A. (2002) Making Connexions: A Case Study in Contemporary Social Policy. *Critical Social Policy* 22 (2): 376–88.

Allport, G., Vernon, P. and Lindzey, G. (1960) *Study of Values*, 3rd ed. Boston: Houghton Mifflin.

Alvarez, S.A., Barney, J.B. and Anderson, P. (2012) Perspective: Forming and Exploiting Opportunities: The Implications of Discovery and Creation Processes for Entrepreneurial and Organizational Research. *Organization Science* (articles in advance) (April 3): 1–17.

Alvord, S.H., Brown, D.L. and Letts, C.W. (2003) Social Entrepreneurship: Leadership That Facilitates Societal Transformation – An Exploratory Study. Center for Public Leadership, Working Paper 5.

Anand, V., Ashforth, B.E. and Joshi, M. (2004) Business as Usual: The Acceptance and Perpetuation of Corruption in Organizations. *Academy of Management Executive* 18 (2): 39–52.

Anastasiadis, S. (2006) Understanding Corporate Lobbying on Its Own Terms. *ICCSR Research Paper Series* 42: 1–42, 1479–5124.

Anderson, C., Spataro, S.E. and Flynn, F.J. (2008) Personality and Organizational Culture as Determinants of Influence. *Journal of Applied Psychology* 93 (3): 702–10.

Anderson, D. (2007) Sustainable and Responsible Finance in the UK: Celebrating 15 Years of the UK Social Investment Forum: Promoting Sustainable and Responsible Finance (1991–2006), in UK Social Investment Forum (UKSIF) (ed.), *Ethical Savings and Investment: The Rise of the Ethical Saver*. London: UKSIF: 12.

Andersson, L.M. and Bateman, T.S. (2000) Individual Environmental Initiative: Championing Natural Environmental Issues in US Business Organizations. *Academy of Management Journal* 43 (4): 548–70.

Angelidis, J. and Ibrahim, N. (2004) An Exploratory Study of the Impact of Degree of Religiousness upon an Individual's Corporate Social Responsiveness Orientation. *Journal of Business Ethics* 51 (2): 119–28.

Archer, M.S. (1995) *Realist Social Theory: The Morphogenetic Approach*. Cambridge: Cambridge University Press.

Archer, M.S. (1996) *Culture and Agency: The Place of Culture in Social Theory*, 2nd ed. Cambridge: Cambridge University Press.

Archer, M.S. (2000) *Being Human: The Problem of Agency*. Cambridge: Cambridge University Press.

Archer, M.S. (2003) *Structure, Agency and the Internal Conversation*. Cambridge: Cambridge University Press.

Archer, M.S. (2007) *Making Our Way through the World: Human Reflexivity and Social Mobility*. Cambridge: Cambridge University Press.

Archer, M.S. (2012) *The Reflexive Imperative in Late Modernity*. Cambridge: Cambridge University Press.

Argyris, C. (1957) *Personality and Organization: the Conflict Between System and the Individual*. New York, Harper and Row.

Argyris, C. and Schon, D.A. (1978) *Organizational Learning*. Reading, MA: Addison-Wesley.

Ashkanasy, N.M., Windsor, C.A. and Treviño, L.K. (2006) Bad Apples in Bad Barrels Revisited: Cognitive Moral Development, Just World Beliefs, Rewards, and Ethical Decision-Making. *Business Ethics Quarterly* 16 (4): 449–74.

Austin, J., Leonard, D., Reficco, E. and Wei-Skillern, J. (2004) Corporate Social Entrepreneurship: A New Vision for CSR, Harvard Business School, Working Paper 05-021.

Austin, J., Leonard, H.B., Reficco, E. and Wei-Skillern, J. (2006a) Corporate Social Entrepreneurship: A New Vision for CSR, in M.J. Epstein and K.O. Hanson (eds.), *The Accountable Corporation: Corporate Social Responsibility*, Volume Three. Westport, CT: Praeger: 237–47.

Austin, J.E., Leonard, H.B., Reficco, E. and Wei-Skillern, J. (2006b) Social Entrepreneurship: It's for Corporations Too, in A. Nicholls (ed.), *Social Entrepreneurship: New Models of Sustainable Social Change*. Oxford: Oxford University Press: 169–80.

Austin, J. and Reficco, E. (2009) Corporate Social Entrepreneurship, Harvard Business School, Working Paper 09-101.

Austin, J., Stevenson, H. and Wei-Skillern, J. (2006) Social Entrepreneurship and Commercial Entrepreneurship: Same, Different, or Both? *Entrepreneurship, Theory and Practice* 30 (1): 1–22.

Baier, K. (1993) Egoism, in P. Singer (ed.), *A Companion to Ethics*. Oxford: Blackwell: 197–204.

Bailey, F.G. (2001) *Stratagems and Spoils: A Social Anthropology of Politics*. Oxford: Westview Press.

Bandura, A. (1986) *Social Foundations of Thought and Action*. Englewood Cliffs, NJ: Prentice Hall.

Bandura, A. (1999) Moral Disengagement in the Perpetration of Humanities. *Personality and Social Psychology Review* 3 (3): 193–209.

Barnett, M.L. (2007) Stakeholder Influence Capacity and the Variability of Financial Returns to Corporate Social Responsibility. *Academy of Management Review* 32 (3): 794–816.

Baron, D. (2005) CSR and Social Entrepreneurship, Stanford Graduate School of Business, Research Paper 1956.

Baron, D.P. (2003a) Corporate Social Responsibility, in D.P. Baron (ed.), *Business and Its Environment*, 4th ed. Upper Saddle River, NJ: Pearson Education: 642–81.

Baron, D.P. (2003b) Private Nonmarket Action, in D.P. Baron (ed.), *Business and Its Environment*, 4th ed. Upper Saddle River, NJ: Pearson Education: 90–118.

Baron, D.P. (2007) Corporate Social Responsibility and Social Entrepreneurship. *Journal of Economics and Management Strategy* 16 (3): 683–717.

Baron, D.P. and Diermeier, D. (2007a) Introduction to the Special Issue on Non-market Strategy and Social Responsibility. *Journal of Economics and Management Strategy* 16 (3): 539–45.

Baron, D.P. and Diermeier, D. (2007b) Strategic Activism and Nonmarket Strategy. *Journal of Economics and Management Strategy* 16 (3): 599–634.

Batson, C.D. (1989) Personal Values, Moral Principles, and Three-Path Model of Prosocial Motivation, in N. Eisenberg, J. Reykowski and E. Staub (eds.), *Social and Moral Values: Individual and Societal Perspectives*. Hillsdale, NJ: Lawrence Erlbaum: 213–28.

Bennett, A. (2005) *Untold Stories*. London: Faber and Faber.

Berle, A.A. and Means, G.C. (1932) *The Modern Corporation and Private Property*. New York: Macmillan.

Bhaskar, R. (1986) *Scientific Realism and Human Emancipation*. London: Verso.

Bhaskar, R. (1998) Facts and Values: Theory and Practice, in M. Archer, R. Bhaskar, A. Collier, T. Lawson and A. Norrie (eds.), *Critical Realism: Essential Readings*. London: Routledge: 409–43.

Bierhoff, H.-W. (2002) *Prosocial Behaviour*. Hove: Psychology Press.

Bigoness, W.J. and Blakely, G.L. (1996) A Cross-national Study of Managerial Values. *Journal of International Business Studies* 27 (4): 739–49.

Bird, F.B. and Waters, J.A. (1989) The Moral Muteness of Managers. *California Management Review* 32 (1): 73–88.

Böhm, S. and Batta, A. (2010) Just Doing It: Enjoying Commodity Fetishism with Lacan. *Organization* 17 (3): 345–60.

Bohman, J. and Rehg, W. (2007) Jürgen Habermas, in *Stanford Encyclopedia of Philosophy* online. Available at http://plato.stanford.edu/entries/habermas.

Bolger, N., De Longis, A., Kessler, R.C. and Wethington, E. (1989) The Contagion of Stress across Multiple Roles. *Journal of Marriage and the Family* 51 (1): 175–83.

Bondy, K., Crane, A. and Browne, L.M. (2004) Doing the Business: A Film Series Programmed by ICCSR in Conjunction with Broadway Cinema, ICCSR Research Paper Series, 25-2004

Bowie, N. (1999) *Business Ethics: A Kantian Perspective*. Oxford: Blackwell.

Braun, V. and Clarke, V. (2006) Using Thematic Analysis in Psychology. *Qualitative Research in Psychology* 3: 77–101.

Brown, M.T. (2005) *Corporate Integrity: Rethinking Organizational Ethics and Leadership*. Cambridge: Cambridge University Press.

Brown, S. and Locke, A. (2008) Social Psychology, in C. Willig and W. Stainton-Rogers (eds.), *The Sage Handbook of Qualitative Research in Psychology*: 373–89.

Brown, T.J. and Dacin, P.A. (1997) The Company and the Product: Corporate Associations and Consumer Product Responses. *Journal of Marketing* 61 (1): 68–85.

Budhwar, P. and Varma, A. (2011) *Doing Business in India*. London: Routledge.

Buono, A.F. and Nichols, L. (1985) *Corporate Policy, Values and Social Responsibility*. New York: Praeger.

Burawoy, M. (2009) *The Extended Case Method*. London: University of California Press.

Burgelman, R.A. (1983) Corporate Entrepreneurship and Strategic Management: Insights from a Process Study. *Management Science* 29 (12): 1349–63.

Carnahan, T. and McFarland, S. (2007) Revisiting the Stanford Prison Experiment: Could Participant Self-Selection Have Led to the Cruelty? *Personality and Social Psychology Bulletin* 33 (5): 603–14.

Carroll, A.B. (1979) A Three-Dimensional Model of Corporate Social Performance. *Academy of Management Review* 4 (4): 497–505.

Carroll, A.B. (1987) In Search of the Moral Manager. *Business Horizons* 30 (2): 7–15.

Carroll, A.B. (1996) *Business and Society: Ethics and Stakeholder Management*, 3rd ed. Cincinatti: Southwestern Publishing.

Carson, D., Gilmore, A., Perry, C. and Gronhaug, K. (2001) *Qualitative Marketing Research*. London: Sage.

Catasus, B., Lundgren, M. and Rynnel, H. (1997) Environmental Managers' Views on Environmental Work in a Business Context. *Business Strategy and the Environment* 6: 197–205.

Caulkin, S. (7 April 2002) Good thinking, bad practice. *The Observer*: 11

Cespa, G. and Cestone, G. (2007) Corporate Social Responsibility and Managerial Entrenchment. *Journal of Economics and Management Strategy* 16 (3): 741–71.

Chapman, M. (2000) 'When the Entrepreneur Sneezes, the Organization Catches a Cold': A Practitioner's Perspective on the State of the Art in Research on the Entreprenerial Personality and the Entrepreneurial Process. *European Journal of Work and Organizational Psychology* 9 (1): 97–101.

Church, J. (2012) Hegel on the Ethical Individual, in J. Church (ed.), *Infinite Autonomy: The Divided Individual in the Political Thought of G.W.F. Hegel and Friedrich Nietzsche*. University Park, PA: Pennysylvania State University, 56–78.

Ciulla, J.B. (2002) Trust and the Future of Leadership, in N.E. Bowie (ed.), *The Blackwell Guide to Business Ethics*. Oxford: Blackwell, 334–52.

Collins, J.W. and Ganotis, C.G. (1973) Is Corporate Responsibility Sabotaged by the Rank and File? *Business and Society Review/Innovation* 73 (7): 82–8.

Confederation of British Industry (2001a). Issue Statement: Corporate Social Responsibility.

Confederation of British Industry (2001b). Membership, 2001.

Connon, H. (May 2002) Sinners Set to Feel the Heat. *Money Observer* 262: 36–40.

Co-operative Group (2010) Ethical Consumerism Report 2010: Ethical Shopping through the Downturn. Published by the Co-operative Financial Services. Available at www.goodwithmoney.co.uk/assets/

Uploads/Documents/Ethical-Consumerism-Report-2010.pdf?token=
cd7d08c627103ee37b0de8204c0e6151d531e572l1355681941#PDFP.

Corman, J., Perles, B. and Vancini, P. (1988) Motivational Factors Influencing High-Technology Entrepreneurship. *Journal of Small Business
Management* 26 (1): 36–42.

Cornwall, J.R. and Naughton, M.J. (2003) Who Is the Good Entrepreneur?
An Exploration within the Catholic Social Tradition. *Journal of Business Ethics* 44: 61–75.

Corporate Knights Inc. and Innovest Strategic Value Advisors Inc. (2005)
The Global 100 Most Sustainable Corporations in the World. Available
at www.global100.org.

Cox, D., La Caze, M. and Levine, M.P. (2003) *Integrity and the Fragile Self.*
Aldershot: Ashgate.

Cramer, J., Jonker, J. and van der Heijden, A. (2004) Making Sense of
Corporate Social Responsibility. *Journal of Business Ethics* 55 (2): 215–
22.

Crane, A. (2000) *Marketing, Morality and the Natural Environment.* London: Routledge.

Crane, A. (2001) Corporate Greening as Amoralization. *Organization Studies* 21 (4): 673–96.

Crane, A. and Matten, D. (2010) *Business Ethics: Managing Corporate
Citizenship and Sustainability in the Age of Globalization.* Oxford:
Oxford University Press.

Crown Prosecution Service (2013). Corporate Manslaughter. Available at
www.cps.gov.uk/legal/a_to_c/corporate_manslaughter.

Csikszentmihalyi, M. and Csikszentmihalyi, I.S. (2006) *A Life Worth Living:
Contributions to Positive Psychology.* New York: Oxford University
Press.

Curtis, N. (2001) *Against Autonomy: Lyotard, Judgement and Action.*
Aldershot: Ashgate.

Dalton, M. (1959) *Men Who Manage: Fusions of Feeling and Theory in
Administration.* New York: Wiley.

Dancy, J. (1993) An Ethic of Prima Facie Duties, in P. Singer (ed.), *A Companion to Ethics.* Oxford: Blackwell, 219–29.

Darby, I. (August 1999) P&G Unveils Plan to Link Products to Good Causes.
Marketing 1: 1

Darcy, K. (2002) Ethics and Corporate Leadership, in R.E. Frederick
(ed.), *A Companion to Business Ethics.* Oxford: Blackwell, 399–
408.

Davidsson, P. and Wiklund, J. (2001) Levels of Analysis in Entrepreneurship
Research: Current Research Practice and Suggestions for the Future.
Entrepreneurship Theory and Practice 25 (4): 81–99.

Davis, E. (2002) *Big Bad Business*, Parts 1 and 2, BBC Radio 4, presented by Evan Davis, economics editor; edited by Stephen Chilcott.

Davis, I. (28 May 2005) The Biggest Contract. *The Economist*: 87–9.

De Leeuw, E. (1999) Healthy Cities: Urban Social Entrepreneurship for Health. *Health Promotion International* 14: 261–69.

Dent, C.M. (1999) *The European Union and East Asia: An Economic Relationship*. London: Routledge.

Desai, A.B. and Rittenburg, T. (1997) Global Ethics: An Integrative Framework for MNEs. *Journal of Business Ethics* 16 (8): 791–800.

Desmond, J. and Crane, A. (2004) Morality and the Consequences of Marketing Action. *Journal of Business Research* 57; 1222–30.

Di Norcia, V. and Tigner, J. (2000) Mixed Motives and Ethical Decisions in Business. *Journal of Business Ethics* 25 (1): 1–13.

d'Iribarne, P. (2003) The Combination of Strategic Games and Moral Community in the Functioning of Firms. *Organization Studies* 24 (8): 1283–1307.

Dillon, P.S. and Fischer, K. (1992) *Environmental Management in Corporations: Methods and Motivations*, Medford, MA: The Center for Environmental Management, Tufts University.

Drucker, P.F. (1968) Conclusion: The Responsibilities of Management, in P.F. Drucker (ed.), *The Practice of Management*. London: Pan Books: 453–66.

Drumwright, M.E. (July 1994) Socially Responsible Organisational Buying: Environmental Concern as a Non-economic Buying Criterion. *Journal of Marketing* 58: 1–19.

Drumwright, M.E. and Murphy, P.E. (2004) How Advertising Practitioners View Ethics: Moral Muteness, Moral Myopia, and Moral Imagination. *Journal of Advertising* 33 (2): 7–24.

Du Gay, P. (2000) *In Praise of Bureaucracy*. London: Sage.

Dyer, W.G. and Wilkins, A.L. (1991) Better Stories, Not Better Constructs, to Generate Better Theory: A Rejoinder to Eisenhardt. *Academy of Management Review* 16 (3): 613–19.

Easterby-Smith, M., Thorpe, R. and Lowe, A. (2002) *Management Research: An Introduction*, 2nd ed. London: Sage.

The Economist (15 November 2001) Curse of the Ethical Executive: Why 'Corporate Social Responsibility' Is Not a Welcome Fashion, available at www.economist.com/node/863487.

Eisenhardt, K.M. (1989) Agency Theory: An Assessment and Review. *Academy of Management Review* 14 (1): 57–74.

Elkington, J. and Burke, T. (1989) *The Green Capitalists*. London: Victor Gollancz.

England, G.W. (1967) Personal Value Systems of American Managers. *Academy of Management Journal* 10 (1): 53–68.

England, G.W. (1973) Personal Value Systems of Managers and Administrators. *Academy of Management Proceedings* 1: 81–8.

England, G.W. (Summer 1978) Managers and Their Value Systems: A Five-Country Comparative Study. *Columbia Journal of World Business* 13 (2): 35–44.

Erikson, E.H. (1950) *Childhood and Society*. London: Imago.

Erikson, E.H. (1994) *Identity and the Life Cycle*. London: Norton.

Eysenck, M. (2004) *Psychology: An International Perspective*. London: Psychology Press.

Fagenson, E.A. (1993) Personal Value Systems of Men and Women Entrepreneurs Versus Managers. *Journal of Business Venturing* 8 (5): 409–31.

Feather, N.T. (1986) Cross-cultural Studies with the Rokeach Value Survey: The Flinders Program of Research on Values. *Australian Journal of Psychology* 38 (3): 269–83.

Feshbach, S. and Feshbach, N.D. (1991) Aggression and Altruism: A Personality Perspective, in C. Zahn-Waxler, E.M. Cummings and R. Iannotti (eds.), *Altruism and Aggression: Biological and Social Origins*. Cambridge: Cambridge University Press: 189–217.

Festinger, L. (1957) *A Theory of Cognitive Dissonance*. Evanston, IL: Row Peterson.

Fineman, S. (1996) Emotional Subtexts in Corporate Greening. *Organization Studies* 17 (3): 479–500.

Fineman, S. and Clarke, K. (1996) Green Stakeholders: Industy Interpretations and Response. *Journal of Management Studies* 33 (6): 715–31.

Fiol, C.M. (1991) Managing Culture as a Competitive Resource: An Identity-Based View of Sustainable Competitive Advantage. *Journal of Management* 17 (1): 191–211.

Fiol, C.M. and Dunbar, R.L.M. 1990. Identifying the basis for organizational cohesion: The tight side of loose coupling, New York University, Working Paper.

Fishbein, M. and Ajzen, I. (1975) *Belief, Attitude, Intention and Behavior*. Reading, MA: Addison-Wesley.

Fisher, C. (1999) Ethical Stances: The Perceptions of Accountancy and HR Specialists of Ethical Conundrums at Work. *Business Ethics: A European Review* 8 (4): 236–48.

Fisher, C. and Lovell, A. (2003) *Business Ethics and Values*. Harlow: Pearson Education.

Fisher, K.K. (1986) Human Resource Management in Action: Management Roles in the Implementation of Participative Management Systems. *Human Resource Management* 25 (3): 459–81.

Fleetwood, S. (2004) An Ontology for Organisation and Management Studies, in S. Fleetwood and S. Ackroyd (eds.), *Critical Realist Applications in Organisation and Management Studies*. London: Routledge: 27–53.

Fleetwood, S. (2005) Ontology in Organization and Management Studies: A Critical Realist Perspective. *Organization* 12 (2): 197–222.

Foucault, M. (2000) *Ethics, Subjectivity and Truth: Essential Works of Foucault, 1954–1984*, Volume One, ed. P. Rabinow. London: Penguin.

Frank, A.G. (1963) Administrative Role Definition and Social Change. *Human Organization* 22: 238–42.

Frankfurt, H.G. (1988) *The Importance of What We Care about: Philosophical Essays*. Cambridge: Cambridge University Press.

Fredrickson, B.L., Cohn, M.A., Coffey, K.A., Pek, J. and Finkel, S.M. (2008) Open Hearts Build Lives: Positive Emotions, Induced through Loving-Kindness Meditation, Build Consequential Personal Resources. *Journal of Personality and Social Psychology* 95 (5): 1045–62.

French, P.A. (1979) The Corporation as a Moral Person. *American Philosophical Quarterly* 16 (3): 207–15.

Friedland, J. (2009) Doing Well and Good: The Human Face of the New Capitalism, in J. Friedland (ed.), *Information Age*. Charlotte, NC: Information Age.

Friedman, M. (1970) The Social Responsibility of Business is to Increase Its Profits. *New York Times Magazine* 14 (11): 1–13.

Fritzche, D.J. (1995) Personal Values: Potential Keys to Ethical Decision Making. *Journal of Business Ethics* 14: 909–22.

Furnham, A. (2005) *The People Business: Psychological Reflections on Management*, Basingstoke: Palgrave Macmillan.

Gabriel, Y., Fineman, S. and Sims, D. (2000) *Organizing and Organizations*, 2nd ed. London: Sage.

Giacomino, D., Fujita, A. and Johnson, T.M. (2000) Are the Effects of Age and Gender Changing the Personal Values of Japanese Executives? *Business Forum* 24 (1–2): 15–20.

Gilligan, C. (1982) *In a Different Voice*. Cambridge, MA: Harvard University Press.

Ginns, B. (26 February 2009) Sheer Arrogance of Greedy Bank Boss Fred 'The Shred' Goodwin. *Yorkshire Post*, available at www.yorkshirepost.co.uk/news/Fred-the-Shred-refuses-to.5022527.jp.

Gioia, D.A. (1992). Pinto Fires and Personal Ethics: A Script Analysis of Missed Opportunities. *Journal of Business Ethics* 11 (5–6): 379–89.

Goldstein, K. (1939) *The Organism*. New York: American Book Company.

Gond, J.-P. (2006) Contribution a l'étude de la performance sociétale de l'entreprise: Fondements théoriques, construction sociale, impact financier, unpublished doctoral dissertation, Toulouse I – Sciences sociales.

Goodpaster, K. (1991) Business Ethics and Stakeholder Analysis. *Business Ethics Quarterly* 1 (1): 53–73.

Goulding, C. (2002) *Grounded Theory: A Practical Guide for Management, Business and Market Researchers.* London: Sage Publications.

Gray, R., Kouhy, R. and Lavers, S. (1995) Corporate Social and Environmental Reporting: A Review of the Literature and a Longitudinal Study of UK Disclosure. *Accounting, Auditing and Acountability Journal* 8 (2): 47–77.

Grayson, D. and Hodges, A. (2004) *Corporate Social Opportunity! Seven Steps to Make Corporate Social Responsibility Work for Your Business.* Sheffield: Greenleaf Publishing.

Greene, G. (1971) *The Power and the Glory.* London: Penguin.

Guerrier, Y. and MacMillan, K. (1981) Managers' Values and Career Decisions. *Journal of General Management* 7 (1): 22–33.

Gummesson, E. (2000) *Qualitative Methods in Management Research*, 2nd ed. London: Sage.

Gurney, P.M. and Humphreys, M. (2006) Consuming Responsibility: The Search for Value at Laskarina Holidays. *Journal of Business Ethics* 64: 83–100.

Gustafsson, C. (2002) Reading 12.1: New Values, Morality, and Strategic Ethics, in H. Mintzberg, J. Lampel, J.B. Quinn and S. Ghoshal (eds.), *The Strategy Process: Concepts, Contexts and Cases*, 4th ed. Harlow: Pearson Education: 295–9.

Guth, W.D. and Tagiuri, R. (1965) Personal Values and Corporate Strategy. *Harvard Business Review* 43 (5): 123–32.

Haidt, J. (2001) The Emotional Dog and Its Rational Tail: A Social Intuitionist Approach to Moral Judgment. *Psychological Review* 108 (4): 814–34.

Handy, C. (1998) *The Hungry Spirit. Beyond Capitalism: A Quest for Purpose in the Modern World.* London: Arrow.

Hannah, S.T., Avolio, B.J. and Walumbwa, F.O. (2011) Relationships between Authentic Leadership, Moral Courage, and Ethical and Pro-social Behaviors. *Business Ethics Quarterly* 21 (4): 555–78.

Hardigan, P.C., Cohen, S.R. and Carvajal, M.J. (2001) Linking Job Satisfaction and Career Choice with Personality Styles: An Exploratory Study of Practising Pharmacists. *Journal of Psychological Type* 57: 30–5.

Harris, L.C. and Crane, A. (2002) The Greening of Organizational Culture: Management Views on the Depth, Degree and Diffusion of Change. *Journal of Organizational Change Management* 15 (3): 214–34.

Harrison, E.F. (1975) *The Managerial Decision-Making Process*. Boston, MA: Houghton Mifflin.

Hart, C. (January 2009) Saved but Not Free. Book review of T. Buergenthal, *A Lucky Child: A Memoir of Surviving Auschwitz as a Young Boy. Sunday Times Culture Magazine*: 45.

Held, D. (2002) Globalization, Corporate Practice and Cosmopolitan Social Standards. *Contemporary Political Theory* 1 (3): 59–78.

Hemingway, C.A. (2002) An Exploratory Analysis of Corporate Social Responsibility: Definitions, Motives and Values. Research Memorandum No 34, University of Hull Business School.

Hemingway, C.A. (2004) Personal Values as the Catalyst for the Corporate Social Entrepreneur. Presented at the 17th European Business Ethics Network (EBEN) annual conference, University of Twente, Enschede, the Netherlands, 24–6 June.

Hemingway, C.A. (2005) Personal Values as a Catalyst for Corporate Social Entrepreneurship. *Journal of Business Ethics* 60 (3): 233–49.

Hemingway, C.A. (2012) The Three Wise Monkeys as a Useful Metaphor in Behavioural Ethics Research: Theoretical Development Using a Socio-reflexive Approach. Presented at the 10th Anniversary Conference of the International Centre for Corporate Social Responsibility (ICCSR), Nottingham University Business School, 26–7 April.

Hemingway, C.A. (2013), Corporate Social Entrepreneurship, in S.O. Idowu, N. Capaldi, L. Zu and A. Das Gupta (eds.), *The Encyclopedia of Corporate Social Responsibility*. Heidelberg: Springer: 546–53.

Hemingway, C.A. and Maclagan, P.W. (2003) Managers' Individual Discretion and Corporate Social Responsibility: The Relevance of Personal Values. Presented at the 7th European Business Ethics Network (EBENUK) UK Annual Conference, and the 5th Ethics and Human Resource Management Conference, Selwyn College, Cambridge, 7–8 April.

Hemingway, C.A. and Maclagan, P.W. (2004) Managers' Personal Values as Drivers of Corporate Social Responsibility. *Journal of Business Ethics* 50 (1): 33–44.

Hendry, J. (2004) *Between Enterprise and Ethics: Business and Management in a Bimoral Society*. Oxford: Oxford University Press.

Hernandez, M. (2012) Toward an Understanding of the Psychology of Stewardship. *Academy of Management Review* 37 (2): 172–96.

Hertz, N. (2001) *The Silent Takeover: Global Capitalism and the Death of Democracy*. London: William Heinemann.

Herzberg, F. (1966) *Work and the Nature of Man.* Cleveland, OH: World Publishing.

Hibbert, S.A., Hogg, G. and Quinn, T. (2002) Consumer Response to Social Entrepreneurship: The Case of The Big Issue in Scotland. *International Journal of Nonprofit and Voluntary Sector Marketing* 17 (3): 288–302.

Hitlin, S. (2003) Values as the Core of Personal Identity: Drawing Links Between Two Theories of Self. *Social Psychology Quarterly* 66 (2): 118–37.

Hitlin, S. and Piliavin, J.A. (2004) Values: Reviving a Dormant Concept. *Annual Review of Sociology* 30: 359–93.

Hodgkinson, G.P. and Starkey, K. (2011) Not Simply Returning to the Same Answer Over and Over Again: Reframing Relevance. *British Journal of Management* 22: 355–69.

Hoffman, A.J. (1993) The Importance of Fit between Individual Values and Organisational Culture in the Greening of Industry. *Business Strategy and the Environment* 2 (4): 10–18.

Hofstede, G. (1980) *Culture's Consequences: International Differences in Work-Related Values.* London: Sage.

Holland, J.L. (1985) *Making Vocational Choices: A Theory of Vocational Personalities and Work Environments*, 2nd ed. Englewood Cliffs, NJ: Prentice Hall.

Horowitz, M. (2002) Defining Character Integrity. *Journal of the American Psychoanalytic Association* 50 (2): 551–73.

Hosmer, L.T. (2003) *The Ethics of Management*, 4th ed. New York: McGraw Hill Irwin.

Howard, C. (2001) Research and Evaluation: Bureaucrats in the Social Policy Process: Administrative Policy Entrepreneurs and the Case of Working Nation. *Australian Journal of Public Administration* 60: 56–65.

Howard, J.A. and Sheth, J.N. (1969) *The Theory of Buyer Behavior.* New York: Wiley and Sons.

Hsieh, N.-H. (2007) Incommensurable Values. Available at http://plato. stanford.edu/entries/value-incommensurable.

Huefner, J.C. and Hunt, K.H. (1994) Broadening the Concept of Entrepreneurship: Comparing Business and Consumer Entrepreneurs. *Entrepreneurship: Theory and Practice* 18 (3): 61–76.

Humphreys, M. and Brown, A.D. (2002) Narratives of Organizational Identity and Identification: A Case Study of Hegemony and Resistance. *Organization Studies* 23 (3): 421–47.

Humphreys, M. and Brown, A.D. (2008) An Analysis of Corporate Social Responsibility at Credit Line: A Narrative Approach. *Journal of Business Ethics* 80: 403–18.

Idowu, S.O., Capaldi, N., Zu, L. and Das Gupta, A. (2013) (eds.), *The Encyclopedia of Corporate Social Responsibility*. Heidelberg: Springer.

Inglehardt, R. (1997). *Modernization and Postmodernization: Cultural, Economic, and Political Change in 43 Societies*. Princeton, NJ: Princeton University Press.

Insight (5 February 2012) If the Customer Doesn't Make a Complaint, Don't Fix the Car. *Sunday Times*: 12–13.

Irvin, J., Pedro, L. and Gennaro, P. (2003) Strategy from the Inside Out: Lessons in Creating Organic Growth. *Journal of Business Strategy* 24 (5): 10–14.

It's a Wonderful Life, film, Liberty, 1946.

Jackall, R. (1988) *Moral Mazes*. New York: Oxford University Press.

Jacob, P.E., Flink, J.J. and Schuchman, H.L. (1962) Values and Their Function in Decision-Making: Toward an Operational Definition for Use in Public Affairs Research. *American Behavioral Scientist* 10 (10): 4–38.

Janis, I.L. (1982) *Groupthink: Psychological Studies of Policy Decisions and Fiascoes*. Boston, MA: Houghton Mifflin.

Johnson, P. and Duberley, J. (2000) *Understanding Management Research: An Introduction to Epistemology*. London: Sage.

Jones, T.M. (1995) Instrumental Stakeholder Theory: A Synthesis of Ethics and Economics. *Academy of Management Review* 20 (2): 404–37.

Kahle, L.R., Poulos, B. and Sukhdial, A. (February–March 1988) Changes in Social Values in the United States during the Past Decade. *Journal of Advertising Research* 28: 35–41.

Kanter, E.M. (1989) Work and Family in the United States: A Critical Review and Agenda for Research and Policy. *Family Business Review* 11 (1): 77–114.

Kanter, E.M. (2009) *SuperCorp: How Vanguard Companies Create Innovation, Profits, Growth, and Social Good*. New York: Random House.

Kell, G. and Ruggie, J. (2001) Global Markets and Social Legitimacy: The Case of the 'Global Compact', in D. Drache (ed.), *The Market or the Public Domain? Global Governance and the Assymetry of Power*. London: Routledge, 321–34.

Keller, K.L. (1993) Conteptualizing, Measuring and Managing Customer-Based Brand Equity. *Journal of Marketing* 57 (1): 1–22.

Keller, K.L. (1998) *Strategic Brand Management: Building, Measuring and Managing Brand Equity*. Upper Saddle River, NJ: Prentice Hall.

Kim, U., Triandis, H.C., Kagitcibasi, C., Choi, S. and Yoon, G. (1994) Introduction, in U. Kim, H.C. Triandis, C. Kagitcibasi, S. Choi and

G. Yoon (eds.), *Individualism and Collectivism: Theory, Method, and Applications*. Thousand Oaks, CA: Sage: 1–16.

King, P.J. and Roberts, N.C. (1992) An Investigation into the Personality Profile of Policy Entrepreneurs. *Public Productivity and Management Review* 16 (2): 173–90.

Kirkman, B.L. and Shapiro, D.L. (2001) The Impact of Team Members' Cultural Values on Productivity, Cooperation, and Empowerment in Self-Managing Work Teams. *Journal of Cross-cultural Psychology* 32 (5): 597–617.

Kivimäki, M., Nyberg, S.T., Batty, G.D., Fransson, E.I., Heikkilä, K, Alfredsson, L, Bjorne, J.B., Borritz, M., Burr, H., Casini, A., Clays, E., De Bacquer, D., Dragano, N., Ferrie, J.E., Geuskens, G.A., Goldberg, M., Hamer, M., Hooftman, W.E., Houtman, I., Joensuu, M., Jokela, M., Kittel, F., Knutsson, A., Koskenvuo, M., Koskinen, A., Kouvonen, A., Kumari, M., Madsen, I.E.H., Marmot, M.G., Nielsen, M.L., Nordin, M., Oksanen, T., Pentti, J., Rugulies, R., Salo, P., Siegrist, J., Singh-Manoux, A., Suominen, S.B., Väänänen, A., Vahtera, J., Virtanen, M., Westerholm, P.J.M., Westerlund, H., Zins, M., Steptoe, A. and T. Theorell (14 September 2012) Job Strain as a Risk Factor for Coronary Heart Disease: A Collaborative Meta-analysis of Individual Participant Data. *The Lancet*, early online publication.

Klein, N. (2000) *No Logo*. London: Flamingo.

Kluckhohn, C. (1951) Values and Value-Orientations in the Theory of Action, in T. Parsons and E. Shils (eds.), *Toward a General Theory of Action*. Cambridge, MA: Harvard University Press, 388–433.

Koehn, D. (2005) Integrity as a Business Asset. *Journal of Business Ethics* 58: 125–36.

Kohlberg, L. (1969) Stage and Sequence: The Cognitive Developmental Approach to Socialization, in D.A. Goslin (ed.), *Handbook of Socialization Theory and Research*. Chicago: Rand McNally: 347–480.

Kolchin, M.G. and Hyclak, T.J. (1987) The Case of the Traditional Intrapreneur. *S.A.M. Advanced Management Journal* 52 (3): 14–19.

Koltko-Rivera, M.E. (2006) Rediscovering the Later Version of Maslow's Hierarchy of Needs: Self-Transcendence and Opportunities for Theory, Research and Unification. *Review of General Psychology* 10 (4): 302–17.

Kotler, P. (1984) *Marketing Management: Analysis, Planning and Control*, 5th ed. Englewood Cliffs, NJ: Prentice Hall.

Kotler, P. (2000) *Marketing Management: The Millenium*. Upper Saddle River, NJ: Prentice Hall.

Kotler, P. and Fahey, L. (1982) The World's Champion Marketers: The Japanese. *Journal of Business Strategy* 3 (1): 3–13.

Kuratko, D.F. and Goldsby, M.G. (2004) Corporate Entrepreneurs or Rogue Middle Managers? A Framework for Ethical Corporate Entrepereneurship. *Journal of Business Ethics* 55: 13–30.

Kuratko, D.F., Montagno, R.V. and Hornsby, J.S. (1990) Developing an Intrapreneurial Assessment Instrument for an Effective Corporate Entrepreneurial Environment. *Strategic Management Journal* 11: 49–58.

Lacy, P. and Andersen, R.K. (December 2004) Corporate Responsibility: The Company Experience. *EABIS Newzine* 4: 1–17.

Lamb, H. (9 March 2002) New Style of Global Trading Is onto a Winner. *The Independent*: 2.

Lan, G., Gowing, M., McMahon, S., Rieger, F. and King, N. (2007) A Study of the Relationship between Personal Values and Moral Reasoning of Undergraduate Students. *Journal of Business Ethics* 78: 121–31.

Langer, E.J. (1989) Minding Matters: The Consequences of Mindlessness–Mindfulness. *Advances in Experimental Social Psychology* 22: 137–76.

Laroche, H. (1995) From Decision to Action in Organizations: Decision-Making as a Social Representation. *Organization Science* 6 (1): 62–75.

Leana, C.R., Mittal, V. and Stiehl, E. (2012) Perspective: Organizational Behavior and the Working Poor. *Organization Science* 23 (3): 888–906.

Leary, M.R. and Tangney, J.P. (eds.) (2003) *Handbook of Self and Identity*. New York: Guilford Press.

Legge, K. (1998) Is HRM Ethical? Can HRM Be Ethical?, in M. Parker (ed.), *Ethics and Organizations*. London: Sage: 150–72.

Leidtka, J. (1989) Managerial Values and Corporate Decision-Making: An Empirical Analysis of Value Congruence in Two Organizations. *Research in Corporate Social Performance and Policy* 11: 55–91.

Lent, A. (Spring 2012) On Liberty. *RSA Magazine*: 32–4.

Lieberman, S. (1956) The Effects of Changes in Roles on the Attitudes of Role Occupants. *Human Relations* 9: 358–402.

Lincoln, D., Pressey, M.M. and Little, T. (1982) Ethical Beliefs and Personal Values of Top Level Executives. *Journal of Business Research* 10: 475–87.

Lockett, A., Moon, J. and Visser, W. (2006) Corporate Social Responsibility in Management Research: Focus, Nature, Salience and Sources of Influence. *Journal of Management Studies* 43 (1): 115–36.

Logsdon, J.M. and Young, J.E. (2005) Executive Influence on Ethical Culture: Self Transcendence, Differentiation, and Integration, in R.A. Giacalone, C.L. Jurkiewicz and C. Dunn (eds.), *Positive Psychology in*

Business Ethics and Corporate Responsibility. Greenwich, CT: Information Age, 103–22.

Long, J. and Porter, K.L. (1984) Multiple Roles of Midlife Women: A Case for New Directions in Theory, Research and Policy, in G. Baruch and J. Brooks-Gunn (eds.), *Women in Midlife.* New York: Plenium: 109–59.

Longenecker, J.G., McKinney, J.A. and Moore, C.W. (1988) Egoism and Independence: Entrepreneurial Ethics. *Organizational Dynamics* 16 (3): 64–72.

Lovell, A. (2002a) Ethics as a Dependent Variable in Individual and Organisational Decision-Making. *Journal of Business Ethics* 37: 145–63.

Lovell, A. (2002b) Moral Agency as Victim of the Vulnerability of Autonomy. *Business Ethics: A European Review* 11 (1): 62–76.

Low, M.B. and MacMillan, I.C. (1988) Entrepreneurship: Past Research and Future Challenges. *Journal of Management* 14: 139–61.

Lusk, E.J. and Oliver, B.L. (1974) American Managers' Personal Value Systems – Revisited. *Academy of Management Journal* 17 (3): 549–54.

Lussier, R.N. (1995) Startup Business Advice from Business Owners to Would-Be Entrepreneurs. *S.A.M. Advanced Management Journal* 60 (1): 10–13.

Macalister, T. (6 November 2001) Charity Survey a Wake Up Call, Says CBI Chief. *The Guardian*: 2

McCarthy, E. (2 October 2003) Dead as a Dot-Com. *Washington Post*: E01.

Macchiette, B. and Roy, A. (1994) Sensitive Groups and Social issues: Are You Marketing Correct? *Journal of Consumer Marketing* 11 (4): 55–64.

McGregor, D. (1966) *Leadership and Motivation.* Cambridge, MA: MIT Press. .

Maclagan, P. (1991) Learning from an Ethics Workshop in an MBA Programme. *Management Education and Development* 22 (2): 87–96.

Maclagan, P. (2003) Self-Actualisation as a Moral Concept and the Implications for Motivation in Organisations: A Kantian Argument. *Business Ethics: A European Review* 12 (4): 334–42.

Maclagan, P.W. (1998) *Management and Morality.* London: Sage.

Maclagan, P.W. (1999) Corporate Social Responsibility as a Participative Process. *Business Ethics: A European Review* 8 (1): 43–9.

McClelland, D.C. (1986) Some Reflections on the Two Psychologies of Love. *Journal of Personality* 54 (2): 334–53.

McKinlay, A. and Starkey, K. (1998) *Foucault, Management and Organization Theory.* London: Sage.

McWilliams A. and Siegel, D. (2001) Corporate Social Responsibility: A Theory of the Firm Perspective. *Academy of Management Review* 26 (1): 117–27.

Maignan, I., Ferrell, O.C. and Hult, T.M. (1999) Corporate Citizenship: Cultural Antecedents and Business Benefits. *Academy of Marketing Science Journal* 27 (4): 455–70.

Mandoyan (10 May 2012) Has the Shareholder Spring Caught up with Aviva's CEO? *Global Journal*, available at http://theglobaljournal. net/article/view/682.

March, J.G. and Simon, H.A. (1958) *Organizations*. New York: John Wiley and Sons.

March, J.G. and Sutton, R.I. (1997) Organizational Performance as a Dependent Variable. *Organization Science* 8 (6): 698–706.

Marcuse, H. (1969) *An Essay on Liberation*. Boston, MA: Beacon Press.

Marr, A. (22 February 2009) I Revere This Man (and His Book on Earthworms)...Andrew Marr on the Legacy of Darwin. *Daily Mail* online. Available at www.dailymail.co.uk/sciencetech/article-1151579.

Marr, A. (21 May 2012) *Start the Week*: Money and Morality, BBC Radio 4.

Martin, J. (2001) *Organizational Behaviour*, 2nd ed. London: Thomson Learning.

Marz, J.W., Powers, T.L. and Queisser, T. (2003) Corporate and Individual Influences on Managers' Social Orientation. *Journal of Business Ethics* 46: 1–11.

Maslow, A.H. (1943) A Theory of Human Motivation. *Psychological Review* 50 (5): 370–96.

Maslow, A.H. (1959) *New Knowledge in Human Values*. New York: Harper & Row.

Maslow, A.H. (1964) *Religions, Values and Peak Experiences*. New York: Viking.

Maslow, A.H. (2011; first published 1962) *Toward a Psychology of Being*. Blacksburg, VA: Wilder.

Matten, D. and Moon, J. (2004) 'Implicit' and 'Explicit' CSR: A Conceptual Framework for Understanding CSR in Europe. *Research Paper Series* 29: 1–41, 1479–5124.

Matten D. and Moon, J. (2005) Corporate Citizenship: Toward An Extended Theoretical Conceptualization. *Academy of Management Review* 30 (1): 166–79.

Means, J.R., Wilson, G.L., Sturm, C., Biron, J.E. and Bach, P.J. (1990) Theory and Practice: Humility as a Psychotherapeutic Formulation. *Counseling Psychology Quarterly*, 3: 211–15.

Meglino, B.M. and Ravlin, E.C. (1998) Individual Values in Organizations: Concepts, Controversies, and Research. *Journal of Management* 24 (3): 351–89.

Mele, A.R. (1995) *Autonomous Agents: From Self-Control to Autonomy.* Oxford: Oxford University Press.

Menon, A. and Menon, A. (January 1997) Enviropreneurial Marketing Strategy: The Emergence of Corporate Environmentalism as Market Strategy. *Journal of Marketing* 61: 51–67.

Meyerson, D.E. (2001) *Tempered Radicals: How People Use Difference to Inspire Change at Work.* Boston, MA: Harvard Business School Press.

Miceli, M.P., Near, J.P. and Dworkin, T.M. (2008) *Whistle-Blowing in Organizations.* New York: Routledge.

Michalos, A.C. and Poff, D.C. (eds). (2012) *Citation Classics from the Journal of Business Ethics: Celebrating the First Thirty Years of Publication.* Dordrecht: Springer.

Michie, S. and Gooty, J. (2005) Values, Emotions and Authenticity: Will the Real Leader Please Stand up? *Leadership Quarterly* 16: 441–57.

Miles, M.B. and Huberman, M. (1994) *Qualitative Data Analysis: An Expanded Sourcebook,* 2nd ed. London: Sage.

Mitchell, R.K., Agle, B.R. and Wood, D.J. (1997) Toward a Theory of Stakeholder Identification and Salience: Defining the Principle of Who and What Really Counts. *Academy of Management Review* 22 (4): 853–85.

Moberg, D.J. and Seabright, M.A. (2000) The Development of Moral Imagination. *Business Ethics Quarterly* 10 (4): 845–84.

Moir, L. (2001) What Do We Mean by Corporate Social Responsibility? *Corporate Governance* 1 (2): 16–22.

Monbiot, G. (2000) A Troublemaker's Charter, in G. Monbiot (ed.), *Captive State: The Corporate Takeover of Britain.* London: Macmillan: 331–60.

Moon, J. (2001) Business Social Responsibility: A Source of Social Capital? *Reason in Practice* 1 (3): 35–45.

Moon, J. (2002) Confronting the Critics Revisited: The Governance of Corporate Social Responsibility. *International Journal for Corporate Social and Environmental Responsibility* 1 (2): 23–32.

Moon, J. (2004) Government as a Driver of Corporate Social Responsibility. *ICCSR Research Paper Series* 20: 1–22, 1479–5124.

Moon, J. (2010) *Integrating Sustainability into Business Schools,* available at www.nottingham.ac.uk/iccsr/isibs/abouttheproject.aspx.

Moore, G. (1999) Corporate Moral Agency: Review and Implications. *Journal of Business Ethics* 21: 329–43.

Moriarty, R.T. (1983) *Industrial Buying Behavior: Concepts, Issues, and Applications.* Lexington, MA: Lexington Books.

Murray-Rust, D.M. (1995) Quakers in Brief: An Overview of the Quaker Movement from 1650 to 1990. Birkenhead meeting, Merseyside, UK.

Near, J.P. and Miceli, M.P. (1996) Whistleblowing: Myth and Reality. *Journal of Management* 22 (3): 507–26.

Nelson, M.R., Brunel, F.F., Supphellen, M. and Manchanda, R.V. (2006) Effects of Culture, Gender, and Moral Obligations on Responses to Charity Advertising across Masculine and Feminine Cultures. *Journal of Consumer Psychology* 16 (1): 45–56.

Neuhouser, F. (2000) The Place of Moral Subjectivity in Ethical Life, in F. Neuhouser, *Foundations of Hegel's Social Theory: Actualizing Freedom.* Cambridge, MA: Harvard University Press: 225–82.

Newhouse, J.P. (1995) Economists, Policy Entrepreneurs and Health Care Reform. *Health Affairs* 14 (1): 182–99.

O'Fallon, M.J. and Butterfield, K.J. (2005) A Review of the Empirical Ethical Decision-Making Literature: 1996–2003. *Journal of Business Ethics* 59 (4): 375–413.

O'Hear, A. (2000) *Philosophy, the Good, the True and the Beautiful.* Cambridge: Cambridge University Press.

Olson, S.F. and Currie, H.M. (1992) Female Entrepreneurs: Personal Value Systems and Business Strategies in a Male-Dominated Industry. *Journal of Small Business Management* 30 (1): 49–57.

Orange, K. (16 October 2007) personal correspondence via e-mail.

Orlitzky, M. (2008) Corporate Social Performance and Financial Performance: A Research Synthesis, in A. Crane, D. McWilliams, D. Matten, J. Moon and D.S. Siegel (eds.), *The Oxford Handbook of Corporate Social Responsibility.* Oxford: Oxford University Press: 113–36.

Orlitzky, M., Schmidt, F.L. and Rynes, S.L. (2003) Corporate Social and Financial Performance: A Meta-analysis. *Organization Studies* 24: 403–41.

Oulton, W. (2007) Using Indexes and Awards, in UK Social Investment Forum (UKSIF) (ed.), *Ethical Savings and Investment: The Rise of the Ethical Saver.* London: UKSIF: 17.

Painter-Morland, M. (2008) Business Ethics as Practice: Ethics as the Everyday Business of Business. Cambridge: Cambridge University Press.

Palazzo, G., Krings, F. and Hoffrage, U. (2012) Ethical Blindness. *Journal of Business Ethics*, 109: 323–38.

Paxman, J. (17 March 2009) *Newsnight*, BBC2.

Pence, G. (1991) Virtue Theory, in P. Singer (ed.), *A Companion to Ethics.* Oxford: Blackwell: 249–58.

Perry, S.C. (2001) The Relationship between Written Business Plans and the Failure of Small Business. *U.S. Journal of Small Business Management* 39 (3): 201–9.

Peters, T.J. (1980) Putting Excellence into Management. *McKinsey Quarterly* (4): 31–42.

Peters, T.J. and Waterman, R.H. (1982) In Pursuit of Excellence ... How the Best-Run Companies Turn So-So Performers into Big Winners. *Management Review* 71 (11): 8–16.

Piliavin, J.A. (1989) The Development of Motives, Self-Identities, and Values Tied to Blood Donation: A Polish-American Study, in N. Eisenberg, J. Reykowski and E. Staub (eds.), *Social and Moral Values*. Hillsdale, NJ: Lawrence Erlbaum: 253–76.

Pinchot, G. (1985) *Intrapreneuring: Why You Don't Have to Leave the Corporation to Become an Entrepreneur*. New York: Harper and Row.

Posner, B.Z. and Schmidt, W.H. (1992) Values and the American Manager. *California Management Review* 34 (3): 80–94.

Prince-Gibson, E. and Schwartz, S.H. (1998) Value Priorities and Gender. *Social Psychology Quarterly* 61 (1): 49–67.

Pringle, H. and Gordon, W. (2001) *Brand Manners: How to Create the Self-Confident Organization to Live the Brand*. Chichester: Wiley.

Pruzan, P. (2008) Spirituality as a Firm Basis for Corporate Social Responsibility, in A. Crane, D. McWilliams, D. Matten, J. Moon and D.S. Siegel (eds.), *Oxford Handbook of Corporate Social Responsibility*. Oxford: Oxford University Press: 552–59.

Pugh, D.S., Hickson, D.J. and Hinings, C.R. (1971) *Writers on Organizations*, 2nd ed. London: Penguin.

Rabinow, P. (2000) Introduction: The History of Systems of Thought , in M. Foucault, *Ethics, Subjectivity and Truth: Essential Works of Foucault, 1954–1984*, Volume One, ed. P. Rabinow. London: Penguin, xi–xlii.

Rallapalli, K.C., Vitel, S.J.J. and Szeinbach, S. (2000) Marketers' Norms and Personal Values: An Empirical Study of Marketing Professionals. *Journal of Business Ethics* 24: 65–75.

Rand, A. and Branden, N. (1964) *The Virtue of Selfishness: A New Concept of Egoism*. New York: New American Library.

Ranken, N.L. (1987) Corporations as Persons: Objections to Goodpaster's 'Principle of Moral Projection'. *Journal of Business Ethics* 6 (8): 633–37.

Raphael, D.D. (1981) *Moral Philosophy*. Oxford: Oxford University Press.

Raz, J. (2003) *The Practice of Value*. Oxford: Clarendon Press.

Redding, P. (2006) Georg Wilhelm Friedrich Hegel, *Stanford Encyclopedia of Philosophy* online. Available at http://plato.stanford.edu/entries/hegel.

Reed, M. (4 February 1999) Wide Open to the Web Warriors. *Marketing*: 18–19.

Reidenbach, R.E. and Robin, D. (1991) A Conceptual Model of Corporate Moral Development. *Journal of Business Ethics* 10 (4): 273–84.

Relaxnews (9 March 2011) Fairtrade Market Experiencing Explosive Growth in UK and US. *The Independent*, Life section. Available at www.independent.co.uk/life-style/fairtrade-market-experiencing-explosive-growth-in-uk-and-us-2236449.html.

Rescher, N. (1969) *Introduction to Value Theory*. Englewood Cliffs, NJ: Prentice Hall.

Rest, J.R. (1986) *Moral Development: Advances in Research and Theory*. London: Praeger.

Rice, G. (1999) Islamic Ethics and the Implications for Business. *Journal of Business Ethics* 18: 345–58.

Ring, K., Lipinski, C.E. and Braginsky, D. (1965) The Relationship of Birth Order to Self-Evaluation Anxiety Reduction, and Susceptibility to Emotional Contagion. *Psychological Monographs: General and Applied* 79 (10): 1–24.

Robertson, D.C. (1991) Corporate Ethics Programs: The Impact of Firm Size, in B. Harvey, H. van Luijk and G. Corbetta (eds.), *Market Morality and Company Size*. Dordrecht: Kluwer: 119–36.

Robin, D.P. and Reidenbach, R.E. (1987) Social Responsibility, Ethics and Marketing Strategy: Closing the Gap between Concept and Application. *Journal of Marketing* 51: 44–58.

Rokeach, M. (1968) The Role of Values in Public Opinion Research. *Public Opinion Quarterly* 32 (4): 547–59.

Rokeach, M. (1973) *The Nature of Human Values*. New York: The Free Press.

Rokeach, M. (1979) *Understanding Human Values: Individual and Societal*. New York: The Free Press.

Rollinson, D. (2002) *Organisational Behaviour: An Integrated Approach*, 2nd ed. Harlow: Pearson Education.

Rosenthal, S.B. and Buchholz, R.A. (2002) Toward New Directions in Business Ethics: Some Pragmatic Pathways, in R.E. Frederick (ed.), *A Companion to Business Ethics*. Oxford: Blackwell: 112–27.

Rotter, J.B. (1986) Generalized Expectancies for Internal Versus External Control of Reinforcement. *Psychological Monographics* 80 (1): 1–28.

Rowe, D. (2009) *What Should I Believe? Why Our Beliefs about the Nature of Death and the Purpose of Life Dominate Our Lives*. London: Routledge.

Rowlinson, M. and Hassard, J. (1993) The Invention of Corporate Culture: A History of the Histories of Cadbury. *Human Relations* 46 (3): 299–318.

Rubinstein, G. (2003) Authoritarianism and Its Relation to Creativity: A Comparative Study among Students of Design, Behavioural Sciences and the Law. *Personality and Individual Differences* 34 (4): 695–705.

Sandel, M.J. (2012) *What Money Can't Buy: The Moral Limits of Markets.* London: Allen Lane.

Sayer, A. (2000) *Realism and Social Science.* London: Sage.

Sayer, A. (2004) Foreword: Why Critical Realism?, in S. Fleetwood and S. Ackroyd (eds.), *Critical Realist Applications in Organisation and Management Studies.* London: Routledge: 6–20.

Schwartz, S.H. (1996). Value Priorities and Behavior: Applying a Theory of Integrated Value Systems, in C. Seligman, J.M. Olsen and M.P. Zanna (eds.), *The Ontario Symposium: The Psychology of Values.* Mahwah, NJ: Erlbaum: 1–24.

Schwartz, S.H. (2006) Basic Human Values: Theory, Methods, and Applications. *Revue française de sociologie* 4 (47): 929–68.

Schwartz, S.H. (2010) Basic Values: How They Motivate and Inhibit Prosocial Behavior, in M. Mikulincer and P. Shaver (eds.), *Prosocial Motives, Emotions, and Behavior: The Better Angels of Our Nature.* Washington, DC: American Psychological Association: 221–41.

Schwartz, S.H. (2011) Studying Values: Personal Adventure, Future Directions. *Journal of Cross-cultural Psychology* 42: 307–19.

Schwartz, S.H. and Bilsky, W. (1987) Toward a Universal Psychological Structure of Human Values. *Journal of Personality and Social Psychology* 53 (3): 550–62.

Scott, E.D. (2000) Moral Values: Situationally Defined Individual Differences. *Business Ethics Quarterly* 10 (2): 497–521.

Seligman, M.E.P. and Csikszentmihalyi, M. (2000) Positive Psychology: An Introduction. *American Psychologist* 55: 5–14.

Seligman, M.E.P., Rashid, T. and Parks, A.C. (2006) Positive Psychotherapy. *American Psychologist* 61 (8): 774–88.

Selznick, P. (1949) *TVA and the Grass Roots.* Berkeley: University of California Press.

Sen, S. and Bhattacharya, C.B. 2001. Does Doing Good Always Lead to Doing Better? Consumer Reactions to Corporate Social Responsibility. *Journal of Marketing Research* 32 (8): 225–44.

Shah, S.K. and Corly, K.G. (2006) Building Better Theory by Bridging the Quantitative–Qualitative Divide. *Journal of Management Studies* 43 (8): 1821–35.

Shane, S. (2003) *A General Theory of Entrepreneurship: The Individual–Opportunity Nexus*. Cheltenham: Edward Elgar.

Sheth, J.N., Newman, B.I. and Gross, J.L. (1991) Why We Buy What We Buy: A Theory of Consumption Values. *Journal of Business Research* 22 (2): 159–70.

Siltaoja, M.E. (2006) Values Priorities as Combining Core Factors between CSR and Reputation: A Qualitative Study. *Journal of Business Ethics* 68: 91–111.

Silverman, D. (1970) *The Theory of Organisations: A Sociological Framework*. London: Heinemann.

Silverman, D. (2001) *Interpreting Qualitative Data: Methods for Analyzing Talk, Text and Interaction*, 2nd ed. London: Sage.

Sims, P. and Gioia, D.A. (eds.) (1986) *The Thinking Organization: Dynamics of Organizational Social Cognition*. San Fransisco: Jossey-Bass.

Skidelsky, R. and Skidelsky, E. (2012) *How Much Is Enough: Money and the Good Life*. New York: Other Press.

Slavin, T. (1 September 2002) New Rules of Engagement. *The Observer*, Management ed.: 11.

Smart, N. (1989) *The World's Religions*. Cambridge: Cambridge University Press.

Soares, C. (2003) Corporate Versus Individual Moral Responsibility. *Journal of Business Ethics* 46: 143–50.

Social Enterprise Magazine online (2003) FAQ's about Social Entrepreneurship. Available at www.socialenterprisemagazine.org.

Solomon, R. (1992) *Ethics and Excellence: Cooperation and Integrity in Business*. Oxford: Oxford University Press.

Soros, G. (2008) The Crisis and What to Do About It. *New York Review of Books* 55 (19). Available at http://www.nybooks.com/articles/22113.

Stansbury, J.M. and Victor, B. (2008) Whistle-Blowing among Young Employees: A Life-Course Perspective. *Journal of Business Ethics* 85: 281–99.

Stone, A. (6 May 2007) Getting Firms to Do More. *Sunday Times*: 15.

Stormer, F. (2003) Making the shift: moving from 'ethics pays' to an inter-systems model of business. *Journal of Business Ethics* 44: 279–89.

Sull, D.N. and Houldner, D. (2005) Do Your Commitments Match Your Convictions? *Harvard Business Review* 83 (1): 82–91.

Swanson, D.L. (1995) Addressing a Theoretical Problem by Reorienting the Corporate Social Performance Model. *Academy of Management Review* 20 (1): 43–64.

Tangney, J.P. (2000) Humility: Theoretical Perspectives, Empirical Findings and Directions for Future Research. *Journal of Social and Clinical Psychology* 19 (1): 70–82.

Tawney, R.H. (1926) *The Acquisitive Society.* London: G. Bell and Sons.

Tenbrunsel, A.E. and Smith-Crowe, K. (2008) Ethical Decision-Making: Where We've Been and Where We're Going. *Academy of Management Annals* 2 (1): 545–607.

Thompson, J.L. (2002) The World of the Social Entrepreneur. *International Journal of Public Sector Management* 15 (4–5): 412–31.

Thompson, P. (2004) Brands, Boundaries and Bandwagons, in S. Fleetwood and S. Ackroyd (eds.), *Critical Realist Applications in Organisation and Management Studies.* London: Routledge: 54–70.

Thornton, F., Privette, G. and Bundrick, C.M. (1999) Peak Performance of Business Leaders: An Experience Parallel to Self-Actualization Theory. *Journal of Business and Psychology* 14 (2): 253–63.

Treviño, L.K. (1986) Ethical Decision Making in Organizations: A Person–Situation Interactionist Model. *Academy of Management Review* 11 (3): 601–17.

Treviño, L.K. (2002) Business Ethics and the Social Sciences, in R.E. Frederick (ed.), *A Companion to Business Ethics.* Oxford: Blackwell: 218–30.

Treviño, L.K., Butterfield, K.D. and McCabe, D.L. (1998) The Ethical Context in Organizations: Influences on Employee Attitudes and Behaviors. *Business Ethics Quarterly* 8 (3): 447–76.

Treviño, L.K. and Nelson, K.A. (2004) *Managing Business Ethics: Straight Talk about How to Do It Right*, 3rd ed. New York: Wiley.

Treviño, L.K., Weaver, G.R. and Reynolds, S.J. (2006) Behavioral Ethics in Organizations: A Review. *Journal of Management* 32 (6): 951–90.

Ucbasaran, D., Westhead, P. and Wright, M. (2001) The Focus of Entrepreneurial Research: Contextual and Process Issues. *Entrepreneurship Theory and Practice* 25 (4): 57–80.

Unsworth, R. (ed.) (2009) Mini Power Steering Failures. *Watchdog*, BBC, available at www.bbc.co.uk/blogs/watchdog/rob_unsworth_editor.

Velasquez, M.G. (2006) *Business Ethics: Concepts and Cases*, 6th ed. London: Pearson Prentice Hall.

Victor, B. and Cullen, J.B. (1988) The Organizational Bases of Ethical Work Climates. *Administrative Science Quarterly* 33: 101–25.

Visser, W. (2011) *The Age of Responsibility: CSR 2.0 and the New DNA of Business.* London: Wiley.

Wade, D. (2 October 2005) What You Think You Want Makes You Miserable So What Do You Have to Do to Find Happiness? *Sunday Times Magazine*: 34–40.

Walley, L. and Stubbs, M. (1999) 'Greenjacking' – a Tactic for the Toolbag of Environental Champions? Reflections on an SME Success Story. *Eco-Management and Auditing* 6 (1): 26–33.

Walton, C.C. (1988) *The Moral Manager*. New York: Harper Business.

Watson, T.J. (1994) *In Search of Management*. London: Routledge.

Watson, T.J. (2003) Ethical Choice in Managerial Work: The Scope for Moral Choices in an Ethically Irrational World. *Human Relations* 56 (2): 167–85.

Weber, J. (1990) Managers' Moral Reasoning: Assessing Their Responses to Three Moral Dilemmas. *Human Relations* 43: 687–702.

Weber, J. (24 February 2009) Impact of the Economy, the Financial Crisis on Corporate Citizenship [*sic*]. Email communication.

Weber, M. (1947) *The Theory of Social and Economic Organization. Translated by A.M. Henderson and Talcott Parsons*. London: Collier Macmillan.

Webster, A.F.C. and Cole, D. (2004) *The Virtue of War: Reclaiming the Classic Christian Traditions East & West*. Salisbury, MA: Regina Orthodox Press.

Wickham, M. and Parker, M. (2007) Reconceptualising Organisational Role Theory for Contemporary Organisational Contexts. *Journal of Managerial Psychology* 22 (5): 440–64.

Wiley, M.G. (1991) Gender, Work, and Stress: The Potential Impact of Role-Identity Salience and Commitment. *Sociological Quarterly* 32 (4): 495–510.

Williams, O.F. (1997) *The Moral Imagination*. Notre Dame, IN: University of Notre Dame Press.

Williams, R.M., Jr (1979) Change and Stability in Values and Value Systems: A Sociological Perspective, in M. Rokeach (ed.), *Understanding Human Values: Individual and Societal*. New York: The Free Press: 15–46.

Wilson, D. (16 January 2002) This Juvenile Posturing Is for Punks. *The Guardian*: 8

Wojciszke, B. (1989) The System of Personal Values and Behavior, in N. Eisenberg, J. Reykowski and E. Staub (eds.), *Social and Moral Values*. Hillsdale, NJ: Lawrence Erlbaum: 229–49.

Wood, D.J. (1991) Corporate Social Performance Revisited. *Academy of Management Review* 16 (4): 691–718.

Wright, D. (1971) *The Psychology of Moral Behaviour*. Harmondsworth: Penguin.

Zagzebski, L.T. (1996) *Virtues of the Mind: An Inquiry into the Nature of Virtue and the Ethical Foundations of Knowledge*. Cambridge: Cambridge University Press.

Zahn-Waxler, C. (1991) Conclusions: Lessons From the Past and a Look to the Future, in C. Zahn-Waxler, E.M. Cummings and R. Iannotti (eds.), *Altruism and Aggression: Biological and Social Origins*. Cambridge: Cambridge University Press: 303–24.

Zhang, K. and Wen, Z. (2008) Review and Challenges of Policies of Environmental Protection and Sustainable Development in China. *Journal of Environmental Management* 88 (4): 1249–61.

Zhang, Z. (2002) *Confucius – The Oriental Sage and Philosopher*. Jinan: Shandong Friendship Press.

Zimbardo, P.G., Maslach, C. and Haney, C. (2000) Reflections on the Stanford Prison Experiment: Genesis, Transformations, Consequences, in T. Blass (ed.), *Obedience to Authority: Current Perspectives on the Milgram Paradigm*. Mahwah, NJ: Lawrence Erlbaum Associates: 193–239.

Zohar, D. and Marshall, I. (2004) *Spiritual Capital: Wealth We Can Live by*. London: Bloomsbury.

Index